Mike Atherton was born in Manchester in 1968. He began his first-class cricket career in 1987, playing for Lancashire and Cambridge University. Two years later he made his England debut, against Australia at Nottingham, the first of 115 Test caps. He went on to captain England a record 54 times before retiring from the game in 2001. Since then, he has written his bestselling autobiography, *Opening Up*, which was shortlisted for the William Hill Sports Book of the Year prize. After a spell at the *Sunday Telegraph*, he is now the Chief Cricket Correspondent of *The Times*. In 2009 Atherton was named the Sports Journalist of the Year at the British Press Awards, the SJA Sportswriter of the Year and in 2010 he became the SJA Sports Columnist of the year. He lives in north London with his wife and two children.

Also by Mike Atherton

Opening Up: My Autobiography
Gambling: A Story of Triumph and Disaster
Atherton's Ashes

GLORIOUS SUMMERS AND DISCONTENTS

Selected Writings from a Dramatic Decade

Mike Atherton

SIMON &
SCHUSTER

London · New York · Sydney · Toronto · New Delhi

A CBS COMPANY

First published in Great Britain in 2011 by Simon & Schuster UK Ltd
This edition published in Great Britain in 2012 by Simon & Schuster UK Ltd
A CBS COMPANY

1 3 5 7 9 10 8 6 4 2

Simon & Schuster UK Ltd
1st Floor
222 Gray's Inn Road
London
WC1X 8HB

www.simonandschuster.co.uk

Simon & Schuster Australia
Sydney

Simon & Schuster India
New Delhi

A CIP catalogue copy for this book is available
from the British Library.

ISBN: 978-0-85720-349-6

Typeset by Hewer Text UK Ltd, Edinburgh
Printed and bound in Great Britain by CPI Group (UK) Ltd, Croydon, CR0 4YY

Contents

For David de Caires 1937–2008

Acknowledgements

Thanks to the various sports editors who have placed some faith in me along the way and who have been a pleasure to work with: Colin Gibson, Jon Ryan and Peter Mitchell at the *Sunday Telegraph* and Tim Hallissey at *The Times*. Thanks to Chris Lane at *Wisden*. Thanks also to Jon Holmes, Ian Chapman and Ian Marshall for their help in transporting this project from idea to completion.

Introduction

David de Caires, the man to whom this book is dedicated, was an inspiring editor. Trained as a lawyer, but for a long time a frustrated publisher, he founded a newspaper in a country that had been denied freedom of expression for two decades and had suffered social and economic collapse due to a failed socialist experiment.

When journalists complain about how difficult things are for newspapers right now, with a combination of the internet and a collapse in advertising posing severe challenges, I think of the story of *Stabroek News*, the small independent newspaper that David de Caires founded, and that survives him still, despite the most brutal challenges.

His newspaper began as a weekly, with funds scraped together. It was written up by the four or five people then employed, was flown at the weekend in a chartered plane to Trinidad, where the *Trinidad Express* kindly printed the paper, was flown back and sold throughout the week, until the exhausting process began again. Gradually, enough funds were built up to buy a press and the newspaper became a daily, finally printed in its own country, Guyana.

The problems, though, were many and varied, the majority of which would not be appreciated by proprietors and editors in the developed world: the nightly power cuts; an absence of trained journalists; a population that, initially at least, was scared to voice an opinion or even talk to journalists, so threatening was the environment and history of political suppression; an economy that was shot to pieces, and a government prepared to react to criticism by withdrawing state advertising, which accounted for a significant proportion of the newspaper's income.

If this seems an odd way to introduce a compilation of cricket writing, then let me make a confession: David de Caires was my father-in-law and I don't think that some of the pieces that make up this book could have been written in the way they have been written had I not met him halfway through my playing career. It was through him that I began to take an interest in newspapers and the people who work in them. It was through him and his family that I began to understand something of the world outside the boundaries that had hitherto constrained me – a breadth of interest that I hope can be detected in some of the pieces on show.

I've often thought it ironic that David de Caires died the night before the million-dollar match between England and Allen Stanford's superstars. He cared little for cricket – poker, horseracing, football and golf were his preferred sporting enthusiasms – but as a man of integrity, he would have abhorred everything that Stanford stood for, especially since part of the West Indies was likely to suffer in his, Stanford's, wake.

Having covered the Stanford issue at length, from the moment he arrived in his personalised helicopter to the day he was arrested for suspected fraud; having travelled to Antigua and written thoroughly about it throughout the week, I then missed the million-dollar match because I had to fly from Antigua to Barbados where David had died in his sleep the night before.

The Stanford 'issue' – beginning with his arrival at Lord's, on one of English cricket's most shameful days, to his final disgrace – is given full coverage here, and it represents, in microcosm, the shift in the game that is at the heart of this book, as cricket moved into a globalised and market-driven 21st century. The first part of the book deals with many of the discontents that the game has thrown up in the wake of this shift, coincidentally, in the short time that I have worked as the cricket correspondent of *The Times*. In some ways it was a fortuitous start at that paper, since there has rarely been a week with little to say.

Terrorism, match-fixing and financial malpractice are not topics that a cricket writer might think of as his bread and butter, but cricket has suffered a traumatic period of late. Many of the pieces here are an examination of the game and where it is heading, and under whose control, as it faces up to the challenge of retaining its traditions in a rapidly changing marketplace.

I have been acutely conscious that, in the short time that I have been cricket correspondent of *The Times*, the game has undergone profound change and suffered from severe convulsions. In a two-year period there has been, in no particular order, a terrorist attack on a cricket team; bombings that have caused the alienation of a cricket nation; the arrival of franchised cricket which threatens the traditional fabric of the game; match-fixing; drugs; and the influence of a 'fraudster of shocking magnitude', to use the Securities and Exchange Commission's description of Allen Stanford.

It is often overlooked, I think, how important good judgement is to a successful columnist or correspondent. We are there to report, for sure, but in this day and age where 'news' cannot remain 'news' for long, we are also there to give opinion based on experience and, importantly, a feel for the game. I'm pleasantly surprised reading through many of these pieces again how my judgement has been more accurate than flawed, both in a cricketing and a wider sense.

In a world dominated by Twitter, where the rush to judgement is so overpowering, the ability to step back from the fray, and to be able to take at least a short time to organise thoughts and opinions, make some calls and hopefully find out a little more, is important.

To give one brief example from the summer of 2010: when the second match-fixing story about Pakistan emerged after a one-day match at The Oval, many took the view that Pakistan should have been banished for good. And yet, when you stopped to think about it, there had been no evidence produced – nor has there still – that any wrongdoing had taken place. The three players caught red-handed earlier by the *News of the World* had already been sent home, and it would have been wrong to tar the rest with the match-fixing brush on the basis of no evidence. That was the view taken in *The Times* against the rantings of the majority.

Beyond the discontents that make up the first half of this book, there have also been great players and great games, alongside the inevitable dross that makes up the essential experience of watching sport. If many of the pieces here are provocative, because of the issues that have exploded in cricket's face over the last few years, then I hope that I haven't lost sight of the essential beauty of the game and of those who play it. Part two of the book deals with some of the games and the players that have aroused my interest.

There are reports of some memorable matches. Some stick out readily: Tendulkar's match-winning hundred, for example, on the final day of the Chennai Test after England had returned to India following the Mumbai bombings. It was a magnificent innings, and a memorable and moving final day, and I hope the report does it justice.

I was lucky to have played against some of the greatest players to have ever played the game: Brian Lara and Shane Warne to name but two. Since I have stopped playing, I have continued to watch these players with great enthusiasm and I hope my writing about them is informed by the experience of having played against them, combined with the kind of dispassionate observations of a non-trained journalist's eye. Empathy, then, for the players without, I hope, any slavish bias towards them.

But as well as the greats, many of the pieces that I enjoyed writing and that I have chosen to include here are about the not so great: Tendulkar's great friend Vinod Kambli, for instance, who I talked to at length in Mumbai as Tendulkar was notching up another hundred, and who was having to deal with his own shattered dreams; or the West Indian Richard Austin, once a crack international athlete, now living the life of a crack addict on the streets of Jamaica, and known to his street-friends as Danny Germs. Like life, cricket is made up of all sorts, and it has been the struggles and the failures of the many that I have found to be as interesting as the successes and the triumphs of the few.

Newspaper reports and columns are not meant to be collected in book form. They are, by their very nature, almost-immediate, sometimes visceral responses to events as they happen, especially when written for a daily newspaper, which is where I have been lately.

Yet, I am very happy to see these pieces put together in one place: they represent a fraction of the thousands of words written over a decade or more, a decade where I chose to replace one craft with another. I didn't really have a clue what to do when I retired from the game, but I have been lucky enough to be able to broadcast and write about cricket and I have tried to do so with as much enthusiasm as I had when I was playing.

It is a vanity project then, from someone not given to vanity. And if there is no appetite for them, at least I can console myself with the fact that one or two pieces may get a nod of approval from a publisher, his hands still stained with ink, in the press room in the sky.

Mike Atherton
November 2010

PART ONE

Discontents

1

The Best Job in the World?

Australia have chosen four captains in the past two and a half decades; England, having chosen four in 1988 alone, rather more than that. After Graham Gooch's resignation in 1993, though, there was a period of relative stability: myself, Nasser Hussain and Michael Vaughan each lasting about four years – Alec Stewart's reign was a brief one as was Andrew Flintoff's – until exhaustion took over.

With Vaughan's resignation there was a delicious little period when Kevin Pietersen ascended to the top job, only to be sacked months later, taking with him a darling of the England and Wales Cricket Board, Peter Moores. This chapter deals with that period in narrative form, from Vaughan's departure, through Pietersen's ascension and on to Andrew Strauss, with a brief interlude for Alastair Cook when Strauss thought the job too much hassle.

Pietersen's period in office was fascinating. I was convinced at the start that it was a giant mistake and that it would end in tears – which is what happened. In between, though, Pietersen surprised me with how well he did in the job. He was tactically naïve, for sure, as he found out to his cost in Chennai, but he tackled other aspects of the job with a forceful and engaging personality. It is difficult to see how Pietersen will ever have another crack at the England captaincy, which is a shame because he would probably do it well second time around. Now we shall never know.

Michael Vaughan Bows Out with Dignity Intact

Michael Vaughan is often said to be England's best captain since Mike Brearley. Surely, though, this does not go far enough. When Vaughan stepped down yesterday afternoon, after five demanding years in the job, England lost one of the best captains in their history. This, after all, is a man who has six more victories as England captain than anybody else, a man who brought back the Ashes after 16 barren years and a batsman who, when on top of his game in Australia six years ago, could have held a place in any world XI of the day.

The decision, I understand, was his and his alone and on the basis that he felt he believed he could no longer continue, it is hard to argue against. The captaincy of England is just about the best job in the world but it is also an all-consuming one. If you take the job seriously, as Vaughan has unquestionably done, then there comes a time when you simply don't want to do it any more. There comes a time when you don't want to spend every evening at dinner ignoring your companions, or your family, thinking about where your next run is coming from, who should be opening the bowling the following morning or how to tell your mate that he is no longer good enough to be in the team. There comes a time when you want the headlines to be about someone else.

As his voice cracked and chin wobbled with emotion, the tears just about held in check, he said that it was both the hardest and the easiest decision he had ever made: the hardest because of the kudos and sheer intellectual (in cricketing terms) challenge of it all; the easiest because it had simply become too much for him. He said that he was no longer himself at home and that he wanted to get 'back to being me'. As he said that, I was ever-so-briefly transported back a decade; it was a comment that will have resonated with anyone who has held the job and it was the one that was at the heart of his decision.

Although this defeat against South Africa was the tipping point for Vaughan, the job has been eating away at him for a while. He first felt some unease in New Zealand last winter and there were enough signs recently to suggest that the end was coming. He became embroiled in an unseemly post-Headingley selection spat, distancing himself from both Peter Moores and Geoff Miller, and was unusually curt with Jonathan Agnew, the BBC's cricket correspondent, before the Edgbaston Test.

It is Vaughan's association with Moores that should come under the most scrutiny. When Duncan Fletcher resigned in the Caribbean, after eight years in charge, Vaughan was quick to praise the man-management skills of Moores and they enjoyed some early success together. But recently, there were signs that Vaughan's bond with Moores was not nearly as strong as with his predecessor.

Vaughan has been in contact with Fletcher throughout the summer, and when the split opened up after the selection of Darren Pattinson it brought to mind the split between Fletcher and Andrew Flintoff during the last Ashes tour over Monty Panesar's non-selection at Adelaide. Vaughan wanted Simon Jones to play at Headingley but one errant selection and one disagreement should not be enough to break a captain–coach bond that is strong.

The other significant contributing factor in this decision was Vaughan's form with the bat. It becomes incredibly difficult as a captain when you are not doing your job as a player. Successful captaincy springs from the respect you generate from your players – as a leader, decision-maker, human being and as a player – and once you start to worry that the rest of the team are carrying you, then instinctive decision-making becomes near impossible.

So this decision was, in part, to try to get back to being the player he knows he can be. He felt that continuing in the job may have curtailed his career prematurely and now, freed from the burden of captaincy and still young enough at 33 to play for a while yet, there might be another chapter or two to write. Certainly there are enough examples – Ian Botham's renaissance at Headingley in 1981 the game after stepping down from the captaincy being the best – of former captains rediscovering their form.

But Vaughan – who will miss the Oval Test but then make himself available for the winter – is now at the mercy of the new man, who must decide whether he wants to step out of his predecessor's shadow for good, and the whim of the selectors. If the desire is still there, he can play for England again but it will not necessarily be as easy as he thinks.

Who will the new man be? In losing not one but two captains yesterday, Hugh Morris, the managing director of the England team, and Geoff Miller, the national selector, gave the clearest hint that they want to unite the role. In fact, during Miller's opening press conference as David Graveney's replacement, he had said that he felt that the two captains scenario, for the Test and one-day teams, was not ideal. Vaughan agreed with those sentiments yesterday, although he added that the arrangement with Collingwood had worked as well as it could.

If Collingwood did go of his own volition, and Morris insisted that he did, then it is a swift change of heart from him. Only weeks ago, after he had been banned at The Oval, Collingwood publicly stated that the job meant everything to him and that he would not do anything to jeopardise it. Nevertheless, The Oval rumpus scarred him and it was not necessarily clear that he had a great tactical feel for the job. Maybe the decision of his great friend Vaughan prompted his own misgivings.

If the selectors do want one man to take on both jobs, there is only one who fulfils the criteria of being worth his place on merit in both teams. That man is Kevin Pietersen. Andrew Strauss has captained England before, with some success, but does not get in the one-day team; Andrew Flintoff has been too badly scarred by his Ashes white-wash to want to revisit the captaincy, and Alastair Cook is too young and green and might not be around the one-day team for much longer.

As much as the selectors have appeared in the recent past to have been taking a cocktail of hallucinogenic drugs before each selection meeting, they surely would not bring in someone from outside. Robert Key is the only name who springs to mind, but this would be too much a bolt from the azure.

The confusion suggests that there has been little forward planning. Vaughan himself has said in the past that he wanted to go on through the next Ashes series and so his announcement might have taken Morris and Moores by surprise. Certainly, there was little in the way of guidance from the ECB that a change was imminent when after the match they revealed that the team for The Oval would be announced the following morning. And when Vaughan left the field on Saturday, midway through the afternoon, it was Strauss not Pietersen who was put in charge.

If it does turn out to be Pietersen, then it will be an enormous gamble. Not only does Pietersen have next to no experience of captaincy, he is England's best player, and along with Flintoff their greatest match-winner. In the past, flamboyant characters such as Botham and Flintoff have found their competitive edge and brilliance dulled rather than sharpened by the extra responsibility. It may be the making of him; if not it will be the breaking of Morris, the man ultimately responsible for the England team.

Yesterday, though, and probably for the last time in his life, the stage belonged to Vaughan. He was emotional, humble, funny and honest as he reflected upon what he will realise in time to have been the greatest days of his professional life. He thanked his team, the back-room staff, the Professional Cricketers' Association, the fans and, most movingly of all, his family. No, Michael, thank you.

The Times, 4 August 2008

Odds Stacked Up Against First-time Gamblers

Geoff Miller and Hugh Morris are not renowned as reckless gamblers, rather one a slightly dour northerner who tells winsome jokes on the after-dinner circuit, the other a nuggety and down-to-earth Welshman. Yesterday, though, as they installed Kevin Pietersen into the highest cricketing office in the land, they were taking their biggest gamble ever.

Along with Andrew Flintoff, Pietersen is the England team's highest-profile player, their best player and their greatest match-winner. The essence of the gamble is whether the demands of the job – and not only one job but three – will reduce his productive-ness, potency and sheer brilliance as a player. Pietersen at his best is uninhibited and instinctive. If the extra responsibility changes that and affects his game for the worse, this roll of the dice will be a costly one.

Nobody knows how this will play out, not Pietersen himself, not the selectors who picked him and not this correspondent. Given that, is it a risk worth taking? I would say no on the basis that the downside is greater than the potential upside. Nor is it clear why the selectors are desperate for one man to do all three jobs. Michael Vaughan, about as good a captain as it gets, became exhausted during the last year doing just one of them. In time, I would not be surprised to see not only separate captains but separate coaches, too, for forms of the game that demand entirely different qualities.

My own choice would have been Andrew Strauss to lead the Test team and Pietersen the one-day team. Strauss is much more than the 'safe pair of hands' he is so often labelled. When he did captain the side two summers ago against Pakistan, he lifted his game to new heights and, at 31, he is at the right sort of age – mature, steady and experienced – to have flourished in the job. He lost out the last time England gambled – on Flintoff – and now his time has probably gone.

Yesterday, Pietersen insisted that he would try to play in the same instinctive, intuitive manner that has so enthralled England supporters since he made his international debut four years ago. He was absolutely right to say that he doesn't intend to change his style of play – that would be madness – but there is a big difference between confident expressions at your first press conference and the reality of the pressures of the job. Just ask Ian Botham – or Flintoff, for that matter.

Pietersen knows that this issue is at the heart of whether his captaincy will be successful. Walking across Lord's with him at the end of his first press conference, he was honest enough to admit that he didn't know whether or how it would affect his game. He also said that if it did, he would be man enough to say that the whole experiment had been a failure and move on.

Yesterday, Miller, the national selector, expressed full confidence that Pietersen would take to the captaincy in the same successful way that he took to international cricket. Miller hopes that not only will Pietersen continue to inspire, but that the extra responsibility will lift his game to even greater heights. Such as those attained at Edgbaston on Saturday by Graeme Smith, who showed the difference between a brilliant cameo and a truly great innings. Pietersen had the chance to win that game for England before the desire to reach a personal landmark in a certain way overshadowed the match situation.

The appointment of an England captain cannot come without being agreed in the highest echelons of the ECB, so there is some sense of collective responsibility about this decision. Morris, the managing director of England cricket, said yesterday that he and the chairman of the ECB, Giles Clarke, effectively rubber-stamped a decision made by the selectors. But if it all goes wrong, it is inconceivable that this decision will not come back to haunt Morris, the man ultimately responsible for England team matters.

Before appointing Pietersen, the selectors probably asked themselves two questions: could he have played the same way for his first 94 runs at Edgbaston if he had been captain? And, would he have played the same shot on 94 had he been captain? They probably reckoned the answer to the first question was 'yes' and the answer to the second was 'no'. Pietersen was unrepentant about the stroke. 'I didn't see the 94 as a big issue,' he said. 'The way that Colly [Paul Collingwood] and I were playing was exactly the way you have to play against South Africa and Australia. You have got to be positive and you've got to be aggressive and that's the way I'll continue to play and captain.'

Two other issues will determine how successful Pietersen's captaincy will be: his relationship with Peter Moores, the head coach, and whether England can re-create the same kind of potent bowling attack that was at the heart of the Ashes triumph in 2005.

Like Macavity, Moores has been hard to find in the last few days, absent as he was from both Vaughan's departure and Pietersen's coronation. But the best periods in the past few years have come when the captain–coach bond has been unbreakable. It is no secret that Pietersen has not seen eye to eye with Moores of late and so these differences will have to be settled quickly and irrevocably.

It is often forgotten that a captain is no magician. There are many things he can control, such as the style of cricket he wants his team to play, the personnel in that team and how they gel together. But without match-winning bowlers, no captain can flourish. Much will depend, between now and the Ashes in 11 months' time, on whether Stephen Harmison can rediscover his mojo, and whether Simon Jones and Flintoff stay fit. If they do, Pietersen's job will be made much easier.

As for the rest, there are no doubts. He treats his cricket with utter seriousness and has an intuitive feel for the game, as his batting often shows, and a good cricket brain. Forget the bling, the celebrity wife, the tattoos, the earrings and the ridiculous haircuts at the start of his career. They are all irrelevant because where it matters – on the training ground, in the nets and out in the middle – Pietersen sets as good an example as any England cricketer I have come across. Don't expect any Flintoff-like late-night tales from this captain.

Yesterday, he was also certain that the dressing-room would go with him. 'I ummed and aahed last year when they asked me about the one-day job,' he said. 'Now I'm a much more rounded figure and I've got a lot more support from the players. That's one of the most exciting things, the text messages and the phone calls from senior players who support me. Once you've got the support of the players there's nothing more you can ask for.'

Good luck, then, to him as he embarks on the next stage of his remarkable journey. It is an enormous undertaking and he will need all his inner toughness to succeed. Yesterday, he said that Vaughan's were big shoes to fill, but unlike Tiger Woods, who was told the same thing about Jack Nicklaus, Pietersen did not say that he had big feet. I hope I'm wrong, but I have a horrible feeling that this is going to end in tears. But, then again, as Vaughan showed on Sunday, it always ends in tears.

The Times, 5 August 2008

Kevin Pietersen Aims to Turn On the Style

Heavy clouds and drizzle greeted England's new captain at Lord's yesterday. He did not arrive in a gold-plated personalised helicopter, as Sir Allen Stanford had done, and he was forced to climb the stairs to the media centre because the lift was broken. But as he did the clouds parted, as if they, too, were in thrall to King Kev, and the sun shone. The portents were good.

He was dressed soberly in a dark suit, with an embroidered England logo and an England and Wales Cricket Board lapel badge. His hair was cut short and the first signs of a goatee beard were showing; his trademark diamond earring had been put away for the show. It was a rather cramped affair, too, since a horde of schoolboy cricketers had found their way in. There was wonder in their eyes, the England captaincy being the stuff of schoolboy dreams.

Kevin Pietersen, 28, would never have dreamt of captaining England as a schoolboy in Pietermaritzburg, South Africa, and so this must rank among the most dramatic and unbelievable of tales. His first thoughts turned to Pietermaritzburg when asked to take on the job. He rang his mother and father, who still live there, along with one of his three brothers. It was his wife Jessica, though, who provided the final confirmation that, in Harriet Harman-speak, his time had come.

He admitted afterwards that he had never been more nervous, but this was a confident and bullish first performance in front of a demanding audience. He spoke of his pride and his excitement; he paid generous tribute to his predecessor, Michael Vaughan ('I love Michael Vaughan,' he gushed), and revealed that a number of senior players had already texted him their messages of support. It was, he said, a challenge he could not duck.

He said he would captain in a 'spontaneous, gut-instinct' type of way and he hoped that it would not change his style. 'Time will tell, but I hope it won't affect the way I play,' he said. 'If it doesn't work out and affects a few things in terms of my personal life and my batting then I will be man enough to say so.'

Only once did he falter and that was when he was asked about his working relationship with the head coach, Peter Moores, with whom Pietersen and a number of other senior players have had issues of late. 'Peter Moores likes to challenge players, and there are a lot of strong characters, opinionated characters in the dressing-room,' he said. 'My position is totally, totally different now that I am captain from being a player and we now need to unite, get on the same hymn sheet and get this team going forward together.'

The implication was that the England team have not been so much of a cosy club of late as a warring faction – although Pietersen was convinced that he and Moores could work well together. 'I sat down with Peter for a long chat yesterday afternoon and I am 100 per cent confident that we can work together,' he said. 'I wouldn't be sat here now if that wasn't the case.'

Sitting alongside Pietersen were Hugh Morris, the managing director of England cricket, and Geoff Miller, the national selector. Miller used the opportunity to name England's team for the next Test, the squad for the forthcoming one-day series and the England Lions team to play one-day games against South Africa on 14 and 16 August. Ravi Bopara replaces Vaughan in the Test team, Samit Patel of Nottinghamshire and Matt Prior have been selected in the one-day squad, and there is an eye-catching return for Simon Jones in the first of the Lions' matches.

Yesterday, though, was all about Pietersen, a cricketer who has divided more opinion and more dressing-rooms than any other in recent times. It is a remarkable story.

The Times, 5 August 2008

Stephen Harmison Ensures England Live in the Fast Lane

In the build-up to the fourth npower Test match, Kevin Pietersen had not exactly adhered to Brian Clough's philosophy on sporting leadership. 'Say nowt, win it, then talk yer head off' was Clough's dictum, but – and this was unavoidable, given the demands on a new captain – Pietersen had decided in the run-up to the game at The Oval not to bother with the first bit. Yesterday morning, though, the talking had to stop and the doing had to start.

The new era began rather well. Pietersen lost the toss, but this proved to be a good thing, as the pitch offered something all day and South Africa's batsmen gave the impression that they were a unit drained from previous exertions. They lost six wickets in the afternoon session, with the result that a promising 103 for one after lunch became 194 all out, an hour after tea. Only the loss of Andrew Strauss before the close and a funereal over-rate could take the gloss off Pietersen's day.

A captain is nothing without good bowlers and yesterday they made it easy for their new leader. The wickets were shared around and, with the exception of Stuart Broad, who leaked too many boundaries, it was a good day for them all. James Anderson, in particular, had a day to remember when he became, at 26 years and eight days old, the fourth youngest English bowler to pass 100 Test wickets.

It was a good day, too, for the man immediately above him on that list. Over the past couple of years, it has been difficult to watch Stephen Harmison bowl, mainly because, following that horror ball in Brisbane, the spectators' instincts upon seeing him ball in hand have been to cower behind the sofa or place their hands over their eyes just in case. But yesterday we got the pre-2006 version:

20

knees pumping and radar working. He was hostile, fast and, praise be, straight.

He was entrusted with the new ball, the first time he has taken it for England since the Old Trafford Test more than a year ago, and he might have taken a wicket with his first ball, Graeme Smith cutting a rising one straight into, and out of, the hands of Alastair Cook at gully. There was pain and blood, too, although the blood belonged to a team-mate, as Tim Ambrose misjudged Harmison's steepling bounce to end up with a mouthful of leather. The pain was reserved for Smith, who edged into what commentators call the midriff, and spent minutes doubled up while everyone else had a titter.

Thereafter, Harmison bowled a probing eight-over spell from the Vauxhall End, during which he was unlucky not to take a wicket or two, passing the bat on occasions and looking generally in good order. It was a change of ends after lunch, primarily so that the prevailing breeze could help Anderson's outswing, that brought Harmison the rewards that were due to him. He took only two wickets, but they were the key ones of Smith and Hashim Amla, when both were set, and they highlighted the value of having a genuine strike bowler at the captain's disposal.

Smith was first to go, top-edging a weary hook shot straight to Anderson at fine leg. He had battled against himself throughout his 103-ball stay, never finding his fluency or best touch. This was unsurprising, given the amount of mental and physical energy that had gone into his astounding perform- ance at Edgbaston. The only surprise here was that he lasted so long.

Like Basildon in a general election, Smith, in form or not, remains a bellwether for his team, and his departure sparked a downturn in fortunes. Harmison's next ball to Amla was fast and full and it duly flattened the batsman's middle stump. Harmison jumped, punched the air with delight and roared his satisfaction, something we have not really seen since the Ashes in 2005. It was a welcome sight.

Now it was Anderson's turn to join in the fun. Swinging the ball malevolently this way and that, with just the merest tilt of his wrist position, he set up Jacques Kallis with a series of outswingers before he darted one back, late and full, to trap the batsman leg-before. Did the ball strike him outside the line of off stump? It was a marginal call, but one that Aleem Dar got right and it was just reward for a skilful bit of swing bowling.

When Ashwell Prince drove Anderson to Ian Bell at cover point, South Africa had lost four wickets for 15 runs in 33 balls. Mark Boucher became the fifth of the session, feathering another Anderson outswinger through to Ambrose, and A.B. de Villiers the sixth, when he played back to the third ball bowled by Monty Panesar on the stroke of tea. Panesar was an immediate beneficiary of the change in captain, used as he was sparingly and, when he took his second wicket in the first over of a new spell, he would have thought, judiciously.

England's new captain directed proceedings from mid-off just like Vaughan, but that was where the similarities ended. Whereas Vaughan would stand impassively, Pietersen clapped, cajoled and was more obviously emotional. There were hugs for his bowlers and an affectionate pat on the behind for short leg. It was all very touchy-feely. From a man who, in his press conferences, had spread more love around than you'd find in a 1960s hippy commune, this was unsurprising. Let it all hang out, man.

The Times, 8 August 2008

Kevin Pietersen Confident That He Can Walk the Walk

This was not so much 'the shot that was heard round the world', as Bobby Thomson's home run for the New York Giants was immortalised in the autumn of 1951, but a gauntlet thrown down that will be picked up on the other side of the world. Kevin Pietersen's assertion that 'if we play like that, we will beat Australia' will be noted, stored away and then rammed down his throat should the glory that he believes is preordained does not come to pass.

This was pure Pietersen. It was a harmless enough delivery, and one that an 'English' captain would have shouldered arms to and let pass by. The Aussies? We will just concentrate on the next match, thank you very much. Yawn, and dull copy all round.

Pietersen? He saw it as a scoring opportunity and not only for a single, either. He ran down the pitch and thrashed it – one leg in the air, no doubt, flamingo-style – through mid-wicket for four. Thrilling stuff, especially for the marketers, who will not have to do much in the way of puffing hype before next year's Ashes series.

One of Pietersen's great triumphs this week was that he managed to get the assortment of drunks, cynics, skivers, scoundrels, gamblers and geeks collectively known as the press corps buzzing with excitement. Indeed, the uplifting nature of his pre-match message did not inspire only his team. We returned and opened our laptops with something close to enthusiasm.

So it was after the match. The *Guardian* could be heard telling its office that there were three back-page leads in the first five minutes of Pietersen's victory press conference. The *Independent* had an unusual spring in its step, a mood that soon darkened when the office agreed that Pietersen's quotes demanded more space and its workload doubled. It then yearned for a return to Atherton-like obfuscation.

England captains tend to come in two types where the press are concerned. Those who are fearful of them, or at least treat the demands as a tiresome interlude to the important stuff – as I did – and those who use a press conference for their own ends. Recently, Nasser Hussain was particularly adept at understanding the need to give a good line, but no one understood the PR value of a press conference more than Tony Greig. His assertion that India had the best umpires in the world prior to his team's tour there in 1976 was a masterstroke of manipulation.

Pietersen will give better copy than any England captain since Greig, whose bullishness and sense of theatre he shares. Something to do with background, I suppose. A captain of a decidedly more English hue tried something similar after beating Australia 3–1 in 1985. David Gower thought that the West Indies captain would be 'quaking in his boots' before England's winter tour of the Caribbean. But this was intended as a quip and nothing in the manner of Gower's statement suggested he believed anything other than the ensuing 'blackwash' was a possibility.

The danger with opening your mouth too readily, especially if the brain has not been put into gear beforehand, is that you will say something silly that will come back to haunt. Greig's faux pas came when he said that he intended to make West Indies 'grovel'. Coming from a white South African, this carried unpleasant over-tones and was used as a motivating tool by Clive Lloyd.

Rather bold foolishness than timidity, though. When England went to Australia in 2002–03, the message was that they were hoping to compete. This was greeted with scorn Down Under. At the end of the 2006–07 Ashes series, after his team had been thrashed 5–0, Andrew Flintoff was asked whether the expectations on England before the series had been too high. Flintoff agreed. The message was hardly a confident one.

In Australia, when expectations and results diverge they do not dampen down the former, they do something about the latter. Ricky Ponting and his team went away after losing the Ashes in 2005 and worked their butts off to make sure that it would not happen again, but Glenn McGrath still predicted 5–0. He was right, too.

Where Pietersen scores over most of the recent incumbents of the England captaincy is that the Australians do not so much respect him as fear him. As one of a handful of players to have sent Shane Warne on to the defensive – as he did when Warne was forced to bowl Ashley Giles-like, two feet outside leg stump in Adelaide two winters ago – the Australians know that Pietersen will back up his press conferences with appropriate action on the field.

It was Mike Denness who once received an envelope from Australia marked 'Mike Denness, England cricketer'. Inside, the letter simply stated: 'Should this reach you, the post office clearly thinks more of your ability than I do.' There is no chance of that happening to Pietersen, one reason why his optimism where the Ashes are concerned will be respected Down Under. For his sake, and for ours in the press box, he should keep on singing.

The Times, 14 August 2008

Kevin Pietersen Learns from Mike Brearley

The odd couple. It was an incongruous sight on the flight to Mohali to see Kevin Pietersen sitting next to Mike Brearley. Brearley, looking every inch the university professor – white-haired, scruffy blue sweater, cords and Hush Puppies – next to the personification of the modern international sportsman, Pietersen, wearing his Vodafone (but not for much longer) tracksuit, noise-emitting earphones and iPod, playing, no doubt, his pop-star wife's latest offering.

Can there have been two more different England captains? Brearley: quiet, contemplative, bookish, tactically supreme but always aware of having to justify his place as a batsman. Pietersen: outwardly confident and brash, the best player in the team by some distance but learning the 'captaincy thing', as he once referred to it, as he goes along.

With his 'degree in people' (something Rodney Hogg, the former Australian fast bowler, attributed to Brearley) nobody would have been better suited to accompanying Pietersen on the long flight north. Brearley would have trodden carefully, knowing exactly how Pietersen would have been feeling on the day after the defeat in the first Test match in Chennai. In itself, becoming only the third England captain after Norman Yardley and David Gower to declare and lose is not a problem, but having the fourth highest successful run chase in history against your name is not great for the CV.

I chatted to Brearley on the morning of the fifth day in Chennai and we both agreed that it was the kind of day you lived for as a captain, the knowledge that you could make a difference but also that awful, nagging feeling in the pit of your stomach that you might mess it up. So Brearley would have been aware of the angst that Pietersen would have been feeling on that flight. Equally, there would have been no better brain for Pietersen to tap into for an insight into how he might have done things differently. It would have been good to talk.

Had I been sitting in Brearley's place, what would I have said in reply to the inevitable question, 'How did I do?' I would have first recalled the numerous days when I felt I got things wrong. How could I not have helped to find a way to dismiss Danny Morrison, cricket's biggest rabbit, as he batted for two sessions against us in Auckland in 1997 to save a Test? How did West Indies, on a shocking pitch in Trinidad in 1998, chase successfully on the final day to win? Captaincy is partly about making mistakes. On any given day, a captain will make hundreds of decisions, some more important than others, and he cannot get them all right. The key is to learn but to try not to torment yourself and wonder: 'What if?'

I don't think Pietersen got things quite right on the final day in Chennai. I felt he was too concerned with saving boundaries at the start. Was this a reflection of England's caution the day before? Yuvraj Singh, for instance, was allowed to get off the mark with a push to deep point. When Andrew Flintoff, rightly, was brought back to attack him early on, the deep-set field did not help Pietersen to keep the left-hander on strike.

To give a small example of how the desire to stop boundaries impinged on the need to get wickets: in the first session, Monty Panesar went over the wicket to Sachin Tendulkar to bowl into the rough. There was a man at deep square leg saving the four and one at square leg stopping the single. Fine. Tendulkar tried a risky slog-sweep out of the rough. He missed. Immediately, the square leg went back to deep mid-wicket and the next ball Tendulkar eased it to where the man had been and scampered up the other end.

Tendulkar's game plan was to play in a risk-free manner, nudging into the gaps, and the 'in-out' field (close catchers and boundary savers) allowed him to do this without taking many chances. It was easier, surely, in those conditions to work the ball around rather than hit over the top. As a result, there was never any sense that England had control in the field, the singles flowed and, with a left-hander and right-hander at the crease, this made it difficult for the spinners to settle.

Peter Moores, the head coach, defended Pietersen on the day after the game, reflecting primarily on his positive attitude in returning to India: 'He remained completely positive about the trip from Day One and that helped us get into a very good mindset,' said Moores.

Captaincy, for sure, is as much about leadership off the field as tactical nous on it and so far Pietersen has been an outstanding leader of men. Not everything went wrong tactically, either. Pietersen did as well as he could – staying calm and trying to take the sting out of the situation – under the onslaught from Virender Sehwag on the fourth evening.

'He tried just about everything on that last day, changing the fields, changing the bowlers and on a day like that there are always people going to say you might have done something different,' said Moores. But did he try everything? Not once, for example, did Graeme Swann bowl round the wicket to Tendulkar. Not once did England veer from the in-out field to a more traditional squeezing field, forcing the batsmen to hit over the top. When you have five sessions to bowl out a team, you want to have come off the park knowing that every option has been exhausted.

Maybe it was written in the stars that Mumbai's favourite son would hit the winning runs and a less rigid tactical approach would not have made any difference. But as a captain, you still want to feel you got things right. Even so, the biggest lesson Pietersen can learn from defeat is how quickly momentum can change in a Test match and how dangerous it is for a team to retreat into their shell. It is said that the best captains produce teams that play in their image. If England's meandering fourth-day performance reflected their captain, then Pietersen has been fooling us all along.

But any criticisms of Pietersen's tactics on the last day should be tempered by the knowledge of how inexperienced he is. The match in Chennai was only his second Test in charge. One of the problems identified in the Schofield report after the 5–0 whitewash in Australia in 2006–07, now gathering dust somewhere in the ECB vaults, was one of leadership. Given that the contracted England players play so few county games, there is precious little opportunity for them to gain any meaningful captaincy experience. They come to international cricket fully prepared from a playing point of view; totally unprepared for leadership.

And what help within the set-up can Pietersen expect? As he looks around the team for advice at a sticky moment in the game, who is there to guide him? Paul Collingwood, by his own admission when he stood down from the one-day job, was unsuited to the demands of captaincy; Flintoff has enough on his plate, bowling his overs and those of others, which leaves Andrew Strauss. And on the sidelines, everything is catered for – batting coach, bowling coach, physical conditioners, masseurs – but nobody to help Pietersen in what Brearley called the art of captaincy.

Pietersen has generally made an outstanding start as England captain, but the last day in Chennai also illustrated how much he has to learn. There were echoes of Brearley in Pietersen's perform-ance, but it is the sage's captaincy, not his batting, that Pietersen must aim to emulate.

The Times, 18 December 2008

Kevin Pietersen: Big Gamble That Failed When the Going Got Tough

When Kevin Pietersen was appointed England captain, it seemed to be an enormous gamble that was likely to end in tears. Nobody, though, could have predicted the speed with which Pietersen's captaincy has imploded, nor the scale of the fallout. Barely five months into the job, he has gone and has taken the coach, Peter Moores, with him.

The departure of the two men, and the appointment of Andrew Strauss in Pietersen's place, announced in a statement last night, will raise questions about the competence of English cricket's decision-makers.

What a week. From a snippet about the coach's future, dropped into a conversation with a national newspaper on New Year's Eve by a disgruntled player, a story developed of a coach and captain with little or no professional relationship and a team divided.

The difficulties between Pietersen and Moores were common knowledge. They first surfaced last winter in New Zealand when Pietersen was one of a number of players who felt that Moores's training methods were over the top and that he was 'challenging' the senior players in a disruptive way. Before Pietersen accepted the captaincy, the two had clear-the-air talks, which resulted in Pietersen announcing that the two could work together and that they were now 'singing from the same hymn sheet'.

One business leader I talked to at the time, however, described Pietersen as the type of captain who would be all right when things were going well, but likely to implode if things started to go wrong. And in India, although certain aspects of the trip were a personal triumph for the captain, the team did not win a game, losing the one-day series 5–0 and the Test series 1–0. After India scored 387 to win the first Test in Chennai, the word got out that Pietersen felt short-changed by the tactical advice on offer. Hugh Morris, the managing director of the England team, was aware of the differences between the two, and Pietersen was known to have discussed the matter with Giles Clarke, the ECB chairman.

Once the story gathered pace that Pietersen could not work with Moores, neither went out of his way to deny the rift or reaffirm the promises of co-operation that had accompanied Pietersen's elevation to the top job. Moores said nothing, while Pietersen merely said the situation was 'unhealthy' and needed resolving quickly. Pietersen had, in effect, flexed his muscles, sure of his own power.

Pietersen's mistake was to stay on holiday in South Africa, instead of returning once the rift became public. By not coming home at the first opportunity, his attitude towards the captaincy was revealed as casual.

In his absence, Morris has spent the last few days canvassing the reaction of Pietersen's team-mates. Most of the players like Moores and think that he is a decent and honourable man, but they have reservations that he is the right man to take them to the next level. As for Pietersen, he will now have learnt an expensive lesson: that the players do not always say to a captain's face what they actually think.

And so the story moved again, this time against Pietersen. By the time the ECB's executive board met by teleconference call on Tuesday evening, the mood had hardened against the England captain. While the directors came to view Moores's position as untenable, because he had 'lost' the dressing-room, they were also determined not to allow a new, inexperienced and – let's be honest – foreign captain to decide who the ECB should hire and fire. By the end of the meeting, the ECB was determined to sack both.

Then came the final, dramatic day. First, news spread that Pietersen had resigned. Technically, this was false: Pietersen did not resign in the morning, but his insistence that he could not lead the team under the present management was taken as a *de facto* resignation by his employers. The ECB had called Pietersen's bluff. Pietersen now balked, and refused to carry out his threat to resign until later in the day.

News organisations carried stories of the departures of both men before backtracking, while the ECB denied all knowledge of any resignations. Then Strauss was seen at Lord's with Geoff Miller, the national selector, and when news came of a 6pm press conference, the jigsaw was in place.

By the end of the day, England had a new captain and no head coach. Strauss could not be more different from Pietersen. The sadness is that he doesn't have his predecessor's intuitive brilliance. Pietersen, as a captain, was an outrageous gamble, but there had been signs that he might pull it off. Now, we shall never know.

The Times, 8 January 2009

Andrew Strauss Must Heal England's Rifts

The bulldozers and tractors were out in force yesterday at The Oval when Andrew Strauss was announced as England's new captain. The outfield was undergoing what looked like a complete facelift to incorporate a new drainage system and floodlights. On the day England lost a captain and a head coach – both effectively sacked only five months after agreeing that they could work together for the benefit of English cricket – it was tempting to see in The Oval's condition and the unavailability of Lord's (the banqueting manager was on holiday, apparently) a metaphor for English cricket: forever tearing itself apart and unable to function.

What the downfall of Kevin Pietersen and Peter Moores has shown is just how big a job Strauss has on his hands. It is not just that the team are underperforming – there have been victories only against lower-ranked opposition in the 18 months that Moores has been in charge – but that they are hopelessly divided. Without these divisions, it would have been impossible for a seemingly innocuous story eight days ago to balloon into a monster, devouring the captain and the head coach in the process.

Hugh Morris, the managing director of England cricket, said as much in the key sentence of his short statement yesterday: he said that the ECB had accepted Pietersen's resignation, which was delivered as late as 4.45pm, because otherwise it would become 'impossible to restore dressing-room unity'. In fact, the board had decided on Tuesday evening [6 January] of the need for a fresh start and had decided then to relieve him and Moores of their duties. Pietersen jumped before he was pushed.

Strauss has two immediate tasks on the tour to the West Indies that starts on 21 January, outside of improving results, and both are interwoven: to reintegrate Pietersen into the team after what has been a massive blow to his ego and to heal the dressing-room divisions. Before making his recommendations to the board, Morris canvassed opinion among the players and while he found universal admiration for Pietersen's greatness as a player, such sentiments did not extend to his personality or leadership.

It is no secret that Andrew Flintoff does not like Pietersen. Flintoff, although no longer harbouring leadership ambitions, carries a good number of players along with him, while Strauss has been known to query if not Pietersen's actions then certainly his motives. So when Pietersen flexed his muscles by effectively demanding Moores's removal, there was little support. Strauss now has the unenviable task of trying to harness his two biggest names and two biggest match-winners for the benefit of the team. If he does not do that, his tenure, like Pietersen's, will be a short one.

This will not be easy, now that Pietersen has been made aware that he did not carry the dressing-room as he thought he did. And now that everyone else knows this, too, this is a very public humiliation for him. He will feel diminished next time he walks into the dressing-room and he will also feel personally let down by the likes of Flintoff and Stephen Harmison, players he made a great show of showering praise on when he accepted the job. When an ego as big as Pietersen's is punctured in such a spectacular way, who knows what the consequences?

Yesterday, Strauss was given two pieces of good news in his quest to bring some ballast to a sinking ship. First, Pietersen reaffirmed in the strongest possible terms, according to ECB sources, his desire to represent England in all forms of the game. Pietersen needs the kudos that international cricket brings, and he is smart enough to know that without it, his value would quickly shrink.

Second, Strauss has a much better chance of getting Pietersen onside now that Moores has been relieved of his duties. There is no doubt that the loss of three captains and modest results have not helped Moores hold on to his job, but there is no doubt also that the biggest reason for his removal is the fear of Pietersen inhabiting the same dressing-room as someone whom he would perceive as being responsible for his sacking. After a divorce, distance is a good thing.

The departure, then, of Moores and Pietersen from positions of responsibility could strengthen England in the medium term. Rather get the problems out of the way now, with six Tests (scheduled) against West Indies, before Australia arrive, than defer them down the line and have them blow up on the eve of English cricket's most eagerly awaited rivalry. And in Strauss, England have given an opportunity to a man who always looked, to some of us, the likeliest candidate to succeed Michael Vaughan.

Moores's removal is harsh in the sense that he is a decent, hard-working and loyal man, who has behaved throughout this past week with great dignity. Nor should it be forgotten that he inherited something of a disaster: a team that had been whitewashed in Australia, in which discipline had broken down and in which factions were rife. But he failed to arrest the decline and the divisions, as showcased in the last week, have got worse. Pietersen by his very nature exacerbated them; it is to be hoped that Strauss, the moderator, may heal them.

In a sense, Moores fell victim to the cult of the coach. High profile, with salaries to match, coaches are now expected to be alchemists, turning dust into gold at the tap of a keyboard. It is depressing that a bunch of England cricketers were looking to find fault with someone else for their own poor performances. Any captain who blames a coach for not defending a target on a wearing pitch is pretty feeble.

For the moment, England do not have a head coach, although the ECB has indicated a desire to find one before the winter is out. The best first move that Strauss could make is to not ask for one. After all, with a batting coach, bowling coach, fielding coach, and computer analyst, how many coaches does a team need?

The Times, 8 January 2009

Cut-out-and-keep Recipes for Alastair Cook to Follow

One of the least remarked upon conclusions of the now dust-laden, moth-eaten Schofield report into the 2006–07 Ashes defeat was the captaincy conundrum. How, said Schofield, can England expect to produce good leaders when, because of their absence from county cricket, the best players are no longer getting any meaningful captaincy experience? It was a prescient point.

With Andrew Strauss lukewarm about Bangladesh, England have earmarked Alastair Cook for the job. He has little to no experience of leading and is unlikely to get any before England come calling. As a result, the management team, fretting about 'succession planning', are aware that they have to find a way of improving Cook's leadership skills.

I am sceptical as to how well such skills can be taught or learnt, and am certain that a feel for the game, in any tactical sense, is either present or not. But there is no harm in aiming for self-improvement and so, in the spirit of generosity, I offer Cook an annotated version of a talk given by Mike Brearley (if not the best

England captain, then surely the man who has thought about captaincy more and written about it better than anyone else) at the Festival of Free Thinking in Gateshead last month:

1) *Good captains must be true to themselves*
Brearley quotes Joseph Conrad, the writer, referring to a sea captain of his acquaintance, who, although normally conservative by nature, suddenly changed course. Suddenly he 'hankered after the meretricious glory of a showy performance' but 'through a touch of self-seeking, that modest artist of solid merit became untrue to his temperament'. Naturally, he failed in his task.

As a young captain of England, and a little adrift, I looked around for a role model and fell upon Allan Border, who had been in an analogous situation with Australia some years before. Initially slavish adherence to his style brought upon myself the sobriquet 'Captain Grumpy', which was also Border's and which might have suited his temperament, but certainly did not suit mine. Best to stick to who you are.

2) *Narcissists make dreadful captains*
Brearley identifies two kinds of narcissist: the first is the glory seeker, the addict to power and control, who sees success only in terms of what it means for himself; the second is someone for whom the desire to be loved and admired becomes too overwhelming and paralyses their decision-making.

An example of the former is Napoleon, who saw himself as above others but was undone by his vanity and self-regard, the needs of his men secondary to the pursuit of glory. Brearley used an unnamed former England captain as an example of the second kind: this was a captain who dithered and vacillated and consulted endlessly, but could not make a decision for fear of how it would look. When, in one match, a tailender showed him up for scoring slowly even though this benefited the team, the captain was resentful of the, as he saw it, humiliation and criticised the tailender for his actions.

Both are completely different characters but both are united by the need to be seen to be wonderful, which distracts them from the task in hand and the needs of their team. No doubt Brearley would not have recommended Kevin Pietersen for the captaincy of England.

3) Good captains encourage others to think for themselves

'Give a man a fish and you help him for a very short while; teach him the art of fishing and he can help himself all his life; teach him to make his own fishing tackle and you've helped him to not only become self-supportive but also self-reliant and independent.' After the suffocating experience that was Peter Moores's schoolmasterly regime, it has been the central theme of Andrew Strauss's captaincy. Brearley would approve.

4) Good captains treat players as individuals

Brearley was fortunate to have at his disposal one of the great opening bowling partnerships, but few have been as dissimilar as Ian Botham and Bob Willis. Brearley would goad, prod and provoke Botham. 'My aunt can bowl faster than you,' he told Botham frequently. But Willis, despite appearances, was a sensitive soul who needed reminding constantly of his ability. Obvious maybe, but when ignored the consequences can be dramatic, as they were between David Gower and Graham Gooch.

5) A good captain's skin is neither too thin, nor too thick

It is often said that leaders need thick skins, but they also need skins thin enough to allow the anxieties of their team-mates to register, but thick enough to contain them within, without then betraying their fears to others. Good captains neither fret nor flap under pressure, but nor are they insensitive to the situation.

According to Brearley, Frank Worrell gave such a display of containment during the nail-baiting conclusion to the Lord's Test of 1963, when England, with a broken-armed Colin Cowdrey at the crease, were closing on victory. With Brian Close winding up Wes Hall to fever pitch, Worrell remained calm and impassive, 'almost removed from the storm and tempests of drama'. It allowed his team to remain controlled, focused and disciplined. Michael Vaughan had those qualities in 2005, too.

6) *Good captains recognise that good teams are like families*
The best teams might give an impression of unity, but more often than not they are like families who bicker and argue, and a good captain allows, even encourages, disparate voices to be heard. The great Australia team circa 1995–2001 was a superb example: Shane Warne disliked(s) Steve Waugh and Adam Gilchrist intently, but there was enough mutual respect to paper over the character clashes. Mark Taylor, a fine Australia captain, managed a dressing-room full of flaming egos brilliantly: when they took the field they gave an impression of unity.

7) *A good captain doesn't demand respect, he earns it*
Sporting dressing-rooms are notoriously disrespectful to authority and a captain must acknowledge this lack of deference and see it as a strength. Just because he wears the stripes, he cannot assume he will be respected, because, said Brearley, 'the name on the box is often not the same as the contents inside it'. A captain earns respect through his performances, his decision-making and his qualities as

a human being. It can, as Cook will find out, be a long, hard and lonely road.

The Times, 3 December 2009

Andrew Strauss Wrecks England Selection Policy

The first time that Ricky Ponting took a break from the Australia captaincy he was publicly censured by Steve Waugh, his predecessor. 'The Australia captain is the benchmark of resilience and mental toughness,' Waugh said, and ought to be seen to be 'almost indestructible'.

As one of the most cussed performers ever to pull on a baggy green cap, Waugh was speaking from a position of strength, although it did not affect Ponting, who has continued to take what Australian observers have come to term his 'annual mid-summer break'. He was at it again last summer, going home at the end of the Ashes for a couple of weeks before returning for the fourth one-day international at Lord's, refreshed and ready to contemplate another gruelling few months on the international treadmill.

Andrew Strauss has argued recently that he is more in step with the modern reality of international cricket than his predecessors, who, with the exception of Michael Vaughan, have criticised him for missing the tour of Bangladesh next month, so he can spend a couple of months in Australia with his wife (who is Australian) and his young children. 'If you accept the principle that resting players is a good thing, then the captain should not be exempt from that,' said Strauss.

This represents a fundamentally different view of leadership from Waugh, who believed absolutely in a top-down, hierarchical approach. Strauss, from everything that he has said and done, embraces a different philosophy, a more inclusive style of management. When asked before the Johannesburg Test last week what were the secrets to his early success as captain, Strauss talked of removing what he thought previously to be a 'top heavy' style of leadership. Strauss's England, we are led to believe, is a happy commune, where the most junior man's thoughts carry equal weight to the captain's and where the leader's actions are not to be divorced from the rest.

No doubt, though, the junior mess were not asked what they thought of their captain pulling rank and missing what is known on the circuit to be the least glamorous and most arduous of tours. It is a bit like India 30 years ago, one correspondent said to me recently when I asked about what was in store for those of us who are going, and he did not mean that in a complimentary way. We can safely assume that, when Strauss broached the subject, it was not a case of 'hands up who wants to miss out on Bangladesh, lads?'

England's policy towards modern touring was set by Duncan Fletcher, the former coach, at the end of the summer of 2001. It was a policy that was carefully thought out and has been the cornerstone of decision-making since. It came about when Darren Gough and Alec Stewart asked to miss the first half of England's winter that year (a tour of India), but to be included in the second half (a jolly to New Zealand).

Fletcher had a problem on his hands: both were senior, influential players – Stewart a former captain – both were match-winners and Stewart had not missed any international cricket by choice since his debut in 1989. In one sense, it was a reasonable request, but everyone knew that they wanted to miss the 'hardship' tour (England had not toured India since 1993 and were unaware that the 'hardship' no longer existed) in favour of one that offered scenery, vineyards and, no doubt, some easy win bonuses. Stewart was also worried about the match-fixing issue, in which he had been unfairly implicated two years before.

Fletcher, who recognised that every decision has unintended consequences, took soundings and decided that he would allow both players to miss either leg (Tests or one-day internationals) of each tour, but not the whole of one tour. In other words, they could play in the one-day internationals in India and New Zealand, or the Tests in both countries, but they could not miss the whole of India and expect their place back in New Zealand.

This was a brave call, given that England were a moderate team at the time, and that a tour to India without Gough and Stewart held little promise of success. But Fletcher knew that, with the importance of the sub-continent to modern-day cricket, he had to find a way of ensuring that England's finest did not routinely pass on the delights of India, Pakistan and Sri Lanka as they used to do. Not only would it weaken England's chances of competing there, it would cause, in the longer term, undue strife in the dressing-room.

Stewart decided against going at all and ceded his place to James Foster. Gough played in the one-day internationals in India and New Zealand, but missed the Tests in both countries. An important principle had been laid down: no matter how big the name, picking and choosing tours was not acceptable. And England competed well in the Tests in India without Gough and Stewart, showing that no one is indispensable.

By touring South Africa and missing the whole of the tour of Bangladesh, Strauss has shattered that policy and laid the foundations for a future in which players pick and choose according to where they fancy spending their winters. Would it have been too much for the England captain to keep faith with a policy that has worked pretty well by missing the one-day games in Dubai and Bangladesh and playing in only two Tests there? After all, two Tests, taking in about three weeks in all, is hardly the stuff from which exhaustion is made. Strauss played just 113 days' cricket, by my reckoning, last year (in 1995 Mark Waugh, brother of Steve, played 170), although I accept that the percentage of international cricket (i.e. high-pressure cricket) is much higher than it was before.

Assuming that Strauss arrived in Bangladesh two weeks before the first Test, he would still have a break of five weeks now, and, given his absence from the World Twenty20, would have a further seven weeks off before reporting for duty a week before the Bangladesh return tour to England. Twelve weeks off in 15 would seem, by most people's arrangements, to be remarkably generous, regardless of the pressures of the job.

Instead, by asking his team to do something he is not prepared to do, Strauss has not only dismissed the first principles of Waugh, he has also undermined England's policy on touring, based upon the principle of fairness, that has worked for the best part of a decade. Mind you, as Graham Onions found out in Johannesburg, fairness is not necessarily part of the new-England lexicon.

The Times, 21 January 2010

Demanding Strauss Sets Impressive Standards for Rest to Follow

To both men it must seem like an age ago. When Andrew Strauss introduced himself to Darren Gough as a Test cricketer for the first time, Gough gave him no more than a cursory nod in return. Thought him to be the new Vodafone representative, the Yorkshireman said subsequently.

With his stiff collars, Windsor-knotted ties and clean-cut dress sense, Strauss has lost none of the qualities that fooled Gough into thinking him more estate agent-cum-salesman than international cricketer. What he has gained in the 18 months since he took on the England captaincy full time, though, is a huge amount of stature.

It is difficult to think of anybody else captaining England right now, so sure is Strauss's hold on the title. In a difficult summer – although surely some of the self-righteousness in the last week has been overplayed – he has handled himself and his team with immense poise. His hoarse voice at the end of the final one-day international on Wednesday [22 September] betrayed the stress that he has put himself under, but at no stage has that affected his batting or his demeanour.

Calmness and strength of mind have characterised his off-field performance throughout the fractious one-day series against Pakistan, as he played a central role in keeping the more militant members of his team on track in the wake of Ijaz Butt's slurs. As public and media opinion swings wildly back and forth, it is not always easy to chart a straight course in such turbulent times, but Strauss has managed it impressively.

He is building an enviable record as captain, too. Only four defeats in 27 Test matches suggests that his toughness as an opening batsman has rubbed off on the rest, so that, as with all good leaders, the team reflects something of the man. England 2010 may not have the flair of Michael Vaughan's 2005 team, but they will not be as flaky as Andrew Flintoff's flops in 2006–07, either. Nor has he let the job affect his own game, his average with the stripes a good six runs better than without them.

The context is important, too, since it is not so long ago that England were reeling from the double sackings administered to Kevin Pietersen and Peter Moores. Since then, the blips have been few and far between – heavy defeats in Jamaica, Johannesburg and at Headingley small stains on an otherwise blemish-free record. Nobody yet has managed to slip any kind of wedge between him and Andy Flower, the team director. It is a terrific partnership.

As Australia looms, it is essential that the team have confidence in its leader, and he has confidence in them. To that end, the summer's six successive series victories are vital. Building up to the Ashes – as the 2005 squad did – with a sustained period of success has enabled Strauss to spend quality time with the same bunch of players. He should know them inside out by now; their foibles, their likes and dislikes and their insecurities. Only two players, Monty Panesar and Chris Tremlett, have not been involved with the squad throughout the summer.

Likewise, the team know how Strauss thinks and how demanding he can be. One aspect of his captaincy has struck me above all – a desire constantly to improve, never to stand still or rest on his laurels. You can see this with his own batting in one-day cricket, which is now a far cry from the one-dimensional, crabby player of before. He sets exacting standards in all areas – personal, physical and cricketing – and his players know that he will not tolerate slackers.

Of course, there are and have been things that grate. His failure to tour Bangladesh last winter was a dereliction of duty and he sometimes needs the opposition to wave the white flag before he goes on to the attack. One former England captain this summer said of him: 'He's got everything but a grasp of tactics.' But anyone in a position of responsibility knows that pleasing people all the time is both impossible and irrelevant. His team play for him and that is all that counts.

England, then, are well placed after a successful and sometimes fractious summer. Strauss has had to look his team in the eye recently to ask them to play for him, and his players have watched in admiration as he has led, literally, from the front. This mutual respect is vital. For no matter how strong the bonds that tie a captain and his team together, a tour of Australia will test them like no other. Why is that? Turn to Mike Brearley, a man utterly comfortable in his own skin normally, but who felt the need to grow a beard Down Under to prove his manliness.

Even Brearley, the great thinker, the great man-manager, felt his equilibrium threatened there. 'The pitches are hard, the weather is hard, the crowds are hard and the Aussies are hard. There is no soft anywhere. That means you have to be hard, too,' he said of captaining in Australia.

In his short time as England captain, Strauss has proved himself as a batsman, leader and human being. English cricket could not be in better hands.

The Times, 24 September 2010

2

The Stanford Affair

Reading through these pieces now, they have a rather surreal tone. Was it really possible that an American 'financier' hoodwinked English cricket, offered the players a million-dollar-a-man match, cavorted around with the players' wives before falling foul of the Securities and Exchange Commission? Did it really happen?

It did, although historians will look back on the episode with a mixture of wry amusement and disbelief. It was a period that belonged to another age, of course, what might be called a Lehman Brothers age, when money was cheap and regulation lax.

I can remember the ECB holding an off-the-record briefing for correspondents in the summer that they signed the contract with Stanford. Just beforehand, the magazine Private Eye *had written a damning assessment of Stanford's business activities. Mike Selvey and I asked the executives of the ECB what they thought of the piece. They had neither seen it, nor did they care much. They had done their due diligence, they said, and they were happy that he could pay up.*

He could pay and did – at least until the authorities caught up with him. But through it all there was little consideration given to English cricket's reputation or, indeed, any fundamental critique of what playing for England meant or what it was all about. In this instance it was solely about money. And if there is one common theme running through this chapter and the one to follow – the rise of Twenty20 – it is how blind administrators, former players and some commentators could become when the dollar signs flashed in front of their eyes.

Lord's Leaping as Allen Stanford Confirms Twenty20 Jackpot

'The only thing I like about rich people is their money,' Lady Astor said, and for the moment the ECB agrees. Not long ago, it would have sprinted across the road to avoid a man such as Allen Stanford, who is rich, American and a self-confessed hater of Test cricket. Yesterday at Lord's, the home of cricket, the governing body embraced him. The reasons? Well, there were 147.5 million of them.

It was confirmed yesterday that England and a Stanford All-Stars XI will play five Twenty20 matches for $20 million (about £10 million) each over the next five years. As revealed exclusively in *The Times* yesterday, the split will be $11 million for the winning players, $1 million for the remaining squad players and $1 million for the management team. The $7 million that remains will be shared between the ECB and the West Indies Cricket Board (WICB). A further $47.5 million has been pledged by Stanford for five annual quadrangular Twenty20 tournaments, which will be announced in the next few days.

As divorce lawyers would confirm, once huge sums of money are involved, things tend to get nasty. Despite the manoeuvrings of the Test specialists, those not involved in Antigua will get nothing. *The Times* can also reveal that serious pressure was brought to bear on the England players on the eve of the third Test against New Zealand at Trent Bridge to sign off the deal, amid acrimonious talks between the ECB and the Professional Cricketers' Association, which was representing the players.

An email from David Collier, the chief executive of the ECB, was sent to the players' representatives the day before the Test holding the players responsible if the deal did not go ahead. In the end the players relented, giving away £1 million in image rights. Even so, as late as 9.45pm on Monday [9 June] the agreement was under threat after the WICB attempted to change its terms at the last minute.

So when Stanford's helicopter landed on the nursery ground shortly after lunchtime yesterday, it was the culmination of an idea, the negotiations for which had long been in existence, but whose time had come. Lord's, perhaps, had not hosted anything like it. Stanford emerged, looked out over the historic surroundings and waved, George W. Bush-style, to the assembled onlookers, including ECB officials, who had gathered in force. Descending the steps, Stanford did what politicians in the United States do when on stage, pointing and smiling, as if to fool people that they have genuine friends in the crowd.

For the moment, the ECB is the best friend he will have. The key players, Giles Clarke, the ECB chairman, and Collier, waited at the foot of the steps in obeisance, their hair buffeted by the helicopter's blades. Then there were handshakes all round and even a billionaire's arm around the shoulder for Collier. Rarely have such levels of fawning been seen.

Then it was off into the Nursery Pavilion for the press conference. It was decked out in black, with the logo 'Twenty20 for 20' emblazoned on the screen at the front of the stage. Various aphorisms had been daubed on the walls to chime with the idea that the winners would receive almost all and the losers nothing. Rudyard Kipling was there ('If you can make one heap of all your winnings and risk it all on one turn of the pitch-and-toss'), as was the South African proverb 'no pressure, no diamonds'.

Stanford spoke of his desire to see West Indies rise from the bottom of world cricket to the top again, of the ECB's first-class

48

management team and how boring Test cricket was. Clarke, Collier and the gathered legends of the game – Sir Ian Botham, Sir Viv Richards, Curtly Ambrose, Desmond Haynes, Sir Everton Weekes and Sir Garry Sobers – and Peter Moores, the England head coach, nodded in agreement (except for the last bit, of course).

Then, as the *pièce de résistance*, a black box containing $20 million was wheeled on to the stage and the legends posed in front of it, staring longingly as if therein lay the secret of everlasting life.

In a beautiful moment, which summed up the contrasting worlds that collided yesterday afternoon, Stanford came on to the stage shortly before the press conference. He waved and smiled and was greeted with an unaccustomed silence. As he turned to go backstage, an ECB official hurried over and, in a timid, frigid kind of English way, stuck out a hand. Stanford looked at the hand for a moment and then gave the startled young lad a bear hug. There is a new man in town, and, as they say in the States, a whole new ball game.

The Times, 12 June 2008

$20 Million Twenty20 Match between England and Stanford Superstars at Risk

A personal deal between two billionaire business rivals will have to be brokered to salvage the $20 million (about £11.4 million) winner-takes-all Twenty20 match between England and the Stanford Superstars after a High Court ruling put its future in serious doubt yesterday.

Allen Stanford will have to reach some form of compromise with Denis O'Brien, the owner of Digicel, the telecommunications company and main sponsor of the West Indies Cricket Board (WICB), if the match has any chance of going ahead in Antigua on

1 November. Among those hoping that a deal will be reached are the England players who stand to pocket about £500,000 a man if they win.

The London International Court of Arbitration ruled that by officially sanctioning the match without granting commercial rights to which Digicel was entitled, the WICB was in breach of contract. The match now has unofficial status – the same as the rebel Indian Cricket League (ICL). However, Stanford's organisation insisted last night that the game would go ahead. According to sources close to Digicel, Stanford and O'Brien spoke for the first time yesterday about the dispute and a compromise appears likely, despite the bad blood between the organisations.

The court ruled that, having made all its contracted players available for a match that had been officially sanctioned, the Stanford Superstars are a West Indies representative team in all but name and therefore, as principal sponsor of Caribbean cricket, Digicel was being denied its commercial rights. Costs running into hundreds of thousands of pounds were awarded against the WICB, money it can ill-afford to lose. It cannot appeal.

The judgement raises the possibility that Stanford will decide to forgo the hassle of further negotiations, withdraw his support and that the match will be cancelled, although that prospect has been described as improbable by Stanford's organisation. He could argue that the incompetence of the WICB would leave him within his rights to do so, but surely there is too much at stake – money and pride – for such an outcome.

More likely is that hastily arranged negotiations between all four parties – Stanford, WICB, the England and Wales Cricket Board (ECB) and Digicel – will find a way round the impasse. The ECB's executive board met yesterday to discuss the matter, although it insists that, as an outsider to the arbitration process, its position remains unaltered. And while Stanford's organisation was not in a position to respond publicly to a judgement it had not seen in full, negotiations with Digicel were continuing.

If the game is to go ahead, one of three things must happen: first, the Stanford Superstars must be seen not to be a West Indies team. This would mean Stanford pitting a substantially weakened team against England. He could, alternatively, rebrand his team as an international Superstars XI.

Secondly, the match could still go ahead as a private arrangement between Stanford and the ECB. This, though, would give the tournament the same status as the rebel ICL, against which Giles Clarke, the ECB chairman, has been stridently opposed. Even in these days of money over principle, Clarke could not agree to that – nor would the players, given the potential pariah status that may result.

Thirdly, and by far the most likely option, Stanford and Digicel will come to a commercial arrangement whereby Digicel allows the game to go ahead in return for the kind of commercial and branding rights to which it is entitled. The ball is now in Stanford's court.

The Times, 8 October 2008

West Indies Cricket Sinks into Further Turmoil

The West Indies Cricket Board (WICB) is discovering a harsh lesson, one that Sir Alex Ferguson learnt a few years ago when he became involved with a racehorse called Rock of Gibraltar – that the billionaires' playground is a rough place to play. Caught between the biggest of rocks and the hardest of places, between Sir Allen Stanford and Denis O'Brien – men worth, according to *Forbes* magazine recently, $2.2 billion (about £1.2 billion) each – the WICB is suddenly looking very vulnerable indeed.

It is quite some achievement to court not one but two billionaires, persuade them to dip into their cavernous pockets and then annoy them both to the extent that one (O'Brien through Digicel) has gone to court, while the other (Stanford), it has been rumoured, is prepared to do so.

Yesterday was a victory for O'Brien and although Stanford was not party to the arbitration between Digicel and the WICB, it was a defeat of sorts for him. Since billionaires do not take these things lightly, the saga, which has had as many subplots and only a little less viciousness than an Elmore Leonard thriller, has some way to run.

No sympathy needs be felt for the WICB, though, since this is a predicament entirely of its own making. Not content with pocketing millions from Digicel – a deal worth $20 million had just been extended to 2012 – it thought it could do the same with Stanford, who has already pumped, according to his own estimates, $80 million into West Indies cricket.

Since the WICB officially sanctioned the match and because part of the WICB's deal with Stanford was to make all its contracted players available, the WICB essentially sold the same set of rights twice. On top of that, Stanford previously had a commercial arrangement with Cable & Wireless, Digicel's telecommunications rival, yet the WICB could not understand why Digicel, which was always confident of the strength of its legal argument, came over all litigious.

Surely a resignation or two from those who purport to lead West Indies cricket will follow. When Stanford arrived at Lord's in midsummer and dumped $20 million in cash on the table, he did so in the presence of Dr Julian Hunte, the president of the WICB, who looked like the cat who had got the proverbial cream. It was, though, the ECB for whom Stanford saved his compliments, saying it was the best-led organisation in cricket.

He did not give his opinion of the WICB, but as the summer progressed his doubts, if they did not already exist, must have begun to grow. Embroiled in an argument over the financial where-withal of the refurbishment of the president's office in St Lucia, the chief executive of the WICB, Donald Peters, was sent on gardening leave. Tony Deyal, a corporate secretary, was also dismissed in the furore and is in dispute over the terms of his departure. Yesterday, in the London International Court of Arbitration, he gave evidence against his former employer. Surely, after yesterday's outcome, the positions of Hunte and Peters are untenable.

Those who have followed the fortunes of West Indies over the years will not be surprised at the WICB's difficulties. It does not always follow that fortunes on the field mirror competence or otherwise off it, but it surely does in the Caribbean. The inexorable decline of a once great team has been accompanied by the most inept administration in cricket. The WICB has given the clearest impression of an organisation that does not know what it is doing.

Unlike football, the involvement of billionaires is relatively new. From Rahul Dravid, publicly excoriated last year by Vijay Mallya, India's richest man, over the performance of Bangalore Royal Challengers in the Indian Premier League, to the hapless if well-meaning WICB, cricket is discovering that it is an involvement that comes with certain risks attached.

The Times, 8 October 2008

Stanford Game Saved to Put England Back on Millionaires' Row

A series of transatlantic phone calls between the billionaires at the head of two warring factions was necessary to ensure that England's winner-takes-all $20 million Twenty20 match in Antigua on 1 November will go ahead as planned. Allen Stanford, head of the eponymous financial services group, and Denis O'Brien, majority owner of Digicel, spoke to each other for the first time about the conflict on Tuesday [7 October] and again on Wednesday, after which they agreed that the wrangling should stop. Then, as billionaires do, they left it to the lawyers to sort out the fine detail.

Although these details will only emerge when the West Indies Cricket Board (WICB) ratifies the deal – and it was meeting in St Lucia to do so yesterday evening – they will be based around the three proposals put forward by Digicel on 11 September. Stanford had already agreed to two of them, namely that Cable & Wireless, Digicel's competitor in the region, would not be brought on board as a tournament sponsor and that Digicel's legal costs would be discharged.

Now the final sticking point – the issue of Digicel branding on the Stanford players' shirts – has been settled. The compromise is likely to allow Stanford's team to wear their distinctive all-black shirts but emblazoned with the Digicel logo. Digicel will also be granted the same branding rights as it would get for a normal one-day international in the Caribbean.

Although Stanford pronounced himself pleased with the process and the outcome, these negotiations were extremely acrimonious and this represents a significant climbdown for him. Digicel has been granted its full commercial and branding rights and, according to reports, only the first three years of the five-year deal have been agreed upon.

Subject to the WICB ratification, though, the match will now go ahead – much to Stanford's relief and, no doubt, England's players', who stand to become dollar millionaires overnight if they win the encounter.

The Times, 10 October 2008

Allen Stanford Builds Legacy in Antigua

Not so much a big fish in a small pond as a whale in a puddle. Allen Stanford's wealth dwarfs Antigua's annual gross domestic product by a cool three-quarters of a billion US dollars. Beyond its shores, Antigua might be known only for producing outstanding cricketers, offshore banks, gambling, tourism and politicians who have sailed not so much close to the wind as into the eye of the storm, but Stanford has an interest in all those areas – although he would insist his $100 million (about £63 million) investment with the ECB and the West Indies Cricket Board for five years of Twenty20 cricket is no mere gamble.

He owns an offshore and an onshore bank here, had a close association for many years with Lester Bird, the former Antigua prime minister, before falling foul of Baldwin Spencer, his successor, and is by some distance its largest private employer. Cricket, though, is his present squeeze and Twenty20 cricket at that, Stanford being as far from a convert to the longer form of the game as it is possible to be. And while his involvement in the game has yet to help to restore the region's cricketing lustre, it has not been for the lack of effort, will or funds.

The most obvious example of his passion is what is sometimes referred to – another snub in the direction of the traditionalists, this – as the SCG, not the Sydney Cricket Ground but the Stanford Cricket Ground. It is, indisputably, the nicest ground on the island, a lush-green, palm-fringed affair conveniently built next to the airport, which services Caribbean Star, Stanford's airline, on one side and the Bank of Antigua, his onshore bank, on the other. The area feels like a private fiefdom.

And for much of the first evening of this week-long event, it was a feeling confirmed whenever the cameras panned on to Stanford, smiling beatifically down from his balcony (he bears an uncanny resemblance to a jowly, middle-aged Basil Fawlty), or mixing with the crowd and cooing in the ear of bemused youngsters. As well as feeding his current obsession, this is a gilt-edged PR opportunity, for himself and his brand, in front of a global audience that his organisation estimates to be about 700 million.

He has said that the inspiration for building his ground came when he saw airport employees playing cricket on scrubland. Not so much scrub now, as a world-class facility. A facility, moreover, that is not what you might expect of a man who, in June, landed a gold-plated personalised helicopter at Lord's, trailing a crate stuffed with $20 million in his wake. It is a rather understated, homely thing – apart from the $50,000 Verdin clock that sits at the top of the pavilion. Rich men's tastes are not hidden for long.

When Stanford first decided to throw his chequebook in with the ECB, toilets, he said, were the clinching factor. After visiting the loos in the ECB offices and emerging impressed by their cleanliness (thank goodness negotiations didn't take place at Headingley), he was sure that he was dealing with a good business. If only today's distressed banks had taken the same precautions with their mortgage offers. Those of you hoping for a little graffiti or mess in the loos of Stanford's fiefdom will be disappointed: they are immaculate. The ground is, too, with hordes of workers swooping down after the final ball, so that within 20 minutes of the close of play not a scrap of litter can be seen. This is a serious operation.

In some ways, the fate of Antigua's three main grounds encapsulates the story of cricket here. The Antigua Recreation Ground, the old Test ground in the middle of St John's, a magnificent ramshackle affair that routinely staged the most atmospheric matches, has been bypassed. The ground that witnessed the emergence of Viv Richards and Curtly Ambrose, giants both, and played host to Brian Lara's twin world-record Test scores, stands as a forlorn monument to an era of West Indies cricket that has passed – and for all Stanford's largesse, is unlikely to be revisited.

Its successor, the Sir Vivian Richards Stadium, is a utilitarian, concrete bowl, built for the ICC World Cup in the middle of no man's land and is inconvenient for the working masses. It stages soulless international matches and stands as a testament to clouded thinking by those who run the game in this region.

Between what West Indies cricket once was and what it has become, Stanford saw a chasm that represented an opportunity. As families watched the opening match on Saturday [25 October] in comfort and in the knowledge that they were partaking in something vibrant, it was clear where the balance of power now lies. Cricket in the Caribbean was ripe for plucking.

The Times, 27 October 2008

English Cricket 'is one of Stanford's WAGs'

When, during the match between Middlesex and Trinidad & Tobago, the camera panned on to David Collier, the chief executive of the ECB, who was sitting on the balcony with Allen Stanford and accepting his hospitality, the picture was an uncertain one. Was that a smile or a grimace on his face? As he jiggled in his seat, with reggae blasting away in the background, was Dave busting his moves (yeah, man!) in a particularly frigid English way or was he wriggling with embarrassment? Because from what we have seen so far, the ECB has pawned the national team off for little more than a rich man's ego trip.

English cricket has become Stanford's WAG.

WAG, of course, a term coined during the football World Cup finals in Germany in 2006, does not really stand for wife and girlfriend; it stands for someone who is noteworthy only for the movements and actions of someone else; someone who is unthinkingly and uncritically admiring. An appendage, in other words. And from the moment Stanford landed his helicopter at Lord's in June, trailing his cash, with the ECB's officials fawning all over him, English cricket has been reduced to WAG status.

The Texan billionaire's canoodling with some of the England players' wives and girlfriends (who proved their WAG status by requiring others to get upset on their behalf) is the moment that has brought the issue into sharp focus, but that is the least of it. There was no intention to offend, just a bit of harmless fun. How lovely it would have been to see one of the women give him a good slap, or tweak his moustache in irritation.

Harmless, then, but once again it concentrated attention on the only person that matters this week. And don't fool yourself that it's any of the players on view. This is Stanford's show. He has a personal cameraman and at least once during every game the attention switches from the cricket (also reduced to WAG status) to Stanford as he makes a tour of his fiefdom, meeting and greeting, lifting children up and cooing in their ears and bouncing good-looking women on his knee.

Then there is his access to the England team – the team photo with the players and the right of entry to the dressing-room; a sacred place, but not this week. Just outside the dressing-room is a sign on which the photos of those allowed in are posted for security reasons. Right in the middle is Stanford. Next time you're at Lord's, why don't you knock on the door, too? After all, what is the difference, in cricketing terms, between you and Stanford? Nothing – except a few noughts on the end of your bank balance.

This is just a modern twist on an ancient tale of temples and the money men. The ECB will argue that all this was not part of the contract, part of the deal. But didn't they read the small print? When rich men get involved in sport this is usually how it ends up. I was at Old Trafford in 1989 when Michael Knighton (a pauper by Stanford's standards) dribbled his way towards the Stretford End and buried one in the bottom corner during his abortive attempt to buy Manchester United, his schoolboy dream.

Sport ought not to be like this, though. We all know that it is a business, of course, but when the action starts and the focus switches from the boardroom to the field, that is when money is supposed to be irrelevant. The playing field and the dressing-room should be two of the few remaining altars over which money has no power. The England dressing-room? You're supposed to get access to that by your talent, your dedication, your passion and willingness to chase a long-cherished dream – not by the size of your bank account. Once such a place loses its mystique, it is cheapened.

Those who run English cricket will justify their involvement with Stanford in many ways. Money is the least of it, actually, since the $3.5 million (about £2.2 million) that goes to the ECB each year is small beer. Sure, the West Indies Cricket Board needs the money more, and there is a genuine desire to help them on the part of English cricket. No, the deal with Stanford was initially about keeping England's IPL-starved cricketers sweet and then, as England and India have begun to squabble more and more, it has morphed into something more political – an attempt to shore up support from the West Indies against increasing Indian dominance.

What is the price of self-respect, though? No wonder Collier may have been squirming: he'd just realised English cricket had become a WAG. Don't worry, David, there's only four more years of bondage left.

The Times, 29 October 2008

Stanford's Twenty20 Circus Proves Worthless

The last time I witnessed an event like the Stanford Super Series was two years ago in Las Vegas. The game was poker – heads-up hold'em – and the venue was the Wynn Casino, a game and a place that exist solely because of money. Without money, poker is a pointless game. After all, how can you bluff without testing your opponent's *cojones* – his willingness to bet big? Gambling oils the wheels of Vegas, and as for the Wynn Casino, the conspicuous consumption of its owner, Steve Wynn, makes Allen Stanford look something of a miser.

There were a lot of similarities between the poker game in Vegas and the 'twenny twenny for twenny' here in Coolidge, Antigua. For a start, one of the poker players was a Texan billionaire banker, a man called Steve Beal, and his opponents were a group of professionals, some of the best players in the world, who called themselves The Corporation. The stakes were familiar, too: $20 million, the only difference being this was $20 million a day for six straight days.

In another similarity to this week, Beal's theory was to raise the stakes so high, to the point at which the professionals could not afford to lose, that it took them out of their comfort zones, so that their normal ice-cool decision-making would be skewed under pressure. And if there is a morbid fascination in watching the cricket here it is to see how cricketers cope with playing for life-changing sums. Creation of heroes is the marketing theme, but really the search is for the villain who cocks up when it matters.

There is one significant difference, though. Nobody in Vegas was under any illusion that this circus was about anything other than money. The chips – in denominations of $50,000 and $100,000 for goodness' sake – were on the table for all to see and at the end of each day the reckoning would be done. It was a dull game to watch – Beal sat all day, every day, in shades, oblivious to the world around him – and the talk around the tables was simply of dollars, not the buzz or the tactics of the game itself. After all, heads-up hold'em is to poker what Twenty20 is to cricket.

But here in Antigua there has been a curious reluctance from those involved to admit why they are here. Of the England players, only Alastair Cook, the least likely to be involved, has spoken of the true nature of this event. Meaningless, he said, without the cheque at the end of it all. He was not exactly slapped down by Peter Moores, the England head coach, for his honesty, but Moores was quick to paint a different picture: pride, the badge, honour and all that guff.

In his press conference prior to leaving for Antigua, even Kevin Pietersen, the captain, who is usually the least bashful of the players, warned his team not to clown around if they won the million bucks lest they be frowned upon at a time when the economy is collapsing. This was an understandable and mature response, but one that has had the effect of making the players even more reticent to talk about the money. As the week has progressed, each press conference has been an exercise in concocting ever more ridiculous justifications for being here, 'Good preparation for a big winter of cricket' being just about the craziest of all.

There is one other difference. The poker game between Beal and The Corporation has been going on for years. I'd lay a very large wager – not perhaps large enough to get a place at Beal's poker table, but a large one nevertheless – that the Stanford Super Series will be a one-off event.

I understand that the ECB has been horrified by the nature of the coverage it has generated and by the reaction back home. As reluctant as the players are to acknowledge the real reasons for being here, Giles Clarke, the ECB chairman, continues to insist that the prime reason for signing a five-year deal with Stanford was charity: to help the West Indies Cricket Board out of its financial problems, and to roll out the Chance to Shine campaign (cricket in schools) throughout the Caribbean. One man's charity, though, has become another man's ego trip.

If some good comes out of this week, it will be that the Stanford Series will force us to re-examine the meaning of sport. Because when you stop and think about it, when you look beyond the grand titles, the personalised helicopters, the crates of cash, the fawning ECB executives and all the hype, this week goes to the heart of what watching sport is all about. It asks the most fundamental questions of this circus, with which some of us have been involved for all our adult lives.

What is the point of it all?

Why do media moguls spend millions, sometimes a billion, hoovering up sports rights? Why will the sports editor of this newspaper send his minions forth to every corner of the world this winter, at enormous expense, to file dispatches? Why do you, the supporters, shell out sometimes vast sums, sometimes small, to follow your team? Why will sport endure long after more vacuous forms of entertainment wither on the vine?

Because it matters. Deep down we know that sport is important only because it is totally unimportant when compared with the grim news that greets us on a daily basis. But we realise that for each and every sportsman of note, they undergo, albeit unconsciously, a daily willing suspension of disbelief. They may talk of keeping it all in perspective, but for the time span of the competition, what they are engaged in is the most important thing in the world to them. It is, as George Orwell observed, war minus the shooting – sport's greatest justification; a kind of playground for grown-ups to blow off steam.

If it doesn't matter, why the nerves? Why did Michael Vaughan spend the morning of the last day of the 2005 Ashes series secretly wanting to throw up? Why the sleepless nights? Why did I once bump into Nasser Hussain, wandering around an hotel in Galle in the dead of night, fretting about his form? Why the trauma? Why did the colour drain from Stephen Harmison's face when his first ball in Brisbane ended up in second slip's hands and why did it take him almost two years to recover? Why the reaction? Why did thousands of people line the streets when England won the Ashes? Because it matters.

Stanford doesn't get this bit, which is why his Super Series is unlikely to endure. It matters all right in the sense that, like all entrepreneurs, he can smell a magnificent opportunity. But the sport itself, he doesn't really get. This is cricket as wrestling – mere entertainment. But sport, as Bill Shankly might have said, is more important than that.

Dazzled by the glare from Stanford's crate of dollars at Lord's in June, the ECB was blind to it, too. Nobody gives a stuff whether England win or lose on Saturday [1 November], and Pietersen came close to admitting it on Tuesday when he said that he 'just wanted to get the thing over with'. Once the money has been won or lost, the players won't give the fixture a moment's thought.

Nor should we – except to remember that international sport is more than just about pocketing the dough. Poker is only about money, but as we all know, poker is not a sport. Come to think of it, the Stanford Super Series isn't like that poker game I watched in Vegas at all: this is poker without money; sport without meaning.

The Times, 30 October 2008

Kevin Pietersen Answers Million-dollar Question

So the die has been cast. Kevin Pietersen revealed his hand at pool-side early yesterday morning, dressed in Bermuda shorts and flip-flops, a Joker-like smile never far from his face. If he had spent the night agonising over the decision of who to leave out of today's winner-takes-all $20 million (about £12.4 million) clash, it wasn't apparent. The unlucky quartet is James Anderson, Ravi Bopara, Alastair Cook and Ryan Sidebottom.

Can we call them unlucky? Sympathy will be tempered by the knowledge that for warming up, ferrying drinks and acting as general dogsbodies for the day, they will still pick up $250,000 – should their team-mates be victorious, of course. Despite this, spare a thought for James Anderson, the unluckiest of the four.

Anderson, a slip of a lad in life terms, is something of a veteran one-day cricketer for England. Since his debut six years ago, he has played 97 one-day internationals and boasts an economy rate of less than five – the benchmark of a good one-day bowler. True, his rate in Twenty20 cricket is much higher – whose isn't? – at 8.25, and this, and that he was unconvincing in his only game here this week and the nature of the pitch, have probably counted against him.

But this will be a bitter pill to swallow because Anderson, 26, has played the last 40 one-day internationals, the same number of consecutive games as his captain, both of them last missing a one-day international in February 2007, in Sydney. Sentimentality counts for nothing. Fielding, too, it would seem is irrelevant because Anderson is among England's most athletic movers and safest catchers. Later, in the press conference, Pietersen was asked who he would most like to see under a skyer to win the dough and Anderson was the first name he mentioned.

Of the others, Sidebottom has been walking around all week

with his left calf strapped, and is short of match practice and match fitness, so his omission is no surprise. Pietersen described Sidebottom's fitness as only 'touch and go'. As for the young Essex pair, Bopara and Cook, no one expected them to play. Pietersen seems to have a blind spot as far as Bopara is concerned, even though he is, in my estimation, a better cricketer than, say, Luke Wright. Bopara's time will come.

The blind spot belongs to the selectors where Cook and one-day cricket are concerned. His presence here this week has been viewed with the same kind of incredulity as Sarah Palin's nomination for vice-president: one potentially just a heartbeat away from the presidency of the most powerful nation on earth; the other a stomach bug away from a pay day in Twenty20 cricket. Unbelievable.

The biggest beneficiaries of the selection process are Stephen Harmison, Wright and Graeme Swann. Harmison's selection is no surprise, and fully merited on recent form. His return to one-day cricket has been a recent and well-timed one. But for that, Anderson would certainly be playing. If they were in each other's vicinity last night, Harmy would have been wise to employ a food taster and keep his rum and coke out of Anderson's reach.

Wright has been so invisible this week that his WAG – one of those seen to be enjoying Allen Stanford's charms – has enjoyed more photos and column inches than he has. He hasn't batted or bowled, except in practice, and even then he has not been always present, suffering from the dreaded bug.

'Luke hasn't done anything right this week, but then again he hasn't done anything wrong. There is going to come a time when we need the kind of strength in depth that he gives us,' Pietersen said, struggling to sound convinced. There is a feeling, although it is based on precious little evidence, that Wright enjoys what the pros call a BMT – big-match temperament – and will revel under the kind of unique pressure that tonight's match will bring.

Swann has benefited from the conditions, which, in all but the most recent warm-up match between Middlesex and the Stanford Superstars, have favoured spin. Having not considered two spinners as part of their game plan at the beginning of the week, this is a change of tack. I wonder, though, if England realise how different that pitch for the final warm-up match (the one that will be used today) was from those earlier in the week. It was hard, flat and shiny – the kind on which a spinner could go the distance.

Still, you'll find no one here holding a grudge against Swann. He has been one of the few England players to take wholeheartedly to this whole thing, propping up the bar at night, cracking jokes, doing passable impersonations of all and sundry and generally having a good time. He is cut from the same cloth as Chris Gayle, the Superstars skipper. While Swann has had his eyes on a pink Ferrari from the moment this game was touted, Gayle replied to a question about what he would do with the money, simply: 'Spend it, man.' In these straitened times, the high street needs all the help it can get.

The Times, 1 November 2008

Allen Stanford Calls Time on Twenty-plenty

Whether the announcement comes this week or next, England's cricketers will not get the chance to play for a million dollars a man in November. Allen Stanford's review of his cricket operations has been completed and the result is that the much-hyped '20/20 for 20' will be scrapped, although he will continue to run his domestic Twenty20 tournament, albeit in a reduced form.

The reasons for scrapping the showcase event are numerous. His board, apparently, is uneasy at the level of financial commitment, especially in the present economic climate. There have been signs for a while that Stanford has been cutting expenditure in reaction to the financial downturn. In December he closed his cricket office in Antigua, and dissolved the Stanford board of legends, who were being paid around $10,000 a month. His Antigua-based investment company recently announced a swathe of job losses.

There were also concerns about the level of negative publicity generated by the event. While Stanford's initial involvement with West Indies cricket was well intentioned, it quickly gave way to more global ambitions and it was hoped the publicity would help Stanford's financial services company challenge the mighty names of investment banking. But ever since Stanford landed at Lord's in his helicopter, English sensibilities were offended and the Stanford name became synonymous not with 'hard work, clear vision and value' but with tackiness.

Nor did the players come to terms with the notion of the one-off event for a million dollars a man. Kevin Pietersen, then captain, said that he could not wait for the week to end and there was widespread feeling among players and supporters that they were simply pawns in a rich man's game.

Most importantly, though, Stanford himself is uneasy sharing any of the publicity with Digicel, the main sponsor of West Indies cricket, who won the rights to branding in a court case just before the inaugural event. After arbitration, Stanford was forced to put Digicel branding on the players' shirts and the Digicel logo on the outfield and on advertising boards. This did not sit well with him, and while he realised that the arbitration ruling came too late to affect the inaugural event, he was determined not to let Digicel share the limelight again.

Stanford has already announced that he intends to honour his commitments to the quadrangular event to be held at Lord's in May, although there is some doubt as to whether this will continue beyond the first year. The tournament completes the first of the five-year contract, after which both the ECB and Stanford have release clauses in the contract.

Stanford will continue his involvement with West Indies cricket through his domestic Twenty20 tournament, although the format is likely to be changed to reduce expenditure. It was always this regional tournament that was the most successful part of Stanford's cricket strategy. It gave exposure to parts of the region that had never previously received any and the tournament itself was a tremendous success. It also made wealthy a number of players from Guyana and Trinidad who won the first and second tournaments respectively.

The Stanford Superstars, who thrashed England, also became dollar millionaires overnight. Darren Sammy, who captained the West Indies 'A' team against England in St Kitts, was one such, and his comments on the day after the match were heartfelt: 'The Stanford Twenty20 tournament will change the face of cricket in the Caribbean and could change the lives of many cricketers. It has changed the lives of seventeen of us tonight. Words can't express how I feel now,' he said.

It just may be that if the victory over England in Jamaica last week is the beginning of West Indies' long march back to Test match respectability, then Stanford's largesse will have contributed in some measure towards it, which would be ironic given his loathing of the longer form of the game. His vision of regenerating interest in West Indies cricket may yet come to pass – a significant and worthwhile achievement in itself – but his chances of cracking the American market now look doomed.

The Times, 12 February 2009

Allen Stanford: A Sorry Tale of Greed and Shame

It was like a scene from *Life of Brian*. Allen Stanford stood on the table, like the messiah he thought he was, raised his arms and hushed his disciples – the Stanford Superstars, who had just trounced England and pocketed a million dollars a man – and other invited guests. 'There's been a lot of negativity and bullshit about this week,' he said (and here you have to imagine hearing it in a Texan drawl). 'But I am here to tell you that we're going to carry on kicking some ass!' He got down from the table and walked out, to wild applause.

It was his apotheosis. Here he was, mingling with sporting stars and worshipped by them because he had made them rich overnight. They were wearing his shirts, they had been playing on his ground and they listened to him adoringly. He had a personal cameraman in tow, recording his every move for posterity. The eponymous event had been watched around the world, although the viewing figures of hundreds of millions were, like much to do with Stanford, grossly exaggerated. Front page, back page, he was the talk of the town.

Three days ago, the US Securities and Exchange Commission accused him of a 'massive ongoing fraud' of 'shocking magnitude'. The US Marshals Service in Houston, Texas, sent a 15-man task force into Stanford's offices to secure files and computers. Alfredo Perez, the Marshals' spokesman, announced a very different kind of departure for Stanford than the rapturous one he enjoyed in Antigua in November. 'Once everybody leaves, the offices will be locked down,' Perez said. Last man out turn off the lights.

As queues of depositors appeared yesterday outside the Bank of Antigua and the Stanford International Bank, both situated in a conclave around the airport that is – or was – entirely owned by

Stanford, the first reaction was one of concern for the many who will be affected and, especially, the future of this tiny island, the fate of which is tied up in no small measure with him. Deposits in Antiguan banks are not protected, and do not expect this small, impoverished country to be able to fund a Gordon Brown-style bailout. Stanford is – or was – its largest private employer here, with interests in gambling, tourism, banking and publishing. Unemployment is high and sure to rise.

There may be trouble for some of the cricketers, too, as stories spread that one of the 'legends' employed by Stanford had reinvested with him, as had one of those he had made a millionaire overnight. At least Stanford's fall from grace may be good news for Baldwin Spencer, the embattled prime minister, who has an election to win and who has clashed with Stanford in the past, calling him a modern-day colonialist. The fiasco of the Sir Vivian Richards Stadium [when the Test against England was abandoned on 13 February, after ten balls and 14 minutes, because conditions were unfit for play] can be forgotten now.

What should not be forgotten quickly or easily is the embarrassment suffered by those who run English cricket and, by extension, the embarrassment for the English game. It is not good enough to say in defence of these decisions, as Giles Clarke, the chairman of the ECB, has done, that the contract was signed with 'the best of intentions'. At some stage a judgement must be made on the consequences of actions, not just the rationale behind them. Andrew Strauss has not enforced the follow-on in the third Test [against West Indies] for the best of reasons, but he will judged by whether or not England win.

Nor is it good enough for the ECB to distance itself from the alleged fraud by saying that 'we haven't promoted his products'. What exactly did the chairman and David Collier, the chief

70

executive, think England were doing in Antigua in November? They must have been blinded by the reflection from the plastic box stuffed with the cash that Stanford took to Lord's if they could not see that the whole exercise was about promoting the Stanford name and, by extension, the Stanford business. Stanford's products and Stanford's name are one and the same. The ECB endorsed his financial 'expertise', as did, unwittingly, the England team.

Nor is it good enough to say, as Nigel Hilliard, the Essex chairman, has this week, that due diligence was carried out in the same way as it would be with any other potential sponsor, i.e., on Stanford's ability to pay. Before, and shortly after, the ECB signed the deal with Stanford there was enough in the public domain to raise serious concerns about his distant past and his more recent activities. Years ago, the US Treasury Department warned about the lax regulation of Antigua's offshore banks and their links to money laundering. Concerns were raised with Collier at a private dinner in midsummer and by the time the Stanford week came around there was enough information to make the antennae of even the most naïve sportswriter twitch.

But money can dull the senses. The behaviour of those infatuated by Stanford's riches was, frankly, the worst aspect of the whole thing: from the ECB officials, who fawned over him when he descended the steps of his helicopter at Lord's, to the former greats, who knelt down, licked and polished his boots at every opportunity, to the players' representatives, who did their best to catch the wave of excess.

Take this little sequence from the Professional Cricketers' Association (PCA). Initially it was keen not to miss out on all this largesse and 'congratulated ECB executives for the opportunities it [Stanford] presents for the England players and for the wider interests of cricket'. After the initial criticism of the Stanford week, the PCA's representatives joined in, calling it a 'garden party' and rubbishing the facilities at an on-the-record press conference in Antigua.

Then, when these comments were accurately reported, the PCA sent Stanford a slithery email seen by *The Times*, the beginning and end of which should suffice: 'Dear Sir Alan,' it began (and, lovely this, note the misspelling of his name), '. . . many thanks for your kind hospitality last night. It was a pleasure to meet you briefly and I do hope we will have another opportunity to meet before the end of the week. The game was a great spectacle and the warmth of your hospitality was hugely appreciated. The ugly tone of the reports I have read from the UK take these comments out of the context that they were made and I do hope you will accept my apology for any offence they may have caused.' Ugh.

And the lessons for those running English cricket? When a game is played for money only, it is worthless, and enough people care about the England cricket team not to want to see them playing worthless fixtures. The England cricket team mean an awful lot to an awful lot of people and they do not like it when they see something valuable, something that represents them, reduced to a rich man's plaything.

This column knows little about financial matters – which is presumably why we have business people, not cricket people, running the game – and so was probably blind to the signs that Clarke saw when he said, after announcing the five-year deal: 'Stanford is a great legendary entrepreneur and he has the entrepreneur's ability to spot an opportunity and seize it and take it forward.' Usually, though, it pays to be wary when someone is offering exorbitant rates of interest and massive asset growth at a time when everything is heading south. If it looks too good to be true, it usually is.

It was Warren Buffett, another great and legendary financier, who said that when the tide goes out, you can see who has been swimming naked. The tide has gone out and it is Stanford's ass now giving a great, whopping moonie to English cricket. It is not a pretty sight.

The Times, 19 February 2009

3

Twenty20 – A New Paradigm

If there is one development that I have been ambivalent about, it is the inexorable rise of Twenty20. It has shown itself to be, for sure, an opportunity of a lifetime for the game, appealing to a new audience in a way that meshes with the demands of modern life. With it, though, there are enormous challenges. It is no coincidence, perhaps, that the resurgence of fixing has come in the wake of the rise of Twenty20; that so many players have succumbed to its charms at the expense of the longer forms of the game, or that so many chancers have become involved.

Twenty20 has produced some memorable matches and memorable cricket, though – the fielding and shot-making are often unbelievable and bowlers have had to find new ways to survive. Who would have thought that the slower ball bouncer would become an integral part of a bowler's armoury? One of the pieces here also looks at how the value of a player could change in an open marketplace, as it has done with baseball and American football.

Inevitably, the challenge thrown up by Twenty20 has not been well handled by cricket's administrators. How, for example, did they allow Lalit Modi to take the game's greatest players for a domestic league in return for nothing? And why did the ICC allow themselves to lose control of the fixture list as they did? And could not this short form of the game have been restricted to a domestic level, as a way of reinvigorating the club/county/state game, while leaving the international game alone?

Inevitably, in England the initial success provoked a desire to exploit it to the full, so that the summer of 2010 saw 156 Twenty20 matches being played in the height of summer. It was the definition of overkill. The matches were often dreadful; the players weary and the public at many counties unable or unwilling to support it. It had lost its sparkle in the space of less than a decade.

At the same time, the IPL was undergoing severe convulsions, and currently Lalit Modi looks less the saviour of the game, rather more a fugitive from it. As noted in one of the pieces here, economists will tell you that any mania or bubble comes with, in modern parlance, corporate challenges. As I write, the IPL has banished a couple of franchises, and Modi, and it has much to do to restore its credit rating.

Still, there was a nice symmetry in the early part of 2010, when England became World Twenty20 champions, the first global one-day tournament they had ever won. It was fitting in a way, as England was the originator of this newest form of the game, and it staves off, for a while at least, the hoary old chestnut of England having invented a game that the rest of the world can beat them at.

How this will all play out is anyone's guess, but for a short time, as the ICL and IPL took off, it will be looked at in years to come as a financial golden age for cricketers. Never have so many earned so much from so little.

Twenty20 Opens Up Vision of the Future

The county ground at Bristol was packed yesterday on a glorious morning, as were five other grounds on Friday evening, as a lost generation of cricket supporters gave a wholehearted thumbs-up to the new Twenty20 Cup. It is early days yet, but the signs are good: the first five Twenty20 games attracted 30,050 supporters compared to 6,295 for the corresponding Benson and Hedges games in 2001.

The ECB's marketing department recognised cricket's profile – white, middle-class and old – to be disastrous for the sport. Apparently, any committee man seen wearing a tie to the game between Gloucestershire and Worcestershire was liable to be ejected from the ground, and this deterrent seemed enough: for the most part, the crowd was young and family orientated. As for middle-class and white, well, one step at a time has always been cricket's way.

The atmosphere at Bristol was slightly more low-key than had been apparent for the opening match at Hampshire. This reflected a Saturday morning start rather than the Friday evening opening extravaganza when spectators were treated to the talents of Alesha, Sabrina and Su-Elise – not Hampshire's new overseas players but the band Mis-Teeq – along with D-Side and the United Colours of Sound.

There were no such musical accoutrements to entice the spectators to Nevil Road, but the spectators seemed happy enough to rely on the talents of the cricketers on display. Ultimately, it is the cricket that has to win them over. To their credit, the players threw themselves about with total commitment. Matt Windows said he'd never been so exhausted, but then he's not often batted at the other end from cricket's Peter Pan, Jonty Rhodes.

Eventually, the cricket will have to stand on its own two feet, once the novelty and the razzmatazz has worn off. But there is every chance it will, because finally the game is being played at a time when people can actually watch (i.e. after work) and in a way that more accurately reflects the times that we live in. You can be in and out in three hours and still be home for *EastEnders* or *Corrie*.

As for the cricket itself, there is no reason why it should be detrimental to the development of our game and our players. The fielding throughout the three frenetic hours was outstanding. Jack Russell took to the new game, as does a dog to a bone. He stood up to the bowlers from virtually the first ball – scurrying, scampering, snarling and generally at his irritating best. His wicket-keeping wasn't bad either.

All eyes were on Jonty Rhodes, still the world's best fielder, at backward point. He even agreed to wear a microphone, so that he could relay his thoughts to the television commentators. But, by the halfway stage he had touched the ball only three times and was reduced to shouting encouragement to the bowlers, and badgering Dermot Reeve to shut up when he was asked a question as the bowler was running in to bowl.

The bowlers themselves must have feared for their futures when this competition was announced in midwinter. But in this low-scoring match they found that, by using their brains, they could keep one step ahead of the enemy. Gloucestershire decided that slower balls were the way to go. Mark Alleyne led the way with a variety, front of the hand and back of the hand, getting slower and slower and loopier and loopier.

David Taylor, Worcestershire's new recruit from league cricket, looked bemused as Alleyne's deliveries crept past his bat at a slower pace than he would find at his club, High Wycombe, on a Saturday afternoon. He found Mike Smith a tougher proposition at the other end and was soon gone, but any game that promotes a closer association between the recreational game and the professional game must be a good thing. There will be more league players getting a go in this competition.

Although this game was a bit of a canter for Gloucester, there is every chance that Twenty20 matches will, as a rule, be closer than one-day games of late. In the World Cup, I reckoned there to be only one game in ten that was a tight match. A shorter game means less of a chance for star players to turn a match, to play the match-winning innings or bowl a devastating spell. The opening set of matches on Friday confirmed this trend.

Players, then, will be constantly playing in matches where the winning margins are small. Consequently, they will be learning continually how to play under pressure; how to bowl at the 'death'; how to finish a game with the bat and how crucial one piece of brilliance in the field can be.

All in all, Twenty20 should produce more innovative bowling, better fielding, batsmen who can score quicker and off every ball, and captains who can make decisions on the hoof rather than sticking to pre-determined plans. All that, and played in front of good crowds, too, in a cracking atmosphere – I almost wish I'd have played it myself.

The initial buzz surrounding Twenty20 cricket is vindication for those of us who argued for change, and to English cricket's much-criticised administrators we must doff our caps. In the long run, Twenty20 cricket might not work, but at least they have tried to shake county cricket out of its undeniable decline – it's just a pity it's taken them so long. Oh, and Gloucester won by six wickets.

Sunday Telegraph, 15 June 2003

Indian Cricket League Little Threat to World Game

During the schism brought about by Kerry Packer's hijacking of world cricket in the late 1970s, one statement from Ray Steele, the treasurer of the Australian Cricket Board, was enough to know that the game was up. At the same time that Packer was in the process of spending A$25 million setting up and televising World Series

Cricket, Steele announced that he had not been able to sell the commercial television rights for Australia's 1977–78 international season. The subsequent revelation that he had negotiated a $1,000 increase, from $9,000 to $10,000, for the rights to the domestic limited-overs competition was greeted with great joy by the board members. These dinosaurs were about to suffer extinction.

Packer's name has cropped up again this week in relation to the ZEE TV-backed Indian Cricket League, which a short time ago announced the names of 50 cricketers who have blown a huge raspberry to their respective cricket boards by joining the league. Javed Miandad urged the Pakistan Cricket Board to take a more conciliatory line than their Indian counterparts by not banning those Pakistan cricketers who had joined up, because the ICL had the 'potential to be like the Packer series and snowball into something big'. The general consensus is that the ICL represents a serious threat.

I don't think so. Packer's success in commercialising cricket, and in the process ensuring that cricketers everywhere received a fairer deal, is the very reason why the ICL presents little threat to the stability of the world game. By and large, international cricketers are happy with their lot and, as with the rise of political extremism, the conditions for revolution demand a growing body of people simmering and disaffected with the status quo.

Packer fed upon the disillusioned in the late 1970s. Great cricketers were served by administrators who were so far out of their depth, and out of tune with the changing times, that they could not sense the danger. Dogs and lamp-posts summed up the then relationship between administrators and players. While there will always be some sense of wariness between the two, the modern-day player knows that he gets a much bigger slice of the pie now than ever before. He may be weary with the amount of cricket he must play, but he is weary and wealthy.

That is the reason why, with the exception of Mohammad Yousuf, not one big-name player with a future rather than a past has signed up. Not one contracted player from India, Australia, West Indies or England has been lured. South Africa are hardly weakened by the loss of fading stars such as Lance Klusener and Nicky Boje. (Boje's signing is interesting not from a cricketing viewpoint but because he has refused on numerous occasions in the past to travel to India because of fear of being questioned by Delhi police in connection with match-fixing allegations.) While Packer could call upon Clive Lloyd, the Chappell brothers, Dennis Lillee and the rest of the best, so far the ICL has persuaded a less-than-thrilling combination of international has-beens and domestic players who never-were and never-will-be.

Nor have there been signings of note from Indian domestic cricket. For a time now, it has been easy to argue that the lowly first-class cricketer in India, as opposed to his international cousin, has been badly served, even exploited by the Indian board. The public has been in thrall to the Tendulkars and the Dravids, and the administrators have been preoccupied with exploiting the cash cow that is international cricket. The level below, which produces the former and without which the latter cannot flourish, has been ignored.

But conditions have been improving, and the ICL is likely to force the Indian board to improve them further, reducing the incentive for any domestic cricketer to leave the fold. The board pay domestic cricketers 13 per cent of their net profits. For the year 2006–07, those profits rose from 45 crores to 232 crores, so a domestic player can now expect to earn 25,000 rupees per playing day, equivalent to £22,000 a year, a very good wage in India.

The assembled hacks in Mumbai must have found it hard to suppress a snigger as Kapil Dev announced to the stage the 44 domestic Indian players who have signed up. They were, he said, 'the cream' of Indian cricket; such giants of the game as Reetinder Singh Sodhi, Laxmi Ratan Shukla and Abishek Jhunjhunwala. Sachin Tendulkar and Rahul Dravid must be quivering with fear at the threat to their commercial hegemony.

The 'cream' that Kapil referred to was effectively a combination of a few washed-up international players, like Dinesh Mongia, a number of domestic veterans (about half of the 44 were over 27 years of age, and therefore past the point where they might expect to have a serious international future) and a smaller number of younger players with genuine prospects. A number of state associations have been hit hard, but India may be thankful for the hurricane which is effectively blowing through the system, washing away many cricketers who, since they have no serious international ambitions, are clogging it up. County cricket could do with something similar.

Packer's revolution was born out of a genuine financial need among cricketers, conditions that barely exist today. It was successful because it pitted one shrewd, ruthless and forward-thinking businessman against the dinosaurs of Australian cricket administration. But Lalit Modi, the man who controls Indian cricket's purse strings, is no Ray Steele, and the BCCI are no dinosaurs. They are as financially shrewd and as ruthless as Packer ever was.

An aggressive response from them was always likely. Kapil was sacked almost immediately from his position as chairman of the National Academy, and since the BCCI are not prepared to sanction the ICL, they have effectively branded all those who have signed up as rebels. Already, it has been reported that Shukla has backed down ('What I earn from Bengal is decent enough,' he said) and one or two others are having second thoughts.

More than that, it has been reported that the BCCI are in the process of setting up their own international domestic Twenty20 competition, and that they have been in talks with Australia about this for months. As rumours of the ICL have swirled around, India's administrators have not been idle. Setting up their own competition would completely scupper the ICL initiative. My understanding is that the England and Wales Cricket Board have yet to be approached about this.

In all the brouhaha surrounding the ICL, the suspicion remains that it is not the interests of the Indian first-class cricketers that are at the heart of this venture, or indeed the interests of cricket as a whole, but simply the frustrations of a television owner who cannot slake the cricketing thirst of his viewers.

One man provides the link between the Packer revolution then and the ICL now. Tony Greig cut a rather heroic figure 30 years ago as he accompanied Packer to the famous High Court victory. Greig's latest association with a cash-rich media magnate is likely to have less far-reaching consequences.

Sunday Telegraph, 26 August 2007

Twenty20 Threat to Game's Future

So far, the first Twenty20 (or twennytwenny, as most commentators in South Africa refer to it as) global competition has been everything that the World Cup in the Caribbean was not. With spectators seemingly having riotous fun and the winners to be revealed in just over a week's time, it has looked like an event to be enjoyed, rather than a marathon to be endured.

The appetite for Twenty20 is insatiable. While all eyes have focused on South Africa, there were two developments elsewhere which suggest that eventually Twenty20 cricket could well become the dominant form of the game. I'd certainly lay a large wager that eventually 50-over cricket will be rendered extinct.

On Thursday in Delhi it was announced that a global Twenty20 tournament involving domestic teams would take place in October 2008. Meanwhile, in England a little-commented-upon press release revealed that there will be a 25 per cent increase in the number of Twenty20 games next year. Whatever happened to the softly-softly approach to make sure that the concept remained fresh? Truly, when the nostrils of administrators twitch with the scent of money, they cannot but bury their snouts in the trough.

The Delhi press conference was a hasty, if not necessarily completely thought-through, response to the Indian Cricket League that was highlighted in this column a fortnight ago. It is underpinned by a domestic Indian Twenty20 league, to be played in April 2008, and the aim is to bring together the two best domestic Twenty20 teams from India, Australia, South Africa and England to play for a $5 million (£2.5 million) purse in Abu Dhabi and Dubai six months later. New Zealand will play two teams in Australia's domestic league, while Sri Lanka and Pakistan will send teams to the Indian league. Negotiations are currently ongoing with West Indies to complete the group.

Or should that be coup? For, while Kapil Dev was publicly sanguine about the future of the ICL in the face of this week's developments, he must know that his breakaway group have just been dealt a death blow.

Stephen Fleming, recently touted as an ICL target, appeared at the Delhi launch along with other star names such as Sachin Tendulkar and Rahul Dravid. The tournament was immediately legitimised by the presence of some of the world's leading cricket administrators. It was quite a contrast to the rag, tag and bobtail names paraded by the ICL a fortnight ago and their subsequent cold-shouldering by the establishment. There will be a few play-ers now poring over the small print in their ICL contracts to see if there is any way out. It is certainly difficult to see anyone wanting to throw their hat in with the rebels from here on in. Why would you?

As I suggested a fortnight ago, the Indian administrators are a ruthless bunch and they have not been idle to the threat posed by the ICL. Lalit Modi, the man who controls the purse strings of Indian cricket, is a sharp operator and it is he and the chief executive of Cricket Australia, James Sutherland, who have been the prime movers behind this initiative.

Up until two weeks ago, England were out of the loop, which shows how hasty an arrangement this is. There are obvious snags to be untangled. Some players, for example, represent domestic teams in more than one country. No doubt if Stuart Clark finds himself in the happy position of having the choice between New South Wales or Hampshire, he would revert to his state of origin. And it is difficult to see how the ICC can justify their enthusiastic back-ing, given that reducing the volume of cricket is supposedly high on their agenda.

More important are the knock-on effects of this tournament, which, no doubt, have not been properly thought through. With a $5 million purse at stake, Twenty20 will suddenly become the most valuable tournament to win from a county player's perspective.

Fifty and 40-over cricket have already felt the pinch – they become even less attractive to sponsors now – and this will be exaggerated. County staffs may well be positioned with Twenty20 primarily in mind. Star players may be rested from first-class games in order to be fit and ready for the Twenty20 tournament. Suddenly Twenty20 starts to look like a threat to the primacy of the County Championship. Will a county be more interested in producing Test players for England, or winning a share of a $5 million pot? It doesn't take much of a clairvoyant to see the potential threat to the traditional forms of the game.

As an enthusiastic supporter of Twenty20 from its inception, the success it has generated in such a short time in revitalising domestic cricket has been heartening. But I have always felt that Twenty20 should have remained just that – a vehicle to revive domestic cricket. Fifty-over cricket and obviously Test cricket remain vital to protecting the very essence of the game, which is a contest between batsmen and bowlers, bat and ball. Twenty20 is the equivalent of the gas chamber for a bowler. If the game's future evolves entirely around Twenty20, why would any young, talented cricketer want to become one?

The recently disgraced Shoaib Akhtar might have overstated his case when he slammed the game's administrators for making it into a batsman's game, but he had a point.

Now that Twenty20 has spread to the international arena, its effects could be more wide-ranging than either I or, I suspect, its creators would wish. It is hard to see a future for 50-over cricket and if, as I do, you still love the slower rhythm and sub-plots of Test cricket, you might fear for that, too.

Sunday Telegraph, 16 September 2007

India's Billion-Dollar Twenty20 Revolution

To query whether the increasing dominance of Twenty20 is a good or bad thing for cricket is pointless, rather like ruminating on whether it is good or bad to grow old. It is going to happen; get over it. Get over it quickly, because it is happening right now. Had you been in India last week, you could not have avoided the issue: every day the Indian Cricket League, India's domestic Twenty20 competition, was front-page news, and this despite the national team's resurgence in Australia and another century from the game's greatest current player, Sachin Tendulkar.

This was the week when the scale of things to come hit home. Firstly, the ten-year global television rights to the Indian Premier League were sold for over $1 billion (£510 million). Then, on Friday, the biggest franchise auction in domestic sport's history saw a further $723 million change hands for the eight franchises on offer. It was said after the Ashes victory of 2005 that cricket was the new football; well, the IPL is cricket's version of football's Premier League, and the consequences, in terms of the finances and structure of the world game, are likely to be far-reaching.

Over in the West, meanwhile, the Texan billionaire Allen Stanford has just spent $3.5 million in a town called Fort Collins, Colorado, to promote his second Caribbean Twenty20 extravaganza, which gets under way this week. His is more of a social and marketing experiment; by targeting a specific area and making Fort Collins the only place in the United States where his tournament can be seen on cable TV, Stanford is the latest to attempt to crack the American market.

India is where the action is, though. With big business, sport and a dash of Bollywood thrown into the pot, the IPL has had the most glamorous and successful start. Each franchise was put up for auction on Thursday; each had a base price tag of $50 million. In the end, the cheapest, Jaipur, went for $17 million more than that, and the most expensive, Mumbai, was sold for more than double the initial estimate. India's most valuable business, Reliance Industries, picked up Mumbai; one of Bollywood's biggest stars, Shah Rukh Khan, fronts the Kolkata franchise, and five icons of Indian cricket have already been accounted for. It is a heady mix.

The tournament is to be played in April/May, and now the owners of the franchises must employ coaches before a further auction takes place for players drawn from a list of 88 Indian and foreign cricketers. As many as eight internationals can be purchased for a squad of 16 players, though only four are eligible for any one match.

Because of the calendar clash with English domestic cricket, not one English player is on that list. There is an English link, however, with the IPL, and it comes in the form of one of the new franchise owners. Emerging Media, who picked up the Jaipur franchise, are run by an Indian-born but London-based businessman called Manoj Badale and, with the failure of Deutsche Bank to secure a franchise, Badale's EM (he is joined by Lachlan Murdoch and other investors) became the only non-Indian business to bid successfully.

Speaking to me on Friday from Mumbai, he outlined the economics of the deal. As well as his initial outlay for the franchise, and running costs, he must now employ a coach, bid for players and rent the ground in Jaipur for a two-month period. In return his consortium receive 10 per cent of 80 per cent of the television revenue, an equal share of the sponsorship income (a global sponsor is due to be announced next week) and any further revenue should his team make it through to the international club tournament in October, when the best two teams from England, Australia, India and South Africa will play off. He expects to make a three-to-five-year return on his investment.

If Badale is the only visible English link so far with the IPL, it is difficult to see how, ultimately, English cricket can insulate itself from these winds of change. Not that the ECB have taken a stand-offish view to the IPL at all: this is an ICC-backed event, with the nod of approval having been given by all the major Test-playing nations, unlike the rival Indian Twenty20 operation, the Indian

Cricket League, which continues to have pariah status. But, given the monies being bandied about for such a short span of work, it won't be long before England's players start looking for a slice of the pie.

At the moment, the threat to the availability of England players because of the IPL is non-existent. England players earn well (Shane Bond's current dispute with New Zealand suggests not every country can be as sanguine as England) and would be foolish to jeopardise those earnings. But one could easily envisage a situation where an ageing or frequently injured player decides the offer is just too good to turn down as uncertainty over his international career increases. Andrew Flintoff, for example, is the only England player to have been covertly tapped up so far. It might not take too many further ankle injuries for him to decide a bucketful of money for eight weeks' work is less hassle than repeated injections and rehab.

Further down the line, English county cricket may find itself threatened and the ECB, by sanctioning the IPL, may not so much have kept the barbarians at the gates, as let them through the front door. If the franchise model expands, as is the hope in India, then there will be a limit to how far a market can serve two masters. Even in India, a much bigger market for cricket, there will be a potential conflict between the new and the old. No prizes for guessing where a young, hip Kolkata businessman will want to spend his company's dosh – and it's not with the antiquated Bengal Cricket Association. Shah Rukh Khan's Kolkata Knight Riders has far more appeal.

Such a potential conflict must be a worry for English cricket's traditional power bases. To give one example: the ICL, which completed its inaugural tournament a month ago, has now announced its 2008 schedule, which includes another shindig in April and May. Paul

Nixon, Chris Read and Stuart Law all played in the inaugural tournament and are still contracted. Where do their priorities lie? With the ICL or a pre-season tour with their county?

With rupees swirling around like confetti, private equity now stalking the game, agents desperate not to miss out on the best deals for their clients, and clients wondering which particular horse to back, cricket is entering a new paradigm, in which rupees and the free market are kings and players and entrepreneurs are the beneficiaries. As developments moved on apace, England left for a quaint tour of New Zealand yesterday.

Sunday Telegraph, 27 January 2008

IPL Revolution Offers Golden Opportunity

When Mike Soper, the jolly-faced ex-chairman of Surrey, ran for the top job in the English game six years ago, he was ridiculed for predicting that cricket could become as popular as football. When the same sentiments were expressed last week, in a Texan drawl by a multi-billionaire, any sniggers were decidedly sotto voce. Allen Stanford's claims may yet prove to be drawn from the realms of fantasy, but there is no doubt that cricket has reached a decisive point in its history: the Twenty20 revolution comes with a health warning, but it also represents the greatest opportunity for cricket since Kerry Packer dragged the sport's administrators kicking and screaming into the 20th century.

The combination of a shorter, more popular form of the game, the economic powerhouse that is India, and the free-market winds that have blown through the game are creating an unstoppable force. I do not believe that when the Test-playing nations gave the thumbs-up to the Indian Premier League (IPL), much thought was given to the possible consequences. The administrators walked blindfold into a storm; when the storm passes, the cricketing land-scape is likely to look completely different.

Of course, the essence of cricket will not change; bowlers will still hurl a clump of leather towards batsmen 22 yards away. But many of the assumptions that underpin its structure and govern-ance, the balance of power between players and administrators, the concept of domestic cricket as a mere feeder for the international game, the primacy of Test cricket, and the viability and structure of English county cricket will all be challenged.

It is not that the IPL has been an unqualified success. Clearly the tournament will have to be tweaked as it evolves. It is too long; there are too many matches; there are too many modest players; many of the tickets have been given away, so it is not clear whether the fans have developed an emotional attachment to their clubs; and the franchise owners, like the stuffed shirts you see at an after-dinner auction, allowed their egos to dominate any business sense and overpaid massively for the franchises and the players.

Yet, to set up such a tournament in less than a year is a remarkable achievement. Crucially for its future success, the players have taken to it wholeheartedly. This is not surprising when you consider the financial rewards on offer, but when, after the first match, Brendon McCullum, the New Zealander who scored [a record] 158 for the Kolkata Knight Riders, said that he couldn't feel his legs for the first eight deliveries because of nerves, it was a good sign.

For sports fans are discerning enough to smell a fraud. They need to sense that it matters to players how they perform and whether they win or lose, which is why mere exhibition matches have never really taken off. H.L. Mencken's dictum that you never go broke underestimating the intelligence of the public may work for daytime television producers and Hollywood directors, but not for sport. The players care, the public want it, and on that basis alone Twenty20 is here to stay. It will drive the finances of domestic cricket the world over.

How, then, will it affect the game? Geographically limited at the moment, the principles that underpin the IPL will surely spread, so that cricket will no longer be governed by well-meaning amateurs for whom the game was a passport to a free lunch and pleasant social life, but instead will be run by hard-nosed businessmen for whom the only line is the bottom line. Already, Justin Vaughan, the chief executive of New Zealand Cricket, has talked of looking into a franchise-based Australasia competition, and there will be a beefed-up English Premier League, with private equity supplied by the likes of Stanford, from 2010 onwards.

Domestic Twenty20, then, will question two of the most fundamental principles that have underpinned the modern game; that is to say, domestic cricket will become important in its own right rather than as a mere feeder to the international game (like football and rugby, clubs will become as important as countries), and Test cricket will no longer be seen as the game's defining product.

It is all very well for the likes of Ricky Ponting to say that Test cricket remains the ultimate. But what about the young boy in the Kolkata slum who sees Mahendra Singh Dhoni (Test average 34, one Test hundred) earning nearly four times as much in the IPL as Ponting (Test average 58, Test hundreds 34). At which format of the game will he want to excel?

When Stanford's $100 million (about £50 million) is up for grabs, at which form will a young England player want to excel, and if he has to make a choice, which will he choose? So far, Darren Gough is the only England player to retire from Test cricket to concentrate on one-day cricket. He will not be the last.

The era of player power is upon us. Packer helped cricketers to get a fair deal, but from now on it is administrators who will feel the pain. Last week, Brad Hodge walked out on Lancashire to join the IPL. At the start of the year, David Hussey and Shane Warne thought dollars and warmth more tempting than pounds and April cold. Nottinghamshire and Hampshire were left in the lurch, contracts ripped up and sent floating on the breeze. It is to be hoped that, with riches, players learn certain responsibilities.

As the IPL was gearing up, many thought that English cricket, like a Swiss canton during wartime, would go unaffected. But now it is clear that there will be consequences and the ECB is mulling over changes that will come into being in 2010. Not much can happen next year, given the Ashes and the World Twenty20 tournament, but after that, and to coincide with a new television deal, all options are open. (A leading executive told me this week that 'all sacred cows will be challenged'.)

What is most likely is that the County Championship will be reduced to about half the number of matches that are played now – complaints from the 100,000 or so county members drowned out by the 500,000 or so who watch Twenty20. It is the economic argument that will win the day. An English Premier League, with foreign teams, will dominate high summer and will be the first move away from the 18-county structure that has been the bedrock of English cricket for so long.

The ECB, though, is aware of the pulling power of Test cricket in this country and will try to market England as its natural home. Neutral Test matches, between predominantly Asian teams, will be played in England both to increase the value of television rights and as a way of exploiting the Asian market here.

To many, the increase in Twenty20, and the changes it will bring, will be unpalatable. In this newspaper, William Rees-Mogg has bemoaned the death of cricket. I thought it ironic that his feelings were made plain on the same day that stuffy academics complained that the British Library was becoming too popular and overcrowded. Imagine that – people wanting to read books. People wanting to watch a form of the game that better suits their lifestyle! I disagree with His Moggship that the rustic origins of cricket at Hambledon were more in tune with Tests than Twenty20.

In any case, world cricket is not necessarily in good shape and these changes will give the administrators a perfect opportunity to take stock and re-evaluate. Crowds for Test cricket have been declining everywhere except in England and Australia. Domestic cricket is watched only in England. (When a pundit queried recently why Matthew Hayden crossed himself after making a hundred only in Test cricket, the reply came that not even God watches state cricket in Australia.) The ICC Champions Trophy is an irrelevance. The Future Tours Programme is a joke. The past two World Cups have been shambolic.

I accept that there are inherent dangers in the spread of a format that is, fundamentally, coarser; a spread of a game that could alienate the traditional fan base. A balance is essential. It is time for wise administrators – those who can see the opportunities while smelling the dangers – to step forward. And wouldn't you just know it, at this defining moment in the game's history, cricket's governing body, the ICC, has never been more impotent, more divided or more derided. Right now, it does not even have a chief executive.

The Times, 1 May 2008

Arrogant IPL Owners Must Admit Mistakes

Are the Rajasthan Royals the Oakland A's of cricket? Devotees of excellent sporting literature will need no introduction to *Moneyball*, a terrific yarn about how the A's, a relatively low-budget baseball team ($41 million – about £22 million – to spend on players counts as low budget in American sport), consistently outperformed their more illustrious and wealthier rivals by dint of the unorthodox coaching methods of Billy Beane, their general manager.

The basic premise of Beane's coaching philosophy was that age-old wisdom, in the form of gnarled tobacco-spitting scouts, was subjective and flawed and did not stand up to the scrutiny of statistics and empirical data. And that many of the statistics that were used, such as batting averages, were too general and vague and irrelevant compared with less utilised and understood statistics such as, say, on-base percentage and slugging percentage (don't ask me, either).

By completely changing the *modus operandi* by which a player was evaluated, Beane was able to compete against teams like the New York Yankees, who might have two or three times the amount to spend in the player draft. Essentially, Beane was looking for players rated by his team of statisticians, but whom the market undervalued; what the author of *Moneyball*, Michael Lewis, called market inefficiencies.

Something similar is happening right now in the Indian Premier League, which is finally reaching its climactic phase. Rajasthan, at $67 million the cheapest franchise of the lot, the one that angered Lalit Modi, the IPL commissioner, for underspending on players in the first auction, are top of the league and looking forward to the semi-finals. The most expensive franchises, Mumbai Indians ($111.9 million) and Bangalore Royal Challengers ($111.6 million), are out.

Bangalore, in particular, have had a miserable time; the whipping boys, more chumps than challengers. This has produced some ructions in their camp, since the owner, Vijay Mallya, one of India's richest men, is not used to losing. Mallya has taken on the mantle of the Roman Abramovich of the IPL: he sacked his chief executive, criticised publicly his captain, Rahul Dravid – an icon of the tournament – and let off a head of steam in the media.

Since the chief executive he sacked was a television presenter in a former life, and since his captain, nicknamed The Wall for his defensive prowess, has not exactly shown an aptitude for Twenty20, it was fairly obvious that Bangalore was, by the standards of American sport, an amateurish operation. Mallya's public comments did much to back up this suspicion. 'My biggest mistake,' he said, showing rare humility for a franchise owner, then breathtaking arrogance, 'was to abstain from the selection of the team. Though I watch a lot of cricket I am no expert. I had a separate list of players that I wanted, but I left it to his [Dravid's] judgement. After seeing the list, my friends told me it looked like a Test team.'

Well, with Dravid, Wasim Jaffer, Anil Kumble and Jacques Kallis suddenly on his payroll to the tune of about $3.5 million a year, he got that last bit right. But he did give the impression that, with some mates for company, he had drawn up a list of names on the back of a fag packet, after downing a cask or two of his own brand of whisky, while watching his Formula One team, Force India, on board his luxury yacht. Beane can rest easy.

The cheapskates Rajasthan, meanwhile, have carried all before them. With Lachlan Murdoch, a director of News Corporation, among their backers they can hardly be said to be paupers, but they sat back at the first auction, surveying the ego-driven carnage around them, before nipping in with some bargain-basement buys in the second. Among their shrewd decisions was that captaincy would prove to be crucial. In Shane Warne they have the best leader in the tournament. Statistically, they also have the best player, Shane Watson, who happened to be, at $125,000, one of the cheapest buys.

It is unlikely that Rajasthan were any more professional than Bangalore or anyone else. Given the rushed nature of the tournament, nobody had time to plan properly. They simply had better instincts, sounder judgement and a lighter, tighter wallet. But, with data now available from the first tournament and two years to plan until the next auction this is where things will, or ought to, change.

Because of the similarities between baseball and cricket, a couple of years ago a friend suggested I try to persuade a coach in English cricket to apply *Moneyball* principles and write up the story. There were two problems: in international cricket there is no movement of players because of the restrictions of nationality and birth, and in domestic cricket there is no money and no thriving transfer market. *Moneyball* principles can only be applied in a free market, but English cricket has been generally feudal rather than capitalist in character.

The IPL solves those problems. It is awash with money and player movement is not hindered either by nationality or by feudal ties. The initial auction, where players were bought and sold according to perceived market value, is similar to the draft system in baseball that allowed Beane to seek out market inefficiencies with his pure data.

Instead of buying greater numbers of expensive flops, the smart owners would be well advised to employ some statisticians. In fact, a group of bright young things has already been hard at work, analysing the first year in great detail on a website, rediff.com. It has come up with a list of the Most Valuable Players (Watson is top) and a Player Value Index, where the performance is adjusted according to price-tag (Sachin Tendulkar is next to bottom).

Broadly, its conclusions are these: it is madness to spend up to 25 per cent of the total spend on one iconic player; it is unwise to spend too much on players who offer only one skill; wicket-keepers have little value; bowling all-rounders are better value than batting all-rounders; young and fit all-rounders offer the best value of all, and owners should populate their team with a core of young players and Australians.

But if the latest comment by Shah Rukh Khan, the Bollywood actor and owner of the Kolkata franchise, is anything to go by, winning the IPL is less important than self-deification. And while cricketers have always toadied up to the money men, it seems as if the dash for cash in the IPL has caused a few of them to lose completely their sense of self-worth. 'My team told me that they have yet to meet a better human being than me,' the preening Khan has said.

While Khan busies himself for the afterlife, other owners could start professionalising their operations in time for the next player auction. If Mr Mallya does read *The Times* of London, he may be interested to learn that I happen to know the best cricket statistician in the business. I'm happy to pass on his details; for a small consideration, of course.

The Times, 29 May 2008

Will the Twenty20 Bubble Be Next to Burst?

When Babe Ruth signed a whopping contract for the New York Yankees on the eve of the Great Depression, he was asked what he thought about earning more than the president of the United States, Herbert Hoover: 'What's Hoover gotta do with it? I had a better year than he did,' the Babe said. But three years later his salary had halved, and one of the leading teams, the Cincinnati Reds, had to be bought out of bankruptcy.

In Canada, ice hockey suffered even more from the effects of the Great Depression. In the 1920s the sport had been transformed from a small, provincial tournament into an international (as far as sport across the pond can be described as international) league with new franchises in Boston, New York, Pittsburgh, Chicago and Detroit, values of which had inflated tenfold in the first half of the 1920s. The sport underwent the kind of transformation that has recently affected cricket. But between 1931 and 1942, 40 per cent of these franchises went under.

Yet, interest in hockey, baseball and other sports did not diminish during these economically barren years. If anything, it increased. The public's appetite for fun, frolics and irrelevancy was proportional to their hardship. Seabiscuit, the great racehorse, became popular partly because the story was an unlikely one: a small horse with a poor gait and an alcoholic jockey struck a chord with those fighting against seemingly insurmountable odds. When Seabiscuit faced War Admiral in a race billed as the 'match of the century' an estimated 40 million tuned in to listen.

The business of sport suffers in recession but not sport itself, which is an important distinction to understand. Cricket was barely affected at all in the Great Depression – Don Bradman was Seabiscuit to Australia's hurting masses in the 1930s – or in the stagflationary era of the 1970s. But cricket, then, unlike baseball or ice hockey in the 1930s, was essentially an amateur, non-commercialised sport, run by well-meaning but amateur (in every sense of the word) administrators. There were no franchises and little sponsorship or television money. The game was more pure, which is not to say that it is dirty now, just that it is more complex, there being more vested interests butting in between the performer and those who pay to watch.

Now cricket is a business that, though it cannot match football, baseball and others for financial clout, is run on exactly the same model. Television revenues underpin the finances of the game and from this all else springs – the wellbeing of franchises in India, the health of county cricket in England, ground advertising, perimeter advertising, player wages and sponsorship deals. There is nothing now untouched by exploitation – the next time Andrew Flintoff is about to go in to bat for England, watch how closely and showily he clutches a can of his favourite soft drink. Product placement is not limited to Hollywood.

It was the Packer revolution in the late 1970s that brought about cricket's long march to modernisation and commercialisation. There has not been a serious economic crisis since then to test the viability of the model, and the events of the last few weeks suggest that the Twenty20 revolution will be the first to feel the pinch. The 20-team English Premier League has been stillborn, and the fallout from Allen Stanford's alleged swindle is that the quadrangular Twenty20 tournament will no longer happen in May, nor his week-long festival in November.

If the rest of the world catches a cold when America sneezes, then the cricket world gets influenza when India so much as clears its throat, and the signs are that even cricket in India is feeling the effects of the global downturn. Subhash Chandra's Indian Cricket League, which until now has survived the monopolistic tendencies of the Indian Premier League (IPL) and the supine reaction of the rest of world cricket, has delayed the third season of its Twenty20 tournament and withheld payments from players. It is understood to be reviewing its existing contracts with a view to instigating a player cull.

Even those tournaments with the backing of the Board of Control for Cricket in India, such as the IPL and the Champions League, are suffering. The Champions League did not get past the first hurdle last year due to the Mumbai bombings, but some blushes were spared because of it. Sponsorship had been hard to find, and the television rights tricky to sell on for ESPN Star Sports, the rights holder.

Having purchased the ten-year tournament before the credit crunch hit for close to $1 billion (now about £700 million) there will be some very nervous executives at ESPN Star. When you can watch Flintoff bowling to Ricky Ponting, national pride and the Ashes at stake, why would you want to watch Darren Pattinson bowling at Tyron Henderson as the Bushrangers take on the Crusaders in a tournament with no history, tradition or meaning?

Now all eyes will be on the IPL in April, as the second season gets under way. Already the signs are that franchise-holders are finding things tougher in the second year after an average shortfall in revenues of $4 million last year. Rajasthan Royals, last year's winners, are without a sponsor, while Kolkata Knight Riders and Deccan Chargers have lost principal sponsors. The warning signs were flashing red for the co-owner of King's XI Punjab recently when he said: 'These are difficult times and we need to work out ways to make sure that all the franchises survive.' Another franchise director, unable clearly to grasp that the current crisis is all about the flow of credit, said: 'There is a cashflow crunch, not an endemic problem.'

Is the Twenty20 revolution a bubble on the point of bursting? It was Charles Kindleberger in his seminal book *Manias, Panics and Crashes* who described a paradigm for understanding bubbles. First comes the new investment, whether it be Dutch tulips, Louisiana gold, the internet, housing or Twenty20; the rise in interest attracts new, often inexperienced investors; then a euphoria takes hold that leads to a weakening of rationality; credit becomes overextended; fraud proliferates, leading to a financial crisis and the recriminations that follow. It is possible to make a case for a Twenty20 bubble on all those grounds.

But should we worry if some franchises go under, taking with them investors in for a quick buck with no real feeling or fundamental interest in the game? It is a fallacy, one peddled by Giles Clarke, the ECB chairman, in these pages yesterday, that a sport must continue to make more and more money in order to be successful. As the business of sport suffers under the weight of recession, cricket will have to cut its cloth accordingly.

Surrey, for example, will not be able to spend £25,000 on two games for Shoaib Akhtar, as they did last year. The ECB may have to make its own decisions on appointing a new team director, instead of paying a (no doubt) expensive firm of headhunters to do its work for it. Maybe, just maybe, the players will have to do without a full-time security officer in the Caribbean.

As finances have grown – and English cricket, as Clarke said yesterday, is in a relatively healthy position thank to the early rene-gotiating of the television contract – there have been an awful lot of people who have carved out a lovely niche, none of whom is essential to the game. The business of sport may suffer over the coming year, and a few Johnny-come-latelys may hurt, but sport itself will go on. And people's appetite for the essentials – the passion, the fury, the skill, the controversy and the competition – will probably increase.

The Times, 26 February 2009

Lessons Ignored in the Rush for IPL Cash

Thank God for people like Jamaica Kincaid. The Antiguan-born writer, not known for pulling her punches, attended the ceremony at which Allen Stanford received his 'knighthood' some years ago. She, too, was receiving a national award for her work and when Stanford went to shake her hand, she refused, saying to his face: 'Your honour demeans my own.'

That small snippet comes from a wonderful profile on Stanford and his involvement in cricket in the *New Yorker* magazine (9

March) by Alec Wilkinson, a staff writer, which will be seen to be the definitive piece on that crazy episode. He goes on to quote Kincaid, who likens Stanford to a modern-day pirate: 'He's always been a crook,' said Kincaid. 'And everybody knows it.'

Everybody may have known it, but few were prepared to say it. Because cricket has never been a wealthy game, and because cricketers have never been, by comparison, wealthy sportsmen, the rich have always enjoyed easy access and the benefit of an uncritical eye. Beneficiaries, looking to make good after ten years of toil for meagre returns, are routinely attracted, like moths to the flame, to those with a few quid, no matter what their deficiencies of character. Because of cricket's relative normality, money disorientates those who play it.

The hope was that the lessons of Stanford would make people pause before rushing in at the first scent of money, but the recent stampede to try to cushion the failure of the Indian Premier League (IPL) to establish a second season in its home territory suggests that those lessons have not been learnt. The IPL has found its home in South Africa, but while the negotiations were continuing, where was English cricket's Jamaica Kincaid? Nobody – certainly not the ECB, nor county executives who cannot but see beyond the next rupee – had the clear-eyed sense to say, and loudly, 'thanks but no thanks' and spurn the handshake.

Linking the IPL and Stanford is not to suggest that the Indian tournament or those who back it are crooked or unworthy. Indeed, the IPL was, and may well be again, a magnificent success, bold in its conception, brilliant in its inception and dramatic throughout, a testament to the innovation, drive and financial muscle that sums up modern-day India. Twenty20, the best players in the world and Bollywood proved to be an alluring mix.

But the IPL is not a gift to the game as a whole. Nobody, except the Board of Control for Cricket in India, the franchise investors and the players, makes a bean out of the IPL. It is, put simply, a private commercial enterprise, an utterly ruthless one at that, and, because there can only be one of its kind, owing to the crowded nature of the international fixture list, it is in competition with every other member nation of the ICC.

Especially so with England, who, despite the failure to embrace an attractive franchise-based competition put forward by Surrey and MCC last year, still have designs to set up the English Premier League. When was the last time Lalit Modi, the IPL commissioner, offered a helping hand to this apple of Giles Clarke's eye? Why, then, would the ECB chairman want to give a helping hand to a competitor in trouble?

The interest in the first season of the IPL was not so much the cricket, which was routine, but the way in which the tournament rewrote existing power relationships. This was the free market set to work on a sport that had been feudal for so long. It was the ultimate expression of cricketing capitalism: franchises were sold to wealthy businessmen; players were paid according to their value in the open market, bartered for, haggled over and sold to the highest bidder, a value that then floated, like a stock-market share, according to that player's performance. The winning of games was incidental to both the raging egos of the owners and the return on their investment.

It was soon clear, though, that the IPL was not about to subject itself to the principles of the free market. In particular, it didn't much care for competition. The IPL has attempted to put the Indian Cricket League (ICL), another Twenty20 tournament organised on the same guidelines as the IPL (and, indeed, one that predated it), out of business as surely as if it were a market trader touting for trade on its own patch.

Anybody – cricketers, agents, commentators, umpires – with links to the ICL has been ostracised, the ruthlessness and pettiness of those who run the IPL best summed up recently in New Zealand when Sachin Tendulkar was withdrawn from a charity match because of the contaminating presence of an ICL player in the same fixture.

In time, people will come to wonder how and why, in response to this brazen self-interest, the member countries of the ICC came to give up their best players to a private competition in return for nothing – except a lot of hassle. What does English cricket get in return for allowing Andrew Flintoff and Kevin Pietersen to play in the IPL during the English season? Nothing, except a few weeks on tenterhooks, hoping that neither gets injured before the Test series against West Indies, the World Twenty20 and the Ashes.

Some will regard this argument as petty – an extension of the ridiculous spat recently over whether Phillip Hughes or Stuart Clark should hone their competitive instincts in England before the Ashes – and wonder why cricket cannot move beyond nationalism. If the IPL benefited all, then that argument would hold water. But when Emerging Media sold an 11.7 per cent share of Rajasthan Royals earlier this year, the astronomical profit went to the investors alone.

Fair enough. Emerging Media took the risk and raked in the proceeds. But when the market dips – and one can only imagine the financial fallout if the IPL had not found an ersatz home – the normal rules of the free market (pre-credit crunch, at any rate) should apply. The IPL has played a ruthless game so far, and should not expect anything less in return.

And because commercial language is the only language understood by those such as Andy Nash, the Somerset chairman, who suggested that the ECB should 'move heaven and earth' to host the IPL in England, let us put the argument more simply: why would you risk devaluing your own 'products' – your first-class competition, your premier one-day competition and your opening Test matches of the season – to inflate the value of your prime competitor?

There are other, more compelling arguments, such as the lunacy of seeing Flintoff or Owais Shah playing for franchises down the road from where their counties, who have nurtured them, are playing. But cricketing arguments have long been lost on decision-makers. The IPL in England? Some would call it an opportunity; others of a more clear-eyed persuasion would fashion a rather more damning description.

The Times, 26 March 2009

ICC and ECB Must Look Sharp over Rajasthan Royals Tie-up

There were plenty of sharp suits at Lord's this week. Sharp suits covering shirts with those ridiculously cutaway collars that immediately make you suspicious that the people wearing them know far more about money than you will ever know.

The collars (with matching corporate ties, of course) were being worn by the executives of Rajasthan Royals, the Indian Premier League (IPL) franchise, who were in town to announce a Twenty20 tie-up with other domestic teams that included Hampshire, Trinidad & Tobago, Cape Cobras and, possibly, Victorian Bushrangers. From now on, in Twenty20 matches, these teams will wear the same shirts, play under the same name and share revenues and, possibly, players.

There was Sean Morris, the chief executive who not so long ago was bemoaning the excessive cricket played by those he was paid to represent as head of the players' union, but who now is trumpeting an in-house tournament to be dropped into the middle of the English season. Funny how your views on the amount of cricket that should be played can change so dramatically in a few short months or, in the case of Rod Bransgrove, the Hampshire chairman, a week, since he talked of the dangers of overplaying at the ECB's recent forum on one-day cricket. Alongside Morris was Manoj Badale, the money man behind the Rajasthan franchise.

They were disingenuous when they talked of creating sport's first global franchise (Manchester United have beaten you to that one, boys), but this was another moment that suggested how far and how quickly the sport is changing, and laid out the battle lines for the future. Since the advent of the IPL, those have been obvious to me: traditional international cricket, governed by the ICC and national governing bodies, against newly empowered franchises attempting to run the game along the football model.

In between these two competing forces are the players. On the one hand there is the prestige of playing for your country and of scoring runs or taking wickets in Test matches, the context of which allows you to be compared with the great players of the past. On the other is the wodge; great, dripping oodles of it. Having scored his runs, taken his wickets and contextualised his name in perpetuity, there is no doubting which side Shane Warne is on now: forget the Ashes, he said this week, the IPL was one of the greatest moments of his cricketing career, if not the greatest.

The scramble is on. Paul Sheldon, the Surrey chief executive, has been in India, along with several other county chief executives, gauging reaction and potential tie-ups; Jim Cumbes, the Lancashire chief executive, sounding somewhat late out of the blocks, said that a county of Lancashire's size, reputation and importance would be foolish to overlook the potential. All the while they sounded like newspaper executives did when they talked of the internet not so long ago – that there must be a pot of gold at the end of the rainbow *somewhere* and they had better not be the ones to miss out.

It remains to be seen whether cricket's promised land, like the internet squillions for newspapers, proves to be illusory. There are a number of hurdles to overcome before the Royals can simply play Twenty20 among themselves wherever and whenever they like. Early noises from India suggested that the Board of Control for Cricket in India (BCCI) was less than sanguine about this . . . well, loss of control. The ECB must also sanction any cricket to be played in England (otherwise an unauthorised tournament will mean that the players are unable to play in future ICC tournaments). Then there are television contracts and companies to negotiate with, not to mention visa requirements that may be hard to come by. For the moment, national governing bodies hold sway.

But, make no mistake, this is part of a bigger movement aimed at the wholesale reorganisation of cricket along football lines. The tie-up of the Royals franchise came on the back of Lalit Modi, the IPL commissioner, announcing his plans to take the IPL to the United States. 'We will host a few matches in the US in the next eighteen months or so,' he said this week.

'There are also plans in the works to hold IPL matches overseas and we hope to be able to provide fans all around the world with the live IPL cricketing carnival experience,' said Modi, never one to undersell his product. 'We are looking at a shorter version of the league post the IPL seasons, which will help us take the game to the fans across the globe. Initially we are looking at markets which have large Indian and cricket-loving populations such as USA, Singapore, Hong Kong, Malaysia, Bangkok, Middle East, Canada and others.' The IPL's tie-up with YouTube should be seen in this context.

Like many English counties, the IPL franchises have realised that the model of playing cricket for only a few weeks a year (months in the case of the counties) is financially unviable, especially given the cost of the initial outlay, the increased player power that drives up the cost base and the continuing expense of maintaining a team and a ground. The aim for Hampshire is to break free from the financial shackles that see them reliant on a handout from the ECB.

But the balance of power is clear. Hampshire are a club of massive tradition, founded in 1863 and playing continuous first-class cricket since 1895, with some of the greatest names in the game – Barry Richards, Malcolm Marshall, Warne himself – to have played in their colours. Rajasthan Royals are not yet three years old. Yet it is the Royals name that Hampshire will carry in their Twenty20 fixtures – a microcosm, perhaps, of how far the balance of power has shifted and will continue to shift.

I have felt for a while that, ultimately, the franchises have certain advantages in this battle for power: Twenty20 will continue to be the form of the game that will attract a new audience; sharp-suited, financially acute businessmen face a near-useless opponent in the ICC; while international teams are limited by the talent available within their boundaries, franchises can buy in players from wherever they like, so that competitive cricket must be easier to maintain for the franchise model; and, where players are concerned, money talks.

Of course, men such as Modi, Badale and Morris will continue to talk an appeasing game: that they are not in it to change the face of cricket for good; that franchise cricket and international cricket can exist side by side to the benefit of both. And who is to say, if they get their ultimate wish, that such a future would not be better for the game?

But those running cricket should not be fooled by those sooth-ing words. Monopolies make money, and it is money that Modi and Badale are out to make. Once before, when they allowed their players to play in the first IPL in return for nothing, the game's governing bodies gave an unwitting leg-up to people who would like to reorganise the sport fundamentally for their own benefit. This week there has been another step in that direction.

The Times, 11 February 2010

4

A Dark New World

Ever since the Munich Olympic Games atrocity in 1972, sport has always operated in the knowledge that it could be a target for terrorists. In the main, though, we rather assumed that there would be other, more relevant, targets, and that the piffle and nonsense of sport would keep real life at bay.

This notion was shattered again when the Sri Lanka team bus was targeted by extremists in Pakistan in March 2009. Earlier that winter, the hotel used by many touring teams in Mumbai was decimated by another terrorist attack. This chapter deals with those two incidents and their effect upon the England team, who were involved directly in the first of those and indirectly in the second.

For the game, though, the threat is very real: of the Test-playing nations, four are from the sub-continent. Such a concentration in one unstable region leaves the game very vulnerable indeed.

Atrocity in Mumbai Still Too Close to Home

The images of the carnage that enveloped the Taj Mahal Palace hotel in Mumbai late on Wednesday evening will have struck a deep chord with England cricketers past and present. For decades it has been something of a refuge for tourists in need of a hiatus from the assault on the senses that is an inevitable part of every India tour. Step outside its ochre-coloured walls and you are immediately engulfed in the anarchic chaos that is modern Mumbai, but inside it was always possible to forget about real life for a while.

No longer. A few weeks ago, England's cricketers stayed in the Taj Mahal Palace as they prepared for the one-day series, and they were due to do so again towards the end of December before plans were put in place to relocate the Mumbai Test match. More worryingly, Middlesex were due to stay in the hotel over the next few days as part of their preparations for the inaugural Twenty20 Champions League. If the attacks had been a couple of days later, they could well have been caught up in the bloodbath.

So terrorism, which is ever-present, becomes something more tangible when cricketers are able to contextualise: hotels they have stayed in, cafés they have drunk coffee in (Leopold Café, which was caught up in the mayhem, is a regular haunt just around the corner from the Taj Mahal) and bars where they might have whiled away a few hours before a rare day off. Death, then, is not only something seen on television screens, or in newspapers, but real. Closer. And sport being one of the greatest celebrations of life that we have, you can rest assured that that is not what sportsmen sign up for.

Understandably, cricketers decided yesterday that they didn't want much to do with it all. The one-day series was abandoned and the senior players, as well as the development squad, will come home. Not even Twenty20 was immune: the Champions League was postponed, as was the 'World Series' in the Indian Cricket League, which was taking place in Ahmedabad. Not that the players were considered to be at risk there, but, rightly, the organisers decided that playing cricket would be inappropriate in the circumstances.

That is the easy bit and no doubt the practical considerations, such as the financial compensation owed to the host nation and to television companies, will be less thorny than when moral considerations (Zimbabwe) are the cause of abandonment. Where it gets more complicated is with the realisation that the entire sub-continent is becoming an increasingly risky place to play.

The Champions Trophy in Pakistan was postponed in August, a month before a bomb blast destroyed the front of the Islamabad Marriott in September (another hotel that cricketers worldwide know intimately). Things are not much better in Sri Lanka, where the war between the government and the Tamil Tigers continues. Since the government pulled out of the ceasefire in January, violence has been on the increase. A series of bombs rocked Colombo on Independence Day in February and in May a suicide bomber close to the Hilton hotel (another cricketing haunt) killed nine people and injured 90.

The World Cup in 2011 is a long way off, but as it involves all these nations, this latest atrocity ensures a headache for those responsible for the tournament's security. Between the opening ceremony in Bangladesh and the final at the Wankhede Stadium in Mumbai, the World Cup is to be spread across four nations involving 19 stadiums: a logistical nightmare even before the extra security that will be demanded now. Private security firms, which have already done good business in the last few years advising teams, will continue to flourish.

As violence becomes endemic in the region, no sport will be more affected than cricket, because it is the sub-continent, rather than London or Melbourne – or even Dubai, the headquarters of the ICC – where cricket's pulse beats the strongest. Pakistan, Sri Lanka and Bangladesh may dance to an Indian tune, but taken as a whole it is the most dominant region – economically, politically and numerically – in the sport.

The game's newest, brashest and most commercial offering, the Indian Premier League, is the template of cricket's future and it will be interesting to see whether the clamour to join from foreign players will ease off. As cricketers around the world prepared to pull out of the Champions Trophy in Pakistan, those playing for Rajasthan Royals were happy to ply their trade two days after a series of bomb blasts in Jaipur. Risks are apparently easier to take when more money is at stake.

Amid the depression, it is important not to forget that things on the ground are often much less chaotic than those of us watching images thousands of miles away would believe. Life in parts of Mumbai will go on as normal today, as they did in London after 7 July 2005. And while the situation is not exactly analogous – the London bombings were indiscriminate, whereas the atrocities on Wednesday seemed to be aimed at specific targets – Australia stayed on and a wonderful Ashes series ensued.

So while it may seem inappropriate to say so right now, I hope the Test series in two weeks' time can still go ahead. Unless the Foreign Office advice is to stay at home, I shall certainly be going. One thing is for sure, however: since 9/11, much of the fun and spontaneity of watching sport has disappeared beneath an avalanche of security requirements. Sadly, sport, long regarded as a playground for those who want to abscond from the grim realities of daily life, is no longer immune.

The Times, 28 November 2008

Safety First for England's Return to India

It is understandable, albeit misconceived, to imagine that England's cricketers face a complex decision over the next few days. Images of carnage at an hotel with which you are intimately acquainted are bound to blur the 'should we, shouldn't we' issue. On top of that, it is a time when Anglo-Indian cricket relations are peculiarly fraught, so that any potential leverage between boards at loggerheads will be seized upon. But when you cut through everything, the decision whether England should return to India to play two Test matches is a simple one and should be based on a single question: is it safe to return?

In itself this is a complex issue, since the assassination of presidents down the years confirms that no one's safety can ever be guaranteed. But surely we all understand that: anyone living in London, New York, Mumbai or indeed any nation involved in the so-called war against terrorism must understand that day-to-day living comes with an element of risk attached. What we – players, journalists, supporters – want to know is whether the balance of probabilities is in our favour.

None of us knows, which is why we rely on experts to tell us and why we must respect that advice. Hugh Morris, the managing director of England cricket, confirmed yesterday that this would be the way forward for the ECB, whose directors were meeting last night. He suggested that security reports would come over the next 24 to 48 hours from a variety of sources, from the Foreign Office, from embassies in India and from Reg Dickason, the man who provides daily security reassurance to the players and their families.

Dickason has a crucial role to play, for it is his advice that the players will trust implicitly. Dickason is a jolly, moustachioed Australian who has been a permanent presence on England tours for the last few years. At times, his closeness to the team – he parades around in England team tracksuits and is often seen socialising with the players – raises the question as to how detached a view he is able to take in these matters. But his professionalism must be taken on trust and, since he is paid a princely sum to give advice about a topic in which he is expert, the players and the ECB would be foolish to ignore it.

Sean Morris will co-ordinate the players' response, along with Kevin Pietersen, the captain, who was speaking to his team-mates throughout yesterday afternoon. Morris, the chief executive of the Professional Cricketers' Association (PCA), is due at the Foreign Office this morning with John Carr, the ECB's director of operations. The PCA's concern is that there may be insufficient time to co-ordinate the kind of independent security reports that in the past have provided firm comfort to the players. If the initial time-frame for the Test series is to be adhered to, a decision to travel or not would have to be taken by Wednesday at the latest.

If the advice from security sources hardens in the coming days – which it may well do, given that India was reported to be raising its security levels to 'war footing' yesterday – to the point at which the advice is for England to stay at home, then no one should be accused of a streak of yellowness. Indeed, the ECB would have a duty of care not to place its players in harm's way.

But, if the advice remains, as it is now, that other areas can accommodate cricket safely, then the ECB should send a team, and indeed should expect its players to go. Briefings have indicated that the ECB is considering Kolkata as an alternative venue to Ahmedabad for the first Test.

Geoff Miller, the national selector, indicated yesterday that no player would have his hand forced. 'The players will be left to make their own decisions and they won't be forced to go back even if the security reports are favourable,' he said. 'If some players choose to stay at home, the selectors will have to reassess, but any decision to miss the Test series will not be held against them.'

This would seem to be in response to reports that three players, Andrew Flintoff, Stephen Harmison and an unnamed bowler thought to be Jimmy Anderson (his wife is pregnant), have expressed serious reservations about returning. But it has always been a matter of personal choice whether you accept the invitation to play for England, with all the rewards and risk – personal and professional – that such an undertaking brings.

There cannot be any question of sending a second-string team, since no player's life is more important than another's. So if players decide that they do not wish to tour, then normal principles should apply: no tour fee and an understanding that no place should ever be taken for granted.

One positive development yesterday was the conciliatory tone of Lalit Modi, the vice-president of the Board of Control for Cricket in India (BCCI), a man for whom English cricket has always seemed to be as a red rag is to a bull. He suggested that compensation was the last thing on the BCCI's mind.

'It is not a case of the BCCI against the ECB or the players, that doesn't achieve anything,' Modi said. 'It has got nothing to do with monetary issues, either. We would never pressurise anyone; that is not the way we operate.' That would come as news to the ECB, but welcome news at that. Perhaps the fear of a Pakistan-like isolation has softened Modi's position.

Modi, though, was right when he insisted that 'we can't allow events to deter us'. It was an opinion shared by Haroon Lorgat, the chief executive of the ICC, the world governing body, who implored England to tour if security and safety allowed. As time begins to soften the brutal memory of the last few days, that seemed to be the sentiment gathering momentum yesterday. It all now hinges on the security advice given to the players. Over to you, Reg.

The Times, 1 December 2008

Kevin Pietersen's Strong Lead Buys England Time

'A collective decision' was how Kevin Pietersen described the England team's decision to fly to Abu Dhabi yesterday. And while no player, he insisted, would have his arm twisted to return to India, the clear impression given was that the England team would decide, after discussing the final security report on Sunday evening, to travel onwards together, or return home together. And since no man's life should be considered more important than another's, this, surely, is a step in the right direction.

This development represents something of a triumph for Pietersen himself. Little has been heard publicly from the England captain since the atrocities in Mumbai, but that is not to say that he has not been busy. Throughout the week he has spoken at length to all the players – some needed more airtime than others – and while he reiterated that he has not strong-armed anybody into travelling, it is known that he has been more forceful than his initial laissez-faire attitude suggested.

The departure of the whole squad for Abu Dhabi yesterday is not to say that the India Tests, the first of which is due to begin on Thursday in Chennai, will definitely go ahead. *The Times* has learnt that officials from the Professional Cricketers' Association (PCA) and the players' representatives, who have seen the interim report upon which the ECB directors made their recommendations on Sunday last, still have serious concerns as to its contents. According to the report, there was insufficient time to prepare a thorough assessment and the PCA remains worried that security procedures have been short-circuited because of time constraints and political and financial concerns. The decision to return to India now depends on the final security report that will be submitted to the players on Sunday.

Abu Dhabi, then, as Pietersen admitted yesterday, is an exercise in buying time, while enabling England to get some much-needed outdoor practice. But it will surely be more difficult for Andrew Flintoff and Stephen Harmison to pull out now that they are out of earshot of family and advisers, who cannot be relied upon to give dispassionate advice. Getting the team to Adu Dhabi, therefore, is a shrewd piece of manoeuvring by the ECB.

Speaking in the ballroom of the Renaissance hotel, Heathrow, two hours before departure, Pietersen suggested that although safety and security were the principal considerations for the group, the wider interests of the game and the need to show solidarity with the Indian people were at the forefront of the players' minds. 'It's fantastic that the players want to go back to India to play cricket,' he said. 'It is important that we stand shoulder to shoulder with the Indian people in their time of need. I'm very confident that we'll have a full squad of fifteen players to choose from for the first Test match next week.

'Everyone has become a lot more open-minded over the last few days. They've had a chance to spend some time with their families. And they now realise that it is going to be a huge thing to go back to India, to go back and do what we love doing. We want to make a positive stance and help people out.'

Referring to those such as Flintoff and Harmison who have serious misgivings about returning, Pietersen said: 'I didn't have to persuade anybody. I respected everyone's viewpoints and their individual concerns. They are their own men and are able to make their own life decisions. But it is fantastic that they have decided to come, because they are two big players and we certainly want them in our team. I feel very proud to be captain of such a great bunch of guys who want to play for their country and want to try to make amends for what happened recently in the one-day series.'

Neither Pietersen nor Hugh Morris, the managing director of England cricket, would confirm what would happen if the security advice was positive but one player still had concerns. Morris said that he hoped that if the security advisers, the ECB and the PCA were all of one mind, there would be no dissenters. For those of a nervous disposition, the news that India's international airports had been put upon high alert yesterday because of the threat of terrorist attacks would have come as little comfort. Morris indicated that all these developments would form part of the security audit that will be presented to the players on Sunday evening in Abu Dhabi and that will then end this 'will-they-won't-they' saga once and for all.

The Times, 5 December 2008

England Adjust to India's 'Ring of Steel'

For a virtual war zone – the description of Chennai given by Stephen Harmison as he pondered whether to return – it has been pretty calm here. The nearest thing to a terrorist alert was two days ago, when a local policeman at the railway station raised the alarm about a suspect package, but the potential bomb proved to be a figment of the drunken officer's mind. No bombs, then, and the only thing resembling the sound of gunfire has been the gentle putter-putter of night rain that has fallen on corrugated-iron rooftops.

Much has been made of the 'ring of steel', the *cordon sanitaire* that acts as protective swaddling for the players: the 500 troops ring-fencing the ground, the 300 or so in the hotel and the 1,000 within its vicinity. And what troops they are! The Rapid Action Force (RAF), distinctive in their blue uniforms and carrying snub-nosed guns; the Special Action Group (SAG), whose female officers look very fetching in high black boots and khaki tops; and the Quick Reactive Team (QRT), who must be out on manoeuvres, or under cover, because so far they have been NTBS – nowhere to be seen.

There is, of course, more security than normal. To drive into the Taj Coromandel, the splendid residence at which the team is staying, your car will be checked over at the barricades, mirrors will be placed underneath to look for bombs, and you must walk through a metal detector at the front entrance – and another if you want to get on to the fourth floor, where the players are holed up. And, as one India player found to his disgust a couple of nights ago, no unauthorised guests will be allowed.

On the fourth floor, there are a dozen or so armed and serious-looking guards, about whom it is tempting to be wary, until you remember that all Indians like cricket. Me, I'm staying on the fourth floor of the Taj, too, and so it is assumed that somehow I am involved with the team. One guard insists, despite my protestations, that I am the batting coach and we now engage in small talk about technique while I wait for the lift to come. It is not so bad, really. I just hope KP and the boys get some runs, or I'll be in for a grilling.

The most tempting thing to do in the aftermath of terrorism is to exaggerate the danger and the effects on daily life. After all, if you want to drive into Lord's the day before a Test match, you have to let the sniffer dogs do their bit there as well. As it happened, I didn't have my pass on the day I arrived here, but I managed to walk through the gates of the M.A. Chidambaram Stadium and out to the middle without anybody asking to see it. The chief sports writer from the *Daily Mirror* (and you know it's a big story when the 'chiefs' arrive) got in by showing his FA Cup pass.

Chennai is 825 miles (1,329 km) from Mumbai, more than 12 hours by rail and God knows how long by bus. Language and cultural differences are vast enough to make Lancastrians and Yorkshiremen seem like blood brothers by comparison. Might as well be another country.

There is no sense that Chennai is in mourning. People here have a very matter-of-fact view of life and they are going about their business: earning a crust, cooking meals, playing sport, looking after the kids and generally getting on. Most Indians haven't got time to dwell and ponder.

Sheila, the bookseller in the Taj, reckons that business is a little slow for the time of year, but Haribabu, who has worked here for 18 years, and now mans the patisserie stall, reports a fine trade in chocolate truffles and black forest gateaux.

Outside, on the Nangambakkam road, the sellers of fruit and dhosa (crêpes) are doing good business, girls from the Sacred Heart High School are hurrying to their lessons, people are chatting and spitting underneath the 'do not spit' signs, the drivers of the death-on-three-wheels (tuk-tuks) are winding their way through gaps you don't think exist, and families ride, helmetless, three or four to a bike. 'Elf and safety wouldn't like it.

Down at the Marina beach, which runs the length of the city, all manner of activities are taking place. Joggers are braving the afternoon heat and the air quality, which the World Health Organisation reckons is seven times the recommended levels of pollution. Children are flying kites and there are dozens of cricket matches going on. More than 200 people lost their lives during the tsunami at this beach in Chennai, many of them children playing cricket, so they know a bit about getting on with things here. After the tsunami, the beach was washed away but it is back now, wide and sandy, all seven miles (12 km) of it.

At the ground, K.Parsatharathy, the groundsman of 35 years, sits on his roller looking unconcerned that a Test is about to start. He'd have liked to have had a bit more time to work on his pitch, but he shrugs and says it will be pretty much like all the others he has prepared here: some pace and bounce early on, with plenty of spin later. His staff, women in bright-coloured saris, sit close by, chatting and waiting for instructions.

Cricketers are practising in the nets, but over in the pavilion there is a bit of a commotion, because Kevin Pietersen and Mahendra

Singh Dhoni are about to unveil the series trophy. Before they do, the big cheese from the Royal Bank of Scotland (RBS), the sponsor, wants to say a few words and she blathers on about RBS's wealth management service (as if anybody has got any money left these days), its global portfolio and the important role RBS plays in local communities. You feel like saying, 'Come on, love, forget the cricket and just lower your mortgage rates.'

Then she's done and she asks Pietersen and Dhoni to unveil the trophy. All of a sudden there is an almighty scrum, as dozens of cameramen, photographers and journalists surge towards the captains. Reg Dickason, the England security adviser, has seconded his son into action on this trip (and that tells you all you need to know about how the security business is doing very nicely out of this show), and it is his responsibility to guard the England captain. Dickason Jr has a look of sheer panic as he finds himself on the wrong side and he tries to fight his way through the scrum. James Avery, the ECB's laconic media officer, leans against the wall, smiling. This is India, after all, and chaos is a given.

All this was happening yesterday in Chennai, much like any other day there when Test cricket is on. Cricketers practising, bankers bullshitting, columnists writing, locals getting from home to work and back again in a variety of ways, children playing cricket on the beach and chaos unfolding. That is what happens after the terror. And today, the Test begins.

The Times, 11 December 2008

England Bow to Sachin Tendulkar's Genius

Urged on by the local paper to bunk off work and watch history in the making, they did so in their thousands. They came with their whistles, hooters and horns, with their faces painted orange, white and green and waving their flags of India. And what a day they had: Sachin Tendulkar, one of the greatest players in history, played one of his greatest innings, signing off a script that could have been written for him with a four to end the match, bring up his hundred and win a Test for his country.

This was no ordinary match and no ordinary victory. The score-book will record that India won at a canter, with six wickets and 20 overs to spare. The statisticians will trot out the necessaries – that this was the highest successful run chase on the sub-continent and the fourth highest in history. But that is the least of it. As Tendulkar dedicated his 41st Test hundred to the damaged city of Mumbai and as 30,000 people stayed and cheered both teams for their efforts with almost equal zeal, it was clear that something special had happened in this old, dilapidated stadium.

Nationalism is never far from the surface in India and after the horrors of Mumbai, its intensity has been more apparent. Tendulkar has always been India's equivalent of the late Ken Barrington, of whom it was said that every time he walked to the crease he did so as if the Union Jack was draped around his shoulders. These feelings would have been magnified this week, as Tendulkar revealed in a television address when he reaffirmed publicly why he played the game: 'I play for India, now more than ever.' Yesterday he was as good as his word.

He gave a masterclass in batsmanship: how to pace a fourth-innings run chase, how to play spin on a wearing pitch, how to tailor an innings to the demands of the situation. He went to the crease in the third over of the day after Andrew Flintoff had given England an early tonic with the wicket of Rahul Dravid, searching for form but finding only a thin edge to the wicket-keeper, and he was still there at the end, caked in sweat and dust, now with Yuvraj Singh, a young thruster, for company. He hit nine boundaries in all, but more to the point were the countless singles, which formed the bedrock of his innings, each one manoeuvred expertly into the gaps as if his blade possessed a sat-nav.

England, who had dominated this game until lunchtime on the fourth day, when they led by 319 runs with seven second-innings wickets intact, will wonder how they lost. They would do well to reflect on the three hours after lunch on Sunday, when the run-rate stalled, they lost all sense of purpose and were complicit in allowing Virender Sehwag to blaze India back into contention. Not for nothing was Sehwag made man of the match.

Even so, England began the last day as worthy favourites, needing nine wickets on a pitch that resembled a palaeontologist's excavation site. They took only three. They might have had more; crucially, Tendulkar, pushing forward on ten to the off-spin of Graeme Swann, was dropped at silly point by Alastair Cook. It was a tough chance, as was Matt Prior's missed stumping down the leg side of Yuvraj when the left-hander had scored 80. But this was a day when we expected the bowlers and close fielders to come off the field hoarse from appealing, so promising were the conditions. Three wickets and a couple of missed opportunities represented slim pickings.

Much was expected of England's spinners on this final day and, although they occasionally found some sharp turn and bounce, they disappointed. Allowing the India batsmen to play on the back foot too often and setting fielders deep as if in fear of leaking boundaries, they could never pin them down and create enough pressure. Monty Panesar, in particular, looked short of form, match practice and confidence. He finished wicketless and dispirited from 27 repetitive and unimaginative overs, his trademark enthusiasm buried under brilliant Indian batsmanship.

Gautam Gambhir, who had helped send India on their way with Sehwag, played beautifully until he poked a ball from James Anderson to gully and V.V.S. Laxman showed glimpses of his wristy genius before prodding Swann to short leg. So it was left to Yuvraj to accompany Tendulkar home. He did so, uncertainly at first and then with growing assurance, finishing on 85 and having played the kind of innings of substance that could be the making of him as a Test batsman.

Yuvraj's success will have irritated England, since they regard him as a show pony. As in the first innings, they raised the decibel levels when he came in and they tried to get under his skin. This time, wisely, he did not take the bait and turned his back on them. With his languid swing of the blade, cocky manner and locker full of strokes, he will always score quickly and, as victory loomed, he threatened to overtake his partner.

By now, Tendulkar was batting not only for his country and himself but for Yuvraj, too, because every time the left-hander played a loose shot or made a grand gesture, Tendulkar admonished him and reminded him of his responsibilities. This was no time for flightiness; there was a match to win. No doubt Tendulkar was reminded of his own century in a losing cause on this ground against Pakistan a decade ago. He had a ghost to exorcise.

Had Yuvraj been batting with anyone else, he would have hogged the limelight and taken India to victory in a blaze of boundaries. But now he had to tread a fine line because the crowd wanted a Tendulkar hundred as well as victory. Such is Tendulkar's standing that Yuvraj retreated from centre stage, gave up the strike and allowed Tendulkar his moment.

Swann served up something juicy on leg stump and Tendulkar, down on one knee and watching the ball like a hawk, paddle-swept it for four. Yuvraj, bad back and all, hoisted Tendulkar into the air, the little maestro clenched a fist in salute and the noise from the M.A. Chidambaram Stadium echoed all the way to Mumbai.

The Times, 16 December 2008

1st Test. At M.A. Chidambaram Stadium, Chennai, on 11–15
December. Toss: England. India won by six wickets. England 316
(A.J. Strauss 123, M.J. Prior 53*, A.N. Cook 52) and 311–9d (A.J.
Strauss 108, P.D. Collingwood 108). India 241 (M.S. Dhoni 53) and
387–4 (S.R. Tendulkar 103*, Yuvraj Singh 85*, V. Sehwag 83,
G. Gambhir 66).

Cricket Shudders on Day It Becomes Terror Target in Lahore

Stuart Broad was fast asleep in his Barbados hotel room at 2am
when he had a phone call from his father. The England fast
bowler was a bit disorientated and confused as to why his old
man should be ringing at that hour and why he had a missed
call from him on his phone. He found out the reasons quickly
enough.

None of us knows how we will react in extraordinary circumstances, but it was clear that Chris Broad, the ICC match referee in
Lahore, in shielding Ahsan Raza, the fourth umpire, from further
gunfire, had behaved heroically. Not that this was a time for talking
about heroics.

Half a world away from the West Indies, Thilan Samaraweera,
at 32 some ten years older than Broad Jr, was also disorientated,
but only because his body was full of drugs. He had just scored
231 in Karachi and 214 in Lahore – only the sixth batsman in Test
history to achieve double hundreds in consecutive matches – and
was looking forward, no doubt, to the felicitations in Colombo on
his return. Instead, he spent yesterday in hospital, heavily sedated
with shrapnel in his leg.

He was not the only one with shrapnel wounds: the captain,
Mahela Jayawardene, the mildest and most pleasant of men, who
has already experienced his share of tragedy in life when he lost his

brother to a brain tumour at 16, had fragments removed from his shoulder, Tharanga Paranavitana, the opening batsman, some from his chest, and Ajantha Mendis, the mystery spinner, shrapnel from his neck and scalp.

As a sports writer, you do not expect to be using the words mystery spinner and shrapnel in the same sentence, but, as the horrendous attack on the Sri Lanka team in Lahore demonstrated yesterday, things have changed. I was one of those who argued consistently that cricketers should go and play in the sub-continent, that England should go and play in India after the Mumbai attacks and, yes, even go and play in Pakistan. Clearly, I was wrong – at least about Pakistan.

Most of us who have played in the sub-continent, who have witnessed the almost religious passion for the sport there, could not envisage a scenario in which cricket and cricketers would be targeted. It is difficult enough to bracket terrorism and sport together in any case, the aim of the first being to end life, the second to celebrate it. The act of killing is contrary to the very idea of sport, and so even though a sportsman's life is no more valuable than any other, the fact that these attacks were aimed directly at sport makes the idea somehow even more shocking.

Occasionally, cricketers have found themselves caught up in events in the sub-continent, but only in the sense that they were in the wrong place at the wrong time. In 2002, the New Zealand team were staying in the Sheraton hotel in Karachi when a bomb went off on a nearby bus, killing 14 people. More recently, the England team's kit – but thankfully not the players – were in the Taj Mahal Palace hotel in Mumbai when the terrorists struck last November.

This, though, is the first direct attack on cricket. It is also a direct attack on Pakistan itself. By targeting something that is so dear to the hearts of most Pakistanis, the one thing that allowed Pakistan normal engagement with the West, this attack has ensured further isolation there. Certainly cricket isolation, which will be the sad but inevitable result. It is no longer safe to play in Pakistan.

There will be no international cricket played there for the foreseeable future. New Zealand were due to go in November and December, England for a four-Test series in February 2010. The entire cricketing community was due there in 2011, Pakistan being co-hosts of the World Cup along with Sri Lanka, India and Bangladesh. Yesterday it was too soon, and inappropriate, for governing bodies to make immediate decisions, but none of these events will take place. Of the leading Test-playing nations, Sri Lanka was Pakistan's last ally, the only country prepared to play there.

Cricket did not wither and die in South Africa during the years of isolation and it is unlikely that it will do so in Pakistan during the exile that will inevitably follow. Anybody who has witnessed the passion of street cricket and tape-ball cricket in urban Pakistan would understand that. Pakistan will continue to play abroad and play home games in Abu Dhabi or Dubai. They may play neutral games in England, as Giles Clarke, the chairman of the ECB, has suggested. These matches will be seen in Pakistan and new heroes will be created, so the aspirations of urban cricketers in Islamabad, Lahore and Karachi will not be completely deflated.

The great fear for cricket, though, is that this new phase of terrorism will spread throughout the sub-continent. India is the financial and political powerhouse of world cricket and yesterday Lalit Modi, the commissioner of the Indian Premier League (IPL), was quick to offer reassurances that the tournament will go ahead.

The dates may be shifted, though, partly because of the need to beef up security and partly because of the elections in India, due to start at the same time as the IPL in mid-April, which will overload the security forces. This shift may affect the England players' participation.

How can decisions be made by players now on where they should play? How is India safer than Pakistan? And what about war-torn Sri Lanka? It is a deeply unsatisfactory answer, but it must be a matter of degree and based on the advice given by security personnel. There is always an element of risk in any walk of life. Where possible, the show must go on.

From a cricket perspective, the increased involvement of security will be the greatest sadness of yesterday's events. Many of us scoffed in India before Christmas when the England team travelled around in a motorcade in the style of a tin-pot Third World dictator, sirens blaring, outriders shooing pedestrians, cyclists and cars out of the way. Was it really necessary? Sadly, it seems as if it was. Events have proven Reg Dickason, the ECB security adviser, right. In Barbados yesterday he said: 'The notion of sporting teams being a protected species was held by many but it was not a view we shared.'

Cricket and cricketers are no longer a protected species and although events in Lahore seemed a world away from the England and West Indies teams who were en route to Trinidad, yesterday's events affected them all.

Broad, of course, was relieved that his dad was unhurt and, no doubt, a little proud, too. Owais Shah's thoughts turned to Lahore and Karachi, where many members of his family live. The thoughts of Aleem Dar, the Pakistani umpire who stood in the fourth Test [in Barbados], were with Raza, a friend and club team-mate. Others, inevitably, began to think about how their possible IPL involvement would be affected and whether they would have to make difficult decisions about whether to travel. The mood was subdued.

The Times, 4 March 2009

5

The Fix Is In

I was on air when Mohammad Amir, the young and impossibly talented left-arm quick bowler from Lahore, overstepped the front line by a huge margin. I commented on the size of the no-ball, but not for one minute did I think of spot-fixing. I have wondered to myself since what this said about me: whether I am simply too naïve or whether the cynicism hasn't yet overshadowed an optimistic outlook on the game and the people who play it.

I hope it says more about the latter than the former, although some would disagree. I still maintain, even after the discouraging events of last summer, that the game is by and large a clean one. There is no doubt though that the rise of Twenty20, and the ICL and IPL, have encouraged a return to previous lax attitudes and regulation. The first two versions of the IPL were not monitored and few were surprised when rumours of wrongdoing surfaced during the second edition in South Africa.

But back to Pakistan and Mohammad Amir. I still take a charitable view towards him on the basis of his age and vulnerability. Many argue differently, and have called for a life ban if found guilty, and objectively it is difficult to argue against that point of view. If the game is to remain/become clean then firm action is essential. Somehow, though, I hope a way can be found to make Amir a part of the solution.

One thing is for sure: the day after the News of the World's revelations was the strangest atmosphere I think I have ever experienced at a cricket match. People were genuinely upset – which, in a way, is a positive thing. People still care about the game.

Nothing to Celebrate as Dark Cloud Looms Large over Lord's

There was cricket at Lord's yesterday but no one really cared. Least of all a Pakistan team that lost their last six wickets in 95 soul-destroying minutes on the way to their heaviest defeat in Tests, by a whopping innings and 225 runs.

Only Umar Akmal, with a spunky 79 from 68 balls, showed any stomach for the fight, although there was more than a hint of desperation about some of his swashbuckling strokes. The boat was sinking and Akmal was determined to enjoy his last dance. His team-mates had long since thrown the lifeboats overboard and disappeared.

The last ball of a match that started and finished in the most dramatic circumstances came when Mohammad Asif, one of the players implicated in the spot-fixing allegations overnight, swatted at Graeme Swann, only to have an inside edge cannon on to his boot and pop to Paul Collingwood at slip.

It was Swann's fifth wicket of another outrageously successful campaign for him and the last in an emphatic series win for England, moments both that would usually spark raucous celebrations. Instead, England's and Swann's were muted, just handshakes all round, and Andrew Strauss was quick to concede that the allegations against their opponents had knocked considerable gloss off his team's achievements.

On the back of those spot-fixing allegations, it looked as though Pakistan were embarrassed to show their faces at all, which might have explained the brevity of their innings. They turned up barely an hour before the start, stayed in their changing-room behind closed doors until play began – just a cuppa and the crossword for a warm-up – did not appear at the post-match presentation and scurried off quickly after the match, leaving Yawar Saeed, the manager, and Salman Butt, the captain, to answer the inevitable questions. Neither did so with any sense of conviction.

The questions are likely to come thick and fast now: from Scotland Yard, initially, from the Pakistan Cricket Board, which has, time and again, failed to act to root out this particular cancer within its cricket team, then from a general public, disillusioned with the notion that too many teams and players, in the past and possibly still now, are perpetrating the worst of sporting deceptions.

Any sport is based upon the simple but crucial premise that the participants are giving of their best and while there is a distinction to be drawn between match-fixing and spot-fixing (the latter being an attempt to manipulate small passages of play rather than the result itself), essentially they are one and the same thing.

What if, for example, one of the no-balls in question had knocked Jonathan Trott's middle stump out of the ground at the start of that world-record stand? Games are won and lost on the smallest of margins.

Given the serious nature of these allegations, the length of time likely to be needed to look into them and that nobody from the Pakistan team has denied them, it is hard to see how the one-day series against them can go ahead as planned. All the right noises were being made last night, but this will rumble on. It is a far, far worse day for cricket than four years ago when Pakistan forfeited a match.

Watching Test cricket at Lord's has always been an immense privilege. For the first time yesterday, it was hard to conjure up any sense of excitement or expectation. Instead, there was just an enormous sadness that the stirring deeds of Trott and Stuart

Broad and, indeed, of Mohammad Amir would be forgotten all too quickly.

At the heart of everything was the knowledge that an 18-year-old bowler, a boy-man of astonishing talent, someone who only days before had lit up a ground for the right reasons, should be at the centre of allegations that, if proved correct, could finish his career for good. It was the loss of innocence, and the notion that a young cricketer could risk so much for so little, that was so profoundly sad.

Amir, remember, had spilt the guts of England's batting all over Lord's on that second morning, with the kind of bowling seen once in a generation. Now, on the final day, he walked to the pitch, head bowed, a nervous smile on his lips, to one or two boos, then silence. Just silence. A game that started so brilliantly ended in ignominy as Swann pegged back his off stump to the fifth ball he faced. A pair and the long walk back, again to silence. There could have been no worse feeling.

If found guilty of the allegations – and the evidence of his two no-balls looks damning indeed – any moral judgement is a clouded one.

At 18, he is old enough to vote and to make his own decisions in life. Yet which one of us at 18 had a supreme sense of right and wrong and the strength of character to ignore the voices of older, supposedly wiser men? More than that, how many of us can appreciate the difficulties of the life that he has led; the impoverishment that forced his parents to send him away from home, unable to clothe, house, feed and educate him. How many of us know the unique pressure placed upon cricketers who are part of a system in which certain actions become expected of them?

Look at what surrounds him. Coaches such as Ijaz Ahmed (married to the sister of Salim Malik – banned for life for

The Fix Is In

match-fixing) and Waqar Younis, who were part of the Pakistan
team in 1990s upon which Justice Qayyum delivered a thundering match-fixing report. Consider this, too: when he received his
man of the series award yesterday, a cheque for £4,000, it was three
times his monthly retainer from the Pakistan Cricket Board.

Pakistan and England are worlds apart politically, economically
and socially and the contrast between Pakistan cricket and English
cricket has never been greater: the order, the structure, the success
and wealth of English cricket; the chaos, the failure and the impoverishment of Pakistan's.

If the rush to judgement of Amir comes any time soon, remember that. Remember that.

The Times, 30 August 2010

The Great Cricketing Casino in the East

Consider this for a moment: Mazhar Majeed, the so-called 'fixer'
in the latest betting allegations to rock cricket, has been arrested
on suspicion of 'perpetrating a fraud against bookmakers'. Yet
the only bookmakers that could possibly have been the subject
of such a fraud are themselves illegal. The only bookmakers who
offer markets on elements of the game open to so-called micro-
manipulation are those in India, where bookmaking is illegal and
designed to avoid tax and service the black market. You wouldn't
get a price on Mohammad Amir bowling a no-ball in his third
over down at Ladbrokes.

The sub-continent, now the financial and administrative powerhouse of the world game, is where betting on cricket is at its fiercest, with hundreds of millions of dollars wagered on each one-day
international. It is for that reason that most of the corruption in
cricket has sprung from there.

135

Some history. India's 1983 World Cup triumph sparked a massive surge in interest in the one-day game on the sub-continent. Over the next decade, the numbers of one-day internationals increased exponentially, along with spurious and unsupervised tournaments in Sharjah and elsewhere. And although Kerry Packer's involvement in cricket had resulted in increased salaries for players, cricketers were still the poor relations of sport and vulnerable to the pressures applied by bookmakers eager to know in advance the make-up of a team, for example, the result of the toss even, and then the results of the matches themselves.

And so match-fixing was born. The game, we subsequently found out, was little more than a giant casino in which the players were the croupiers, controlling the cards and the spin of the roulette wheel and taking a decent cut on top. If this came as news to those of us in the England team it was not because of any naïvety, simply because between 1993 and 2000 England did not tour the sub-continent, save for the World Cup in 1996, when the bookmakers had plenty of other flesh on hand that they had already got their hooks into.

The Test match that blew the whole scam wide open was one that I played in at Centurion Park in South Africa in 1999. Then, the South Africa captain, Hansie Cronje, accepted a leather jacket and a few thousand dollars to ensure that the match would not be drawn since, because of the heavy rain over the first three days, the bookmakers' liability on the draw was massive.

Phone conversations between Cronje and Sanjay Chawla had been taped by the Delhi Police and subsequent work by India's Central Bureau of Investigation revealed Cronje to have been heavily implicated in match-fixing on the sub-continent during the previous four years. Further investigations, in particular by Justice Qayyum in Pakistan, painted a picture of a game that was, according to Lord Condon, the first commissioner of the International

Cricket Council's (ICC) Anti-Corruption Unit (ACU), institutionally corrupt.

Although the ICC took immediate measures to stamp out corruption – players were no longer allowed phones in dressing-rooms, for example – it could be argued that the germs of the allegations of the last two days at Lord's could be found in the ICC's refusal to take stronger action against all those implicated. Instead, it was happy to finger one or two high-profile players while ignoring calls to delve deeper, hoping that by doing so they could stamp out the problem without castrating the game.

A similar situation occurred in Pakistan where, despite the thoroughness of the Qayyum report, few of those implicated by Qayyum had action taken against them. Mushtaq Ahmed, for example, is England's bowling coach and yet Qayyum found that there were 'sufficient grounds to cast doubt' on him on a tour of Sri Lanka in 1994–95. Wasim Akram, later inducted into the ICC Hall of Fame, was found to be 'not above board' and it was recommended he should never hold a position of responsibility again. Players who were part of the Pakistan team throughout the 1990s hold coaching positions within the team now.

After this mini-purge by the ICC, and after it installed Lord Condon as head of the ACU, it was assumed that the problem had disappeared. Condon, who has now been replaced by Ronnie Flanagan, a former Home Office chief inspector, warned on numerous occasions of the dangers of complacency and of 'spot-fixing'.

Two factors made a resurgence of corruption more likely. One was the rise of Twenty20: franchise tournaments in India such as the Indian Cricket League and Indian Premier League were unsupervised by the ICC's ACU and, with franchise holders having spent millions on buying their franchises, rumours abounded of match-fixing.

Second, was a change in betting patterns. It was no longer necessary to fix the result of a match, rather a specific element of it. So, for example, a batting team might determine how many runs they would score in a portion of five overs in a one-day game; or, as the allegations this week suggested, a bowler might suggest how many no-balls he would bowl and when. It is this so-called micro-betting that is at the heart of any corruption now.

Given the shift of cricket's power base to the East, given the way cricket is uniquely placed to offer betting opportunities, given that it is a game played by human beings and given that the governing body of the game is weak, it is unlikely that an absolute end to corruption will come any time soon.

The ICC had its chance to stamp it out ten years ago, but it is a far less powerful organisation now, having lost control of the fixture list on the back of the rise of Twenty20. Illegal bookmaking and the shift of cricketing power to the East: a potent combination whose chickens came home to roost again this week.

The Times, 30 August 2010

Mohammad Amir Can Come to Symbolise Reform If Proved That the Mark Was Overstepped

The England captain, a number of his predecessors, the Pakistan manager, Yawar Saeed, and the greatest Pakistani cricketer of them all, Imran Khan, were of one voice on Sunday: if the allegations are proved to be accurate then the punishment should fit the crime.

'If someone is proven to be categorically guilty then the only way is for them never to play international cricket again,' said Strauss in a flawless post-match performance. In a different way, Saeed agreed: 'If I have stolen one shilling from you, you punish me for a shilling not for a million pounds,' he said. And if fixing is the greatest crime a sportsman can commit, the punishment, in Saeed's view, should be suitably harsh.

The crime, if proven, is obvious. What is not so straightforward is who perpetrated it and who the victims are. Clearly, the paying public would be victims, deceived into thinking that Pakistan's cricketers were giving their all; England's players would be victims, too, because the Spirit of the Game, when you think about it, is about one thing and one thing only: respect for your opponents.

But I would argue that Mohammad Amir, rather than one of those allegedly perpetrating the crime, would be the biggest victim and the focus of any investigation should be on those who felt it necessary, and were able, to take advantage of him and on the culture within the team. On the likes of the middleman who, the *News of the World* reported, had the wherewithal to waken him from his slumbers on the eve of a Test match, address him as 'fucker' and announce that instructions could wait until the morning.

Now think of Salman Butt, the captain, and the nature of authority in Pakistan itself. When a slip catch disappeared through the cordon at The Oval, Butt walked towards them and gave them a very public dressing-down. An England captain might have got a flea in his ear had he done the same; in Pakistan you don't flout authority. Could an 18-year-old resist the wishes of his elders, his superiors?

Yesterday, Amir's coach and mentor from his academy days in Rawalpindi, defended his protégé. 'My school is run very strictly and with discipline, and my boys here would not do such things,' Asif Bajwa said. Maybe true, but Amir has been a part of a very different environment now – the Pakistan cricket team – and it would be the biggest indictment of the culture of them if some-one who has only been around for such a short period has been corrupted in that time.

Think, for a moment, about the no-balls at the heart of the controversy, the two bowled to order, allegedly, by Amir and the one by Mohammad Asif. Amir's were enormous, a good foot or so over the front line. Asif's overstepping of the front line was more measured – an inch or so. If this was deliberate it might be possible to see the difference between a hopelessly naïve young man, drawn into a situation beyond his understanding, and a hardened professional with plenty of previous under his belt. And they say both should face equal punishment.

Clearly, any cleansing of Pakistan cricket will be a long road since the corruption is so ingrained. It is an uncomfortable truth, but one that must be said of a country run by a president, Asif Zardari, whose nickname is 'Mr Ten Per Cent'. Time and again, from Pakistan Cricket Board (PCB) officials to people such as Justice Malik Mohammad Qayyum, who admitted to leniency against Wasim Akram because the cricketer was his idol, people in authority have encouraged appalling behaviour.

There is a Pakistan Task Team in place, headed by Giles Clarke and including luminaries such as Mike Brearley and Greg Chappell. Their influence must be brought to bear, with the full backing of the ICC, in trying to help purge the PCB of incompetence and corruption.

There are good people in Pakistan cricket. As it happens, during the evening before the allegations became public, I was dining with Ramiz Raja, the former Pakistan batsman and former chief executive of the PCB. We got talking about Imran Khan and Ramiz's view was that fixing did not happen, would not have happened, and could not have happened while Imran was in charge. Leadership is everything here. People such as Ramiz and Imran have to be persuaded to get involved again.

Admittedly, if these allegations are proven accurate, to reprieve

Amir at the expense of anyone else involved would be completely arbitrary and, in a sense, unfair. It would give succour to those who argue – rightly – that the events of the past few days are a direct consequence of a failure to act on the excesses of the past. Yet that would be to ignore the obvious: that Amir is a potent symbol right now, of what was, what is and what might be.

He should not be punished as an example to the rest, as everyone seems to suggest, rather he should be made aware of the issues, educated, rehabilitated and held up as an example of what can be achieved. Amir's rehabilitation should be at the heart of the cleansing of Pakistan cricket. The brilliant young bowler is not the cause of the problem but the most tragic consequence of it.

The Times, 31 August 2010

Why the Culture of Greed Has a Vice-like Grip

Imagine the scene. You are an inexperienced player on your second tour. The captain, a revered figure, calls a team meeting without the presence of the coach. He tells everyone that there has been an offer to throw the next day's match, a one-day international, for $200,000, and a unanimous decision must be made whether to accept. All for one, one for all.

It is hard to imagine how a meeting such as this could take place in professional sport. But it did, in Mumbai in December 1996, the night before a one-day international between South Africa and India. Of all the match-fixing stories, this is the one that has most intrigued, horrified and, in a dark way, amused me.

The circumstances and the narrative show how easy it is for the culture of a team to become corrupted. The match in question was one that was tacked on to an already full itinerary, played to benefit the former India cricketer Mohinder Amarnath. This was much to the disgust of a weary South Africa team, who had been in India for two months and wanted to get home. They were tired and irritable and, as events would show, not thinking clearly.

We know that Hansie Cronje had already received money from M.K. Gupta, a bookmaker, for information during the Test series that preceded the match in question. Gupta, having made his downpayment during the Tests, now offered Cronje $200,000 for his team to throw the match.

The subsequent team meeting that South Africa held to discuss the offer was eventually reported, but sketchily. Colin Bryden, the cricket correspondent of South Africa's *Sunday Times*, wrote about it after the allegations against Shane Warne and Mark Waugh in 1998, although the headline, 'Proud South African Cricketers Hit Match-Fixers For Six', could be said to be laughably ironic in due course. Players involved also gave sparse testimony to the King Commission later, after the outing of Cronje as a match-fixer.

Over the years, this particular team meeting has fascinated me. I always wondered how such a meeting could come about – the awkwardness of the topic, the conversations involved and, since it transpired that only three players spoke out vehemently against the offer (which was ultimately rejected on a one-for-all or all-for-one basis), how it could be contemplated by any self-respecting team.

Over time, I've spoken to many of those who were in that room. Most say that Andrew Hudson, Derek Crookes and Daryll Cullinan were the only ones to recognise the issue for what it was; the only ones who were able, as the dollar signs whizzed in front of their eyes, to know right from wrong. But for them, the money could have been accepted.

Others found ways to convince themselves to take the offer seriously. One talked of the healthy exchange rate against the rand;

another thought it a chance to make some easy cash at the end of his career; another spoke of the anger the squad felt at being forced to play another game; another, unbelievably, asked whether any gains would be tax free; and another voiced a triumphant opinion that they had finally made the big time now that they, too, were being offered the kind of money he had heard other teams talking about. Unbelievable, but true.

A core of senior players held a second meeting privately. Gupta was then asked whether he would up his offer. During the King Commission, Cronje admitted he was sore with himself for not accepting money for losing a match they lost anyway.

Nevertheless, that it was contemplated at all and debated at length is remarkable. This from a team, excluded from international cricket since 1970 over apartheid, who had only been readmitted four years earlier, who had a reputation for godliness and, under Kepler Wessels, for outstanding professionalism.

We are talking about the culture of sporting teams here. South Africa's changed within the space of two years, from the moment that Wessels stood down as captain to Cronje first accepting money from a bookmaker on that tour to India. So when people say that the culture of the Pakistan cricket team cannot change, I don't agree. Any team can change their culture if the right people are in charge.

The drinking culture at Manchester United, prevalent under Ron Atkinson, was quickly stamped out by Alex Ferguson after his arrival in 1986. The losing culture of the England cricket team was ended by a fortunate marriage, one that brought together Duncan Fletcher and Nasser Hussain ten years ago. South Africa's descent into moral relativism was brought about by the susceptibility of one man, Cronje, to money.

As the culture of a team can change rapidly, so can the culture of an entire sport. The recent Bloodgate scandal in rugby union suggested strongly that the move to full-on professionalism has changed the sport to a point where it is unrecognisable from the one played in the amateur age. Bloodgate could not have happened at that time, when players and coaches – and supporters, no doubt – had their sport in proper perspective.

Few could argue that cricket's culture has not changed in recent years and this is about more than the Pakistan team. The pervading culture in cricket now is a grasping one, from administrators to players to commentators. Once money is involved, anything goes. The prevailing culture is one of greed.

The ECB gets into bed with a fraudster of shocking magnitude; a report on the accounts of Zimbabwe Cricket is shredded amid rumours of massive misappropriation of funds; the ICC runs its World Cups with television contracts rather than the public good in mind. At a Test ground recently, wi-fi users were warned against betting, even as the ground in question was fixing the advertising boards plugging the name of a betting company. An Australia player was sent home for drinking as the captain was instructed to wear the team sponsor's cap advertising a brewer. All these things have happened in the last few years.

An England player uses his profile to shamelessly plug a sponsor's product even as he waits in the changing-room as next man in; players involve themselves with benefit sponsors no matter how dodgy the reputation; players hold county clubs to ransom; England players sign central contracts but expect to be able to play in the Indian Premier League (IPL); commentators act as players' agents; an England selector is also a county coach. All these things have happened.

The most egregious example of the present culture is the IPL. Board of Control for Cricket in India officials are also franchise holders; commentators sit on the IPL governing body; the television coverage is not so much about the cricket but about how many sponsors can be satisfied; rumours of money laundering are rife.

Conflicts of interest are wide-ranging and numerous. Taken individually, they might not amount to much. Taken as a whole, they paint a picture of a sport in thrall to money. Is it any wonder, in that atmosphere, that players could be led astray easily? Particularly players from a relatively impoverished country that pays players poorly. If everyone else is on the gravy train, why should they miss out?

It has been said, time and again in this quarter, that cricket will become a great game again only when there is transformation at the very top. While the ICC is run by politicians and businessmen with little feeling for the game and intent only on maximising revenue and politicking to ensure that narrow vested interests are looked after, nothing will change. Their priorities are all wrong.

Leadership is everything. Rotten leadership changed the culture of the South Africa team in the blink of an eye. When Crookes, the young South Africa spinner, spoke up against his hero-worshipped captain in that team meeting in December 1996, it was to anyone from the outside the obvious thing to do. When Cronje asked the team to swear an oath of secrecy and Crookes refused, saying that he was unwilling to keep anything from his wife, it was a brave thing to do.

Within the prevailing culture, which by and large is not crooked but merely grasping, they would be seen as acts of minor heroism.

The Times, 2 September 2010

Unless There Is Hard Evidence to Back Up the Claims, the Show Must Surely Go On

The twitterati were into action quickly again over the weekend after the latest allegations concerning Pakistan's cricketing integrity.

'Enough is enough, call the last two games off,' tweeted the former England captain, Michael Vaughan.

At the risk of vesting something more meaningful into what are nothing more than immediate opinions on a marketing platform, the calls to abandon the last two one-day internationals were a classic case of opening mouth, or twitching typing finger, before engaging brain.

Unlike the initial allegations against the three Pakistan cricketers now suspended, there is, so far, scant evidence to back up the latest claims. An anonymous phone call to a newspaper about alleged conversations between an illegal bookie and a suspected match-fixer is hardly the basis upon which a series can be abandoned. It is hard to believe that if the newspaper in question did have the story absolutely nailed down it would have withheld information to help out the ICC. As Andrew Strauss said yesterday, it could have been, for all we know, a 'crank' call.

The ECB has written to the ICC asking for the hard evidence that the third one-day international was corrupted, but, as yet, nothing has been forthcoming. On what basis should the remaining two games be called off? An anonymous tip-off?

What is clear from the events of the last two days is that Haroon Lorgat, the ICC chief executive, has lost his nerve and his organisation has not the first clue how to engage in crisis management. When Giles Clarke, the chairman of the ECB, wrote to the ICC for information, Sharad Pawar, the ICC president, was not even aware of events. Second, the ICC's press release was vague, implicating everyone, including England's players.

As the ICC has refused to give the ECB any further evidence, we must deduce that it knows little more than the notion that the number of runs in a certain eight- or ten-over spell during the Pakistan innings may have been manipulated. It may well turn out to be that a portion of the match was fixed, in which case the England team and the public have been hoodwinked again, but until the hard facts are ascertained, no cricketer and no team should be prejudged.

It is possible to construct any number of alternatives. Spreads – the number of runs to be scored in a fixed period of time – are available before the match and bookmakers are not normally far out. Anybody, therefore, could ring a newspaper and claim knowledge of how many runs are likely to be scored in a particular number of overs and be not too far wide of the mark.

Why would anybody do that? Again, it is possible to construct any number of reasons. If, as claimed, these sources are coming out of India, it is not implausible that someone in India might want to paint Pakistan in the worst light. Or, what if that someone had placed a big bet on the series being stopped? How better to make that bet pay off?

These are far-fetched possibilities, to be sure, but the point is that until much firmer evidence comes to light, the ECB would be acting on the shakiest of ground to call off the forthcoming games. Certainly, it has been a miserable tour, soured beyond measure, and it is hard not to feel sympathy for Andy Flower and his players. But there is a difference between that sympathy and any curtailing of the tour. The first is understandable; the second is, so far, based on nothing more than a kneejerk reaction to a flimsy story.

The Times, 20 September 2010

ICC Deserves to Be Held as Butt of Derision

Many years ago, in what I always think of as my 'other life', a friend and a colleague from Lancashire and England rang me in a panic. It was a Saturday and a tabloid newspaper had phoned him to say that he, I and another England player were to be named the next morning in a match-fixing scandal. The paper wanted to know if he had any comment to make.

He did not, but he rang me, partly out of consideration and partly to ask what to do. Now I was in a panic. This was 2000, the year match-fixing had come to light after England's tour to South Africa and the Hansie Cronje revelations. You might recall that Chris Lewis, the former England all-rounder, had alerted the ECB – and, unfortunately, the media – to the news that a bookmaker had told him that three England players were implicated in match-fixing.

I rang the chief executive of the ECB at the time, Tim Lamb. What did he know of the story? Was I one of the three names that had been given to him by Lewis? He would not tell me: only he, the chairman of the board, Lord MacLaurin of Knebworth, and the in-house lawyer knew who the names were, and that was the way it was going to stay. That was that; Saturday passed slowly.

To say I was upset at Lamb's initial reaction would be an understatement. I had never, in more than a decade as an England cricketer, been approached by a bookmaker and I had never been involved in receiving money for information or for fixing. And yet, for the rest of that day, I was in limbo, not knowing whether I was about to be named or indeed even if mine was one of those names that Lewis had passed on. It would have been nice to know, if only to prepare a reaction.

Nothing came out in the newspaper the next day. To this day I do not know whether they were merely trying to frighten my friend, whether they were trying it on to flush out some information, or, indeed, whether we were two of those named by Lewis. Later that summer I was interviewed, as was every other England player who played that year, by Scotland Yard. I still do not know who the three names were, although I have heard rumours that included any number of players who played regularly throughout the 1990s (England players in the 1990s paid to lose: shock, horror!). Years later, I asked Lewis, but he was not for telling.

Looking back, I realise that Lamb handled the issue rather well. Lewis had passed on information – as he was bound to do – and that information was presumably checked out by the ECB but without the smearing of any innocent cricketers. Of course, it could have divulged three names to the media while it went about the business of checking things out. No doubt that would have pleased those who thought the ICC acted with due care and attention on Saturday when it released a statement casting suspicion on Pakistan's victory at The Oval on Friday [17 September].

When Haroon Lorgat, the ICC chief executive, rang Giles Clarke ten minutes before the off at The Oval and asked the ECB chairman to consider cancelling the match, it was the action of a man who had lost his nerve. What did he expect Clarke to do? Get the announcer to say to thousands of supporters that, sorry, an anonymous call to a newspaper has highlighted the possibility of some spot-fixing, according to an illegal bookie and a known fixer. And then hand back a couple of million quid? Get real.

And then when the ICC issued the press release the next morning to accompany the story in the *Sun*, it did both sets of players a grave disservice. If England's players have been reduced to apoplexy by Ijaz Butt, they ought to have been even more incensed by the ICC. No one takes Butt seriously, but to have the game's governing body issue a press release that implicates you ought to give everyone pause for thought as to whether the game is in good hands. Since then, the ICC has assured the ECB that no England player is under suspicion.

Pakistan's cricketers remain under suspicion, though, for that Oval match; and because fixing is just about the worst thing of which you can accuse a sportsman, you had better be damn sure of your facts. As yet, even now, the ICC has provided no information to the ECB that it would have acted properly to cancel that match or indeed that anything untoward happened. It is not good enough to say that 'broadly speaking' the information appeared to be correct. The Anti-Corruption and Security Unit gets hundreds of thousands of dollars a year to be more accurate than 'broadly speaking'.

Those who felt that Pakistan's tour should have been cancelled after the revelations during the Lord's Test had a strong point. It would have been understandable to abandon a tour during which players had been caught red-handed, while preaching about giving a portion of their match-fees to charity. But there is a huge difference between the *News of the World* sting – a proper investigation – and the anonymous call to the *Sun*. To have overreacted to these latest claims that, as yet, lack credibility would leave the game dangerously vulnerable to any crank call.

Everything since – the intervention of Butt, the scuffle in the nets between Wahab Riaz and Jonathan Trott, and the almost delicious tension that presented itself at Lord's – followed on from the ICC's clumsy and panic-ridden handling of that episode. The captains, Andrew Strauss and Shahid Afridi, had the look of men who knew too little and yet had the eyes of the cricketing world upon them when they met for the toss. They were put in an invidious position by the game's governing body.

England, with Strauss and Andy Flower to the fore – could there be two better men to have in a crisis? – have handled themselves impressively, although it would have been preferable to have risen above Butt's rantings on the morning of the fourth one-day international.

Many feel indignant on England's behalf, as the team themselves said they were, but there is no one in the cricketing world who takes the chairman of the Pakistan Cricket Board seriously. 'Buffoon' is a dangerous word to use in a Pakistan context, so it is fortunate that the former chief executive of the ICC, Malcolm Speed, has beaten me to the description where Butt is concerned.

By responding, rather than laughing off his accusations, England gave his comments unnecessary credence. If they decide to sue, they will be lowering themselves to Butt's level. Better to forget the ramblings of an old fool and move on. It could be argued, though, that England's players now know what it feels like to be an innocent in the Pakistan dressing-room as accusations are passed back and forth without a shred of evidence.

There are those who feel that enough is enough, that Pakistan should be summarily dismissed from world cricket. Perhaps they forget that John Higgins was found to be not guilty of fixing after a similar sting. And how would they feel if they were in that dressing-room, clean and incorruptible, but tarred with the fixing brush, a whole career, a livelihood ruined on the basis of a team-mate's poor choices?

Individuals, and only those proven guilty, should pay the price, not good men, not a whole team and not a whole country. Nor is it good enough to banish a team on the back of incompetent administrators – we have had enough of those ourselves. Is this the view of a dreamy-eyed romantic who cannot see what is obvious to everyone else? No, simply that respect for individual rights and justice goes way beyond the importance of sport.

Your reaction to this one-day series depends on whether your point of view is optimistic or cynical. The doubters will argue that Pakistan's only impact on this tour has been to increase the level of cynicism. But the past week, at least, has been characterised only by mischief, poor leadership and buffoonery, and not, as far as anyone knows yet, crookedness. Sport, all sport, requires a degree of trust from its supporters.

The Times, 23 September 2010

6

The World Game

Cricket is poorly served by its administrators. The International Cricket Council, the focus of a couple of pieces here, masquerades as a governing body, but it is really just an amalgam of vested interests. As a result, the game is poorly organised and the interests of spectators are secondary to those of television and sponsors.

An overcrowded fixture list, resulting in tired players and meaningless matches, is the most obvious sign of this incompetence. Into this mess, Lalit Modi was allowed to brazenly hire many of the world's best players for the Indian Premier League in return for very little.

The resolutions concerning Zimbabwe down the years, with Zimbabwe retaining their Full Member status, with all the financial advantages that accrue, despite the overwhelming evidence that those monies cannot have been spent on cricketing facilities or infrastructure, suggest strongly that the ICC cannot govern in the best interests of the game in its current form. Malcolm Speed, the former chief executive of the ICC, stepped down eventually when it was clear that politicking would override cricketing interests on the Zimbabwe issue.

Nor, if these pieces here are any reflection of the state of affairs, is the game in rude health. Pakistan cannot play at home, and have been involved in numerous scandals; West Indies appear in terminal decline; Bangladesh are uncompetitive and Zimbabwe have been paralysed by inept and possibly corrupt administration. West Indies and New

Zealand in particular, because of their small populations and lack of financial muscle, are uniquely vulnerable to the power of the IPL.

Who are the good men who, in the years to come, will step forward to run the game more competently than now?

Zimbabwe

On Cricket Alone, Zimbabwe Is in Disgrace

So let us talk not politics but cricket. After all, that is what Peter Chingoka and Ozias Bvute want, is it not? Those twin pillars of the crumbled edifice called Zimbabwe Cricket (ZC), who have presided over a most disgraceful decline while all the time enjoying the benefits that Full Member status of the ICC brings, called upon the international cricket community this week to consider only cricketing matters when Zimbabwe's position at the high table is discussed. We shall grant them their wish.

Chingoka called the move to table a resolution on Zimbabwe as 'unethical', which is a bit like being lectured on fidelity by a sex addict. He reminded Ray Mali, whose last act of a thoroughly undistinguished presidency this was, that the ICC has agreed in the past that 'sport and politics, like oil and water, do not mix'. The thuggish Bvute, the man responsible for kicking Henry Olonga off the team bus after his black-armband protest during the 2003 World Cup, bragged that the 'so-called current worries' in Zimbabwe are an irrelevance to its cricketing status.

That delicious little prefix 'so-called' is all the evidence needed that oil and water do mix and that there is an all-too-close association between ZC and Robert Mugabe's ruling Zanu (PF) party, as outlined last week by Andy Burnham, the Secretary of State for

Culture, Media and Sport. 'So-called'? Tell that to the family of Ben Freeth, the farmer whose horrors at the hands of Mugabe's henchmen *The Times* has chronicled in grim detail this week.

But back to the cricket. You would think that a Full Member of the ICC would need to have a functioning and competitive cricket team. Not necessarily world-beating, but functioning and competitive. But Zimbabwe, of their own accord, have not played a Test match since September 2005. In the past seven years the team have won one Test match. In the 32 one-day internationals since August 2006 they have won only two, losing 28. The figures reflect the reality that the Zimbabwe cricket team are a bunch of schoolboys masquerading as an international side. Most of the good players have left.

As we have seen this past week, with Ireland thrashed by a world-record margin [of 290 runs] by New Zealand; one-day international status given to a game between Bermuda and Canada in King City, Ontario; and Hong Kong and the United Arab Emirates involved in games in the Asia Cup with similar status, the ICC cares more about the push for globalisation and making money than upholding standards.

But while the ICC spreads the gospel far and wide, its members do not want much to do with Zimbabwe. England and South Africa have cut bilateral ties and India, Zimbabwe's greatest ally, pulled out of their most recent tour there on the grounds that they could not be bothered.

And what of the next generation? In the most recent Under-19 World Cup, Zimbabwe won one match – against Malaysia – and finished twelfth out of 16 teams, losing on the way to Nepal by 99 runs. They also failed to send a team to compete in the Clico Under-15 international championship in the Caribbean. The official reason given for Zimbabwe's absence was a visa problem, but no formal application for visas was submitted.

But surely, given the millions of dollars passed on by the ICC down the years, there is a competitive cricket structure within Zimbabwe? Some months ago Steven Price, a brave freelance journalist based in Harare, wrote a series of articles about the state of the game in Zimbabwe at national, club and school levels. Collectively, they presented a disturbing picture of a sport that is in a state of decay. Bvute, by the way, had tried to bully Cricinfo, the website, into revealing Price's whereabouts in 2005. 'What has he got to be afraid of?' Bvute said when he did not get his way.

There was a picture of a club ground near Harare called Selous, with knee-high grass and derelict facilities, a club typical of many others that cannot afford tractors and mowers to cut the outfields. There is the odd club in Harare – well connected, of course, and therefore well funded – who thrive, but players from one of those clubs were sent home from national practice by Geoff Marsh, the former coach, for wearing Zanu (PF) T-shirts. In 2005–06, the Logan Cup, the premier first-class competition in Zimbabwe, was cancelled without notice and this year the Twenty20 competition was suspended with less than 24 hours' notice.

Some club matches in Matabeleland were cancelled this year because there were no cricket balls. Umpires are scarce, as is basic equipment. Grant Flower, the former Zimbabwe batsman, had this to say about domestic cricket: 'I speak to players who pitch up at games and there are no umpires, they are struggling to find six stumps, some of the wicket-keepers don't have gloves and there are no lunches or teas provided and there is no diesel to fuel the tractors and mow the outfields.' No team, no structure, no hope.

So what has happened to the millions of dollars given to ZC by the ICC? If only we knew. On the ICC's website there is a mission statement of values, one of which, under the heading 'Openness, honesty and integrity', reads: 'We work to the highest ethical standards. We do what we say we are going to do, in the way we say we are going to do it.' Presumably, because the ICC is simply an amalgam of its constituent parts, these constituent parts sign up to such mission statements, too.

But ZC has issued no accounts for public consumption since 2005. When the ICC became suspicious and held an internal inquiry, some of its findings were leaked. The leaks were damning: 'It is clear that the accounts of ZC have been deliberately falsified to mask various illegal transactions. It may not be possible to rely on the authenticity of its balance sheet.'

On the back of this, an independent audit by KPMG was commissioned. Despite the ICC's mission statement, this audit has not been released and when the British government asked for a copy it was refused. It has been reported that the KPMG audit noted 'serious financial irregularities'.

A country serious about its cricket must have administrators who treat the game with the respect it deserves. So we come back to Chingoka and Bvute, respectively the chairman and managing director of ZC, who have been instrumental in leading the organisation into this maelstrom of bullying, racism and decay. Any cricketer with the courage to speak out, as Tatenda Taibu, the former captain, did in 2005, is hounded out. Taibu left before returning two years later. In November 2007, life presidents of ZC were stripped of their positions so that they could not cause trouble at the annual meeting. A purge took place; hand-picked cronies from the provinces were unlikely to ask awkward questions.

Last week, Andy Flower, brother of Grant and the finest player that Zimbabwe has produced, was collared by journalists at The Oval. He looked briefly at the ECB's media relations man, to check that he was not about to embarrass the organisation that employs him as a coach, and gave a withering verdict on Zimbabwe Cricket's administrators. 'Peter Chingoka is part of Mugabe's despicable plan and the fact that he is allowed to prance around the ICC committee is embarrassing for the ICC.'

The Times, 3 July 2008

Calls to End Zimbabwe Test Exile Persuasive

Some years ago, when his ambitions extended beyond the presidency of the International Cricket Council, John Howard, the former Australian Prime Minister, referred to Robert Mugabe, in unusually blunt, non-diplomatic terms, as a 'grubby dictator'. Later, he banned the Australia cricket team from playing in Zimbabwe.

Yet last week, Howard flew to Harare to talk to those still running cricket there and Andy Flower [who had previously condemned Peter Chingoka, the chairman of Zimbabwe Cricket (ZC), in the strongest terms] gave a considered and articulate presentation to the MCC World Cricket Committee during which he encouraged a reappraisal of the boycott of Zimbabwe.

The actions of the first man can be swiftly dismissed – politicians will do anything for votes and Howard needed Zimbabwe's support for his failed bid for the vice-presidency of the ICC – but the words of the second, less so. By wearing a black armband at the 2003 World Cup, Flower made a stand against the situation in his homeland that resulted in a premature end to his international career and the relocation of his family. Until recently, he has remained a consistent critic of those running cricket in Zimbabwe and he cannot, like Howard, be criticised on the grounds of self-interest.

So what has changed? Superficially, much has. The Movement for Democratic Change (MDC) is in a power-sharing arrangement with Mugabe's Zanu (PF). The economy has stabilised, is now dollar denominated and hyperinflation is a thing of the past. In cricket, accounts have been produced and independently verified, the team have won matches with an XI chosen strictly on merit and 'good people', such as Dave Houghton, the former Zimbabwe batsman, have returned to get involved and bring credibility. A newly created franchise system offers hope for a competitive future.

Yet nobody would be foolish enough to argue that the serpents have vanished from what was previously Africa's Garden of Eden. Mugabe remains firmly in control. Torture, murder, repression, starvation and corruption are still rife. Only this month, Amnesty International said: 'We remain concerned about persistent abuse of the law against perceived opponents of the former Zanu (PF) government' and urged 'the unity government to end all malicious persecutions of people exercising their rights to freedom of expression and peaceful assembly'.

Last month a documentary called *Mugabe and the White African*, highlighting the struggle of a white farmer's family to hold on to their land, was released to much acclaim. It was an appropriate moment, because as the world's eyes and ears were on another sporting event in Africa, Mugabe embarked upon another round of land-grabbing. Hillary Clinton said last month that the ruling clique within Zanu (PF) 'continues to benefit from the diamond trade and benefit from corruption to a very significant degree'.

The links between cricket and Zanu (PF) remain strong. Ozias Bvute, the man who kicked Henry Olonga off the team bus during his protest with Flower and whose bullying, unpleasant and seemingly racially motivated policies became such a feature of Zimbabwe Cricket, is still the managing director. Chingoka remains as chairman. Their political links to Zanu (PF) are well known, hence their inability to travel to places such as the United Kingdom and Australia, and hence the ICC's need to relocate meetings to non-cricketing destinations such as Singapore. And if no one has yet been able to prove any corruption, it has been widely suspected and they retain little or no credibility within the cricketing fraternity.

Despite these problems, the time has come to listen to those in Zimbabwe, those whose lives have been affected and those who have had the guts to stand their ground. David Coltart, a human rights lawyer, MDC politician and Minister for Education, Sport, Arts and Culture, is one; David Ellman-Brown, a life president of ZC and a qualified chartered accountant, is another. This week I spoke to both as they argued the case for Zimbabwe's return to Test cricket.

First, Coltart: 'It has been very difficult for us in the human rights community because we came to a position that unless we reached an agreement [with Zanu (PF)], Zimbabwe could become another Liberia or Somalia. The agreement provided a non-violent evolutionary means of achieving a transition to democracy. Inevitably that meant that some of our goals of holding people to account for terrible crimes committed will not be achieved. It was a choice for a better future.'

As with politics, so with cricket. 'Things are not perfect,' he said. 'Chingoka and Bvute are still running the game, although whatever their failings, their sins are not at the same level as Mugabe's. But we are making progress. I'd say we are at a similar stage that South Africa was at in the early nineties before Mandela's release. Transition was by no means certain then, either, but sport had a big role to play.

'The Howard issue was unfortunate, but they [ZC] publicly abstained rather than voted against him. India was running that show and I don't think Zimbabwe's future should be decided by Howard's failure to get nominated. The cricket team is certainly improving, good people are involved again and all those developments have flowed from the improvements in the political situation.'

But what of the ICC funds that went missing and the report by KPMG, the auditors, into 'financial irregularities'? Ellman-Brown has gone through the report and insists that there is no evidence to finger Chingoka or Bvute.

'There were certainly weak areas of financial control and exchange control irregularities but you have to remember that they were trying to run a business in a hyperinflationary environment,' he said. 'Because of hyperinflation, those accounts were meaningless. There were certainly grey areas but nothing that you could substantiate as incriminating. There is much more transparency now.'

Why then has the ICC not released the report? 'You'll have to ask them that,' he said.

Ellman-Brown favours a return to Test cricket against the weaker teams initially, such as Bangladesh and West Indies. This gradual repositioning would help to strengthen ZC for the inevitable, long-awaited moment when Mugabe steps down or dies. It is inconceivable that the British government would sanction a return of the England team until then, but Coltart argues that involvement with Zimbabwe now would encourage the moderates within Zanu (PF), so when that moment comes, it is they rather than the hardliners who have the upper hand.

Principles or pragmatism? It is easy to be principled from thousands of miles away; easy to feel indignant on behalf of others. For those on the ground, who have been through the worst of times, the only thing that matters is the future. Coltart has been threatened with imprisonment, survived an assassination order and seen numerous clients disappear for good. If he can put aside rancour, it should be easy enough for the rest of us.

'One cannot live in the past,' he said. 'You have to move on. As in South Africa, cricket can play a role in helping a peaceful means to transition and a better future. It is one of the few things we have got.'

The Times, 8 July 2010

Pakistan

Hair Trigger for Drama which Became a Crisis

At least Malcolm Speed, the chief executive of the International Cricket Council (ICC), got one thing absolutely right. At the beginning of the most explosive and jaw-dropping press conference that I can remember, he said that the whole episode was due to a series of 'entirely avoidable and unnecessary overreactions'. This is not the biggest crisis that cricket has ever faced. It is not even the biggest crisis that cricket has faced in the last decade – match-fixing, the greatest possible fraud on the paying public, was a far graver threat to the game – and, in time, people will look back in amazement at how one little pimple was allowed to grow and fester into a boil that finally burst at Friday's press conference, spreading pus all over the game.

Hair's midweek madness gifted the ICC with a convenient way out of the impasse that threatened to engulf the one-day series between England and Pakistan and, by extension, the wider international game. By releasing the details of three private emails that Hair sent to his employers in the early part of last week – the first proposing a payment of $500,000 with conditions attached, the second, more sinister email, holding the ICC to ransom for a 'revised amount', and the third which revoked the two earlier emails and cheerily hoped that life would 'go on regardless' – the ICC were able to lay responsibility for the whole sorry mess at the feet of one man.

Speed may have couched Hair's assassination in a caring, paternal tone, arguing that the umpire sent the emails at a time of great mental turmoil, and that there was no malicious intent involved, but it was, ultimately, a calculating and brutal act of self-preservation from an organisation noted more for their lawyerly rigidity (think back to the Zimbabwe furore) than their humanity. The events of last Sunday at The Oval are now likely to be forgotten as Hair's madness takes centre stage. The most likely result of it all – though making predictions is a fool's game in the current climate – is that the meeting of the ICC's executive committee in Dubai will dismiss Hair from their employment and subsequently the hearing against Inzamam-ul-Haq is likely to be concluded in Pakistan's favour.

It is a rough kind justice on Hair, but justice nonetheless because if there is one man who could have stopped this episode from escalating it is him. If a more sensitive, pragmatic and less dogmatic umpire had been standing alongside Billy Doctrove then the full house at The Oval, and millions watching around the world, would have been allowed to enjoy a splendid contest reach its natural conclusion. The day before Hair sent his emails to the ICC, he told the *Brisbane Courier Mail* that he stood by his actions at The Oval. I bet he wishes he could now jump back in time and revisit the decision to charge Pakistan with ball-tampering, applying a little more of the wisdom and humanity he might have subsequently hoped for from his employers.

So let us revisit that afternoon at The Oval, the point of origin of the whole affair – the first entirely avoidable and unnecessary overreaction. For nothing that I have seen, heard or read in the interim – not the apologists for Hair who sprang up midweek, nor the conspiracy theorists who fretted over whether Duncan Fletcher did or did not see the match referee, nor those who slammed Pakistan for their undoubtedly disproportionate response – has convinced me of anything other than that the whole sorry mess was caused by the crassest and most insensitive piece of umpiring I have ever seen. By applying the law to the letter, Hair enslaved us all to the rule book instead of allowing us to enjoy the fascinating contest between bat and ball that was so clearly developing.

Despite the subsequent threats in his emails to take civil action against the Pakistan team, I do not believe Hair to be biased against the sub-continental teams. I believe that he tries to do his difficult job without fear or favour. But I also believe that he made a catastrophic error of judgement last Sunday. It wasn't inevitable that his grand gesture would lead to the first ever forfeiture of a Test match, but it was inevitable that the accusation of ball-tampering against Pakistan would dominate that day, and days to come, to the exclusion of everything else.

Why? Because of the complex history between these two teams – the undercurrent of empire and race that has always added a certain tension to the confrontation – and because both these teams, especially Pakistan, have previous where ball-tampering is concerned. In short: because of the context within which a modern-day England–Pakistan series is played. Hair's action and, in my opinion, his overreaction, paid no heed to anything other than the moment, midway through the afternoon, when he saw what appeared to him to be unusual marks on the ball. His decision was blinkered, it was narrow-minded and, in good time, I have no doubt that it will be considered to have been plainly wrong.

Let us for a moment assume that Hair was right and that the ball had been tampered with. If so, it is surely fair for us to assume that the misdemeanour was relatively minor. How so? The umpires inspected the ball 15 minutes earlier, at the fall of the previous wicket, and must have been satisfied with its condition. Sky Sports have scoured footage of the intervening 15 minutes and can find no evidence of tampering. Granted, television should not be used as judge and jury (though it is ironic, given last week's events, that 12 years ago a certain England captain was hauled up before the beak on television evidence alone when both umpires insisted that the ball's condition had not been changed), but it is inconceivable that the cameras would not have picked up anything major.

Moreover, it is becoming increasingly likely that Hair cannot have seen anything being done to the ball. How so? Because, until Friday, the ICC had not asked Sky Sports, the host broadcaster, for any footage to be used in the hearing as evidence and because no Pakistani individual, except the captain-cum-scapegoat, had been cited for tampering. It is therefore highly likely that Hair saw marks which concerned him and that he presumed that those marks had been caused by tampering. What a presumption to make!

Let us continue to assume, then, that tampering of the most minor kind – a scratch here, a scratch there – had occurred. You now have a choice. Do you rigidly uphold the letter of the law or do you recognise that a full house and millions around the world are enjoying a fascinating game and take the more pragmatic approach. I hope that you, like me, would take Inzamam quietly aside, register your concerns, ask him to relay those concerns to his team and ask him to put a stop to it. (That no conversation between Hair and Inzamam occurred before Hair changed the match ball was confirmed by Bob Woolmer.) If it continued, you would knock politely on the Pakistan team's dressing-room door during the tea interval and ask them to stop again. If it continued after tea then, and only then, would you put your traffic warden's hat on.

I used the analogy of the traffic warden – the type who slaps a ticket on your windscreen 20 seconds after your time has run out – at the time on television. It provoked a response from a viewer that, while detesting the actions of the warden, most people would simply grumble a bit and then get on with life, rather than beat the warden to a pulp, which was the analogous overreaction from Pakistan. True enough. But if that ticket resulted in a permanent criminal record, with all the attendant problems and damage to your reputation that it caused, then I reckon most people would look to take the matter further.

So did Inzamam. The rest, as they say, is history.

Sunday Telegraph, 27 August 2006

Darrell Hair Tribunal Highlights ICC Flaws

And so it has come to this. A farce whose origins sprang, as Malcolm Speed, the chief executive of the International Cricket Council (ICC), said at the time, from 'a series of entirely avoidable overreactions', has finally reached its conclusion just over a year later at the Central London Employment Tribunal. And if the ICC have many more disastrous days, such as they endured on Friday – the start of, in David Cameron-speak, 'The Great Darrell Hair Fight-Back' – it might be a seminal moment for the future of the administration of the game.

Earlier in the week, Hair had not had a particularly good time of it in his attempt to sue the ICC for racial discrimination. He was cross-examined brutally by Michael Beloff QC and suffered a blow on Thursday when his chief witness, Billy Doctrove, cited 'personal reasons' rather than front up, as he had promised to do.

But on Friday it was the turn of three of the ICC directors – Sir John Anderson (New Zealand), Inderjit Singh Bindra (India) and Ray Mali (then the South African director, now the president)

– to face cross-examination by Hair's lawyer, Robert Griffiths QC. What a time of it Griffiths had! Turning to the gallery with a malevolent grin every time a point was scored, he revealed completely the vacuum of leadership at the heart of the organisation that purports to run the game.

One by one these well-meaning, certainly not racist but undoubtedly bumbling and, on this evidence, incompetent administrators shuffled to the front of the room, raised their right hands and promised to tell the whole truth and nothing but the truth. One by one they were sent packing, lacerated from head to foot by Griffiths's ordered mind and razor tongue. Only Bindra retained any sense of clarity of thought, sticking resolutely to his line that 'the game had to go on!' and 'no man is bigger than the game!' By then it was too late; the damage had been done.

Things began badly. The stenographer failed to turn up and the parties retreated until she did – all except Anderson who, perhaps unaware of the fires of hell he was about to descend into, chose to pass his time playing Sudoku. If it was a ploy to ease his nerves or order his thoughts, it failed miserably. The day before, Anderson had given evidence and, according to one who was there, he didn't wear his pomposity lightly. Now, he visibly shrivelled before Griffiths, refused to look him in the eye, and developed a frog in his throat the size of which Iain Duncan Smith would have been proud of.

Anderson's was the key evidence of the day, because it was his three-man sub-committee who chose to ignore the recommendations of the paid executives, Speed and David Richardson, and decided to remove Hair from the elite panel. Griffiths was not slow to seize upon the bizarre nature of this three-man panel, made up of the representative from Pakistan (who, it might be said, was a little compromised), the representative from Zimbabwe (who had publicly supported Pakistan's stance and who represents one of the most flawed sporting bodies in world sport) and Anderson himself, who had described Hair's action at The Oval a year ago, as one of the most 'appalling' he had witnessed. 'Mr Hair didn't stand much of a chance, did he?' said Griffiths.

Nor did Anderson. Now Griffiths wanted to know how this three-man committee had come to their conclusions. It appears they did so over a jolly lunch. And then, Griffiths wanted to know, how did they persuade the board of directors to accept their recommendations? They did so in discussions that lasted less than five minutes. Griffiths was incredulous. 'Five minutes!' he thundered, leering at the gallery. 'Five minutes! And on that basis Mr Hair lost his status as a Test match umpire!'

Now Griffiths performed the impossible. I had wondered whether Speed might be the villain of this piece, given his undoubtedly shabby treatment of Hair in the aftermath of The Oval fiasco (you will recall how Speed revealed Hair's private emails). 'How much weight,' Griffiths wanted to know of Anderson, 'did you give to Speed's recommendation [not to take further action against Hair] given his immense experience in cricket, and,' Griffiths added in a kind of conspiratorial, Masonic way, 'given his experience in the law?'

'I disagreed with him,' said Anderson.

'You gave his recommendations no weight, then?'

'I disagreed with him.'

It was suddenly apparent that had Speed been making the decisions this whole sorry mess would have been avoided. At a stroke, Griffiths had transformed Speed into an administrative god.

Anderson admitted that Hair was an excellent umpire; that he had not been given due process over his individual rights, and that the code of conduct and the principle of natural justice had been ignored, and that the reputation of the ICC and the game was paramount. Then came the *coup de grâce*.

'Did you attend the final of the World Cup, Sir John?'

'I did not.'

'Is it important that an umpire knows the laws of the game?'

'It is.'

'You are aware, of course, that the umpires who officiated in the final made a complete bodge of it?' (Griffiths spat out the word 'bodge' with great emphasis to the amusement of the gallery.) 'Did they bring embarrassment beyond belief to the ICC?'

'They did.'

'And are they still umpiring?' Anderson mumbled something inaudible in reply after which Griffiths extended his mercy. Anderson went back to Sudoku, a far less taxing undertaking.

I had little sympathy for Hair during the events of The Oval, but I rather hope the tribunal chairman (this whole process has an Orwellian ring to it) finds a way of recognising that Hair has been treated appallingly since then, while throwing out the racism claims. By bringing a claim based on racism rather than constructive dismissal his compensation, if he wins, will be much higher than if he simply sued for constructive dismissal – a weakness that has undermined his stance throughout. But instinctively I find myself sympathising with the individual and the powerless over the corporate and the powerful. This is not about what happened at The Oval, but what has happened since. There is no doubt that Hair has been treated poorly.

Beyond these narrow confines, perhaps the lasting effects of this case will be the governance of the ICC. It was clear on Friday that decision-making should be left to the professionals, to the paid executives, rather than to the well-meaning amateurs.

Nothing summed this up more than the cross-examination of

Mali. He was asked what the primary role of an umpire was, to which he replied that an umpire has certain responsibilities inside the boundary rope and certain responsibilities outside it. Would he like to elaborate? For an instant, Mali looked like he had been asked to describe the internal workings of his wristwatch. Then he declined to say anything further, except that he felt Hair could resume his responsibilities as an elite umpire in the future. At that point every man jack in the room, possibly even Robert Griffiths QC, wondered what the hell they were doing there.

Sunday Telegraph, 7 October 2007

Door Must Not Be Slammed on Pakistan

It is possible to love the Pakistan cricket team, just as it is possible to hate them. They can play sublimely, they can play disastrously; they play within the laws, and break them at will; they have produced some of the game's greatest talents, and some of its biggest villains. Watching Pakistan play cricket is a bit like watching Paul Gascoigne play football. There is always magic, but it is a magic fraught with danger. They force you to the edge of your seat, nails bitten to the quick, never quite sure what crazy thing is going to happen next.

In the late 1990s, if you wanted boring consistency, then watching Australia was the thing: always pressing home the advantage, always winning, usually with a preaching tone to boot. If you wanted textbook cricket, then England was the place to be: left elbow high, and all that, and steady line and length. If you wanted tactical sterility, then you should have gone to South Africa: seam bowlers banging away outside off stump, to rigid field settings. Even West Indies were predictable in their awfulness.

Pakistan, meanwhile, were totally and utterly unpredictable;

beguiling, bewitching and, at times, bloody dreadful. They would win gloriously then lose shambolically, each defeat producing convulsions and factions within the camp, the captain blaming the coach and vice versa, before some government minister stepped in and sacked the lot. In a bizarre period between 1992 and 1995, there were nine different captains of the team, the job little more than a prestigious game of pass the parcel.

A list of Pakistan captains in the 1990s is both a gallery of rogues and a roll call of some of the great players of the period: Imran Khan, Javed Miandad, Wasim Akram, Waqar Younis, Saaed Anwar, Salim Malik. Imran was the father figure by the early part of the decade, the roughest of diamonds who became the most polished of fast bowlers. He was the inspirational figure who urged his team to fight like cornered tigers in the 1992 World Cup when they were on the brink of elimination and who, ultimately, lifted the trophy on a triumphant night in Melbourne. That evening Pakistan showed the rest of the world what was possible if raw, uninhibited talent was given its head.

Imran, and the disciples who followed him, revolutionised the art of fast bowling on dry, unhelpful pitches. Imran had learnt the secrets of reverse swing from another Pakistan fast bowler, Sarfraz Nawaz, and passed them on to Wasim and Waqar, who became one of the great opening partnerships in the history of the game. No other pairing can have been so dangerous with new ball and old, no other fast bowlers have been so skilled at making the old ball move in the air, snaking this way and that, homing in on the toes or the base of the stumps with heat-seeking accuracy. Both had a greater percentage of bowled and leg-before dismissals than any other fast bowlers in the history of the game.

Nothing is ever simple, though, with Pakistan cricket. Rumours circulated that the secrets passed on from generation to generation contained some dark arts, and accusations of ball-tampering flew back and forth. No cricketer who played in that era with eyes open could deny that ball-tampering was rife – Chris Pringle, the New Zealand bowler, admitted to using a bottle top during the tour to Pakistan in 1990 – just as no batsmen would deny that, tampered with or not, the ball did magical things in the hands of Wasim and Waqar.

If Pakistan's quicker bowlers revolutionised the game, so did one of their spinners, Saqlain Mushtaq, the inventor of the 'doosra'. The genesis of the 'doosra', the off spinner's equivalent of the googly, can be found in the dry, parched pitches of Pakistan. While they provided enough natural wear and tear to encourage reverse swing, they also prevented an off spinner finding the degree of curve that, say, an English off spinner would get in more damp and lush conditions. To beat the outside edge of the bat, then, Saqlain came up with the 'doosra', flicked over the top with a cocked wrist. Now, no sub-continental off spinner worth his salt is without a doosra in his armoury: Harbhajan Singh, Muttiah Muralitharan and Ajantha Mendis. But it was Saqlain who paved the way.

How did this team, with wonderful, attacking batsmen and world-class, revolutionary bowlers, have such an indifferent, chaotic record in the mid-1990s? Justice Qayyum was given the task of looking into that and his report into match-fixing was about as condemnatory as it was possible to be. Salim Malik was banned for life (and is apparently writing a book lifting the lid on match-fixing in the 1990s) and found guilty of fixing matches against Sri Lanka and Australia. Wasim, it was recommended, should never hold a position of responsibility again. Qayyum reported that there were 'sufficient grounds to cast strong doubt' on Mushtaq Ahmed, the England spin-bowling coach.

The impression given of cricket on the sub-continent in the 1990s was of a giant casino, in which the players were addicted gamblers, cricket often taking second place to the demands of bookmakers. Investigating a match in Christchurch in 1994, when Pakistan lost against the odds, Qayyum suspected the worst but could not prove it. He came, instead, to a conclusion that could have summed up Pakistan cricket in that period: 'There were misfields, there were wides. The batting collapsed. But then again, that is the Pakistan cricket team,' he said. Indeed.

Nothing, perhaps, sums up the contradictions of Pakistan cricket, and the abyss into which it has descended, better than Miandad. He is the greatest player that Pakistan has produced, without doubt one of the greatest players of the modern era. He is now the director general of the Pakistan Cricket Board, but he has ties, through a family marriage, to a wanted terrorist who was initially at the forefront of match-fixing and who is now linked with the network responsible for the Mumbai bombings in December and who is suspected of carrying out the Lahore massacre. Miandad's eldest son is married to the daughter of Dawood Ibrahim, who the US State Department describes as 'a global terrorist with links to al-Qaeda and Lashkar-e-Taiba'.

Pakistan cricket has faced many hurdles over the last two decades, but none bigger than it faces now. Despite all the problems, the loss of Pakistan to the cricket calendar would be a grievous one, for they have encapsulated all that is good and bad in cricket – all that is good and bad in sport.

When you watch cricket played on the streets in Pakistan, you watch the game played in its purest form. No coaches and no text-books to interfere, just raw talent and passion. That is why it is always likely that Pakistan will produce special cricketers who push the boundaries of what is possible, who perfect the art of something different and who demand that the rest of world catch on or lose out. It makes Pakistan one of the most precious resources the game has to offer.

It is essential that cricket is not left to wither and die, and that the ICC does its utmost to lend support and nurture Pakistan cricket back to life. It is inconceivable that international cricket can be played in Pakistan in the short term [after the terrorist attacks on the Sri Lanka team bus], but there is no reason why we should not delight in watching the next generation of rascals play in Abu Dhabi, Dubai, London and Melbourne. Cricket would be poorer without them.

The Times, 5 March 2009

Bangladesh

Where Poverty Turns Defeat into a Priceless Gift

Athar Ali Khan, the former Bangladesh cricketer, remembers the reception they received after winning the ICC Trophy in 1997: the red carpet that greeted them at the airport, the thousands who lined the streets to the hotel, the breakfast reception at the prime minister's residence, and the half-million people who turned up later to pay their respects along Manik Mia Avenue. It made the celebrations at Trafalgar Square in 2005 look like a demure garden party.

Athar says that they were treated like kings. Each of them received 500,000 taka (now about £4,800) from the prime minister, garlands and flowers from other ministers of state, plus televisions and fridges and sundry other gifts were showered upon them by local businessmen. He says it was manic, unbelievable, way beyond anything that any of them had experienced, even though the celebrations in Dhaka whenever the team won a match were legendary.

Mohammad Rafique, one of the best players that Bangladesh has produced, recalls the journey to practice that he had to take each day across the Buriganga River to get from his home in Jhinjhira. Most of Dhaka's waste flows into the Buriganga, which, accordingly, turns black in the dry months and emits an overpowering stench to the inhabitants of the slums that rise up along its banks.

Rafique still lives there, albeit in a four-storey concrete building rather than a tin hut. If he was still playing cricket, he wouldn't have to suffer the stench on a boat now, because his gift after the ICC tournament success 13 years ago was the construction of the Babu Bazaar bridge across the river. Cricket, he says, has given him everything, so when he was asked what he would like after winning that tournament, he said he wanted to give something back to the only community he knows.

These are small things, perhaps, although not in Bangladesh, where cricketers are revered and where the game's importance is measured not in results, but in a broader, more meaningful context. As we occasional visitors come and pronounce on the standard of cricket here, with the kind of arrogance and certainty that is typical of our trade, we need to remember that our judgements should be made with C.L.R. James's famous aphorism in mind: 'What do they know of cricket, who only cricket know?'

Sport is meaningful on many levels. Those who have played, and those who watch for a living, focus on the search for excellence and the intensity of competition that can produce such gratifying, soul-enriching results. In a celebrity-obsessed world dominated by the fake and the absurd, a certain truth, unadorned and undeniable, always emerges from the field of play – proper reality television, if you like.

But, and let's be honest here, we've seen precious little excellence or intensity on this tour of Bangladesh. Pockets of it, perhaps, in the swashbuckling start to the second Test by Tamim Iqbal and in the stout-hearted resistance of Mushfiqur Rahim and Junaid Siddique on the final day in Chittagong. Graeme Swann's send-off, born out of frustration, when he dismissed Siddique at least suggested things had not been straightforward for England, and in that outburst there was an acknowledgement of some kind of struggle.

Otherwise it has been thin gruel. The pitches have not helped, of course: two strips of rolled snot from which not even Sir David Attenborough could find any life, and cricket more than any other game is dictated to by conditions. Even so, the standard of play at times has been sub-first class, never mind international cricket. Bangladesh's fielding has occasionally been from the village green.

Some of the dissatisfaction is based on the statistical effects of these mismatches. As Ian Bell sent his average against the hosts north of 200 (no blame attached here, because what else is he supposed to do – get out?) and performances against Bangladesh distort otherwise average careers (check out the effect of Jacques Rudolph's double hundred on his career overall), former players feel cheated. Statistics are the only way of comparing today's players with those of the past and when averages become distorted because of substandard cricket, so these comparisons are rendered useless.

But, really, these things are irrelevant when measured against more important considerations. C.L.R. knew a bit about the deeper meaning of sport, writing at a time when the West Indies were moving from colonialism to independence. Cricket played an important role in uniting the islands, fostering a sense of identity and inflating self-esteem. The appointment of Frank Worrell, the first black West Indies captain on a permanent basis, played a vital part in the process of self-determination.

Something similar, if less explicit, is happening here in Bangladesh. Less than 40 years old, it is still a fledgling state and one that has experienced more than its share of disaster and hardship. The only time you hear of the country on the news is when disaster has struck: the monsoons that don't come or come with too much intensity, leading to death and famine; other natural disasters; and, before the restoration of democracy, military coups and political upheaval. All on the back of a long and bloody struggle for independence.

It is a country with little other than enormous manpower. The only positive stories to emerge recently out of Bangladesh are the Nobel prize given to Muhammad Yunus for his revolution in microcredit, and the Bangladesh cricket team. People recall the celebrations after Bangladesh's unexpected victories over Pakistan in the 1999 World Cup and India in 2007, and the outpouring of national pride that followed. Suddenly, people were seen wearing Bangladesh cricket shirts and Bangladesh flags were paraded proudly in the street.

Now Shakib Al Hasan, the captain, is one of the world's leading all-rounders – a great source of shared pride – and his contract with Worcestershire is seen as evidence of Bangladesh's growing influence on the cricket world. Each landmark – Siddique's maiden hundred and Bangladesh's highest Test score against England, for example – is cherished as a step in the right direction. Cricket provides rich nourishment in a diet that is low on self-esteem.

So, certainly the results are terrible and certainly the players are fortunate to be playing Tests. There are legitimate arguments as to whether Bangladesh should have been promoted so quickly without the infrastructure to support them, and there are question marks against India, who pushed for Bangladesh's Test status but have yet to host them. They need more help.

But these are minor quibbles and they miss the point entirely. Set against Bell's average, a nation of 150 million people that loves cricket is too important a resource for the game to lose. As well as the search for excellence and the purity of competition, sport is about more fundamental things: the great triviality can occasionally truly matter.

Here in Bangladesh, cricket transforms, it inspires and it is absolutely central to the very notion of national identity and shared experience. And what can be more important than that?

The Times, 25 March 2010

South Africa

Makhaya Ntini's Absence Raises
Awkward Question for South Africa

One of the iniquitous effects of apartheid – an ideology that is rarely referred to by name in today's South Africa – is that we are encouraged to think continually of sporting teams in terms of race. It is, though, a question that South African cricket must ask of itself, and urgently: why has there been only one black African cricketer of note, when black Africans comprise over 80 per cent of the population?

That cricketer, Makhaya Ntini, is, in international terms, of the past. Friedel de Wet, his replacement, has suffered what is thought to be a serious back injury and De Wet's replacement, Wayne Parnell, is from a township in the Eastern Cape that also produced Alviro Petersen and Ashwell Prince. But none of these is black African and it is a black African that Cricket South Africa (CSA) desperately needs as a role model to help to inspire others.

Fifteen years ago, on England's first tour of South Africa after readmission, Ali Bacher, the chief executive of the South African cricket board at the time, promised that within ten years the home team would be more than half made up of blacks. 'Black' covers a multitude of races here – African, Coloured, Indian – but implicit within Bacher's pledge was the acknowledgement that black Africans would play a central role in cricket over the next decade.

Five years ago Gerald Majola, Bacher's successor and himself the product of a famous black cricketing dynasty, made the same promise. But despite the millions spent on cricket in the African community, the returns have been minimal.

In 1995–96 England helped to increase the visibility of cricket in the townships around Johannesburg. The opening first-class match of the tour was played at the Soweto Oval – still the only first-class match it has hosted – and Nelson Mandela made a grand entrance midway through the first session, bringing the game to a halt. He chatted to us all, but at length to Devon Malcolm, and Bacher had the photo opportunity he craved.

Later that tour, England opened a cricket ground on the outskirts of the township of Alexandra, five square miles of desperate degradation hemmed in by some of the wealthiest suburbs of Johannesburg. Since then, England have played matches, or helped promote cricket, in a number of townships, Alice, in the Eastern Cape, for example, and Galashwe, in the Northern Cape. Last year Australia asked to be taken into Soweto and their players spent the day coaching there.

Zed Ndamane is the development officer in Gauteng, although he comes from the Eastern Cape, and I spoke with him this week about his province's failure to capitalise on these opportunities. 'It is a combination of facilities and investment. We have four township teams in the 16-team Premier League in Johannesburg and they are usually in the middle or lower middle reaches of the league. Four turf pitches is not a lot for the population size. Black schools don't have the playing fields or the space.

'In the 1990s transformation was a buzz word and companies were eager to get involved as it reflected well on them. Now, 15 years later, with the football World Cup looming and a recession biting, there is not the investment that there was. We used to have 127 coaches in the townships and we are down to about 32 now.

'We do have a scholarship scheme in place, whereby we take the most promising and put them in good schools with good facilities. Our budget is limited, though, so we are just scratching the surface. We have just recently produced our first African player to represent South African Schools, which is great, but it is slow and frustrating progress. Cricket is the second most popular sport in the townships, but it is all about investment and facilities and there is not enough of either.'

There are four professional African players in the Gauteng squad: Thami Tsolekile, a wicket-keeper/batsman who represented South Africa briefly on England's 2004–05 tour to the country, Aaron Phangiso (left-arm spinner), Pumelela Matshikwe (right-arm fast bowler) and Grant Mokoena (top-order batsman).

Tsolekile was particularly exciting because he was something of a marketing dream for CSA. He came from the Langa township in Cape Town, raised as one of 14 in a two-room, bricks and mortar house on Harlem Avenue, which is next door to Langa Cricket Club. But at the same time as Tsolekile disappeared from the South Africa team, so did Langa from the first division of the Cape Town league.

Three of Tsolekile's peer group in Langa went on to play for the South Africa football team. Football is an African game here, in a way that cricket and rugby union cannot match. And with the football World Cup coming, and investment aimed almost solely at making sure the tournament is a success [12 billion rands (about £992 million) is being spent on building or redeveloping football stadiums], cricket is likely to fall even farther behind.

For Bacher, whom I spoke with this week, the great tragedy was the injury sustained by Mfuneko Ngam, a black African fast bowler who had the potential to ease Ntini's burden. 'The late Hylton Ackerman was in charge of our academy when I was still involved in cricket here and I would go to him constantly to ask whether there were any black African superstars coming through,' said Bacher. 'He'd always say "no" until one day he told me to come and watch a young fast bowler that he believed could be another Michael Holding. Ngam was beautiful to watch, a real athlete and seriously quick. His back injury robbed us of a potential superstar.'

How does Bacher feel now about his promise all those years ago, and the lack of progress of young black African cricketers? 'I remember going through the villages of the Eastern Cape with the head of Mercedes-Benz and seeing all these villagers playing cricket; I was sure we would produce a steady stream of good black African cricketers,' he said. 'I am still hopeful about the Eastern Cape, where cricket has long been embedded. It's in their blood there. It is more of a struggle here in Gauteng. I hope and trust that South African cricket is doing everything in its power to change that. It is vital for the future health of our game.'

Another cricket club opened their doors yesterday, to more pomp and ceremony, in the heart of Johannesburg, in the shadows of the stadium formerly known as Ellis Park. But here in Gauteng, the home of the most desperate townships, cricket and rugby are just bystanders to football. Mind you, to stand on the Oval in Alexandra and look down into the slum below is to wonder that any kind of sport is played there at all. Sunshine and space are key ingredients for any sport and while there is plenty of the former, there is none of the latter.

The Times, 14 January 2010

West Indies

West Indies Ambling to the Edge of Oblivion

'Some of the old generals have retired and gone
And the runs don't come by as they did before
But when the Toussaints go, the Dessalines come
We've lost the battle but we will win the war . . .
Pretty soon the runs are going to flow like water
Bringing so much joy to every son and daughter
Say we're going to rise again like a raging fire
As the sun shines you know we're going to take it higher . . .'

So goes David Rudder's magnificent calypso to West Indian cricket, one that has become something of an anthem for its diehard supporters. His message, like that of many commentators in the West Indies, is an essentially optimistic one. The empire may be crumbling but it will come again. But why should it? Such lazy assumptions have long been part of the problem within the administration of West Indies cricket and if the largely apathetic response – the weary indifference of the long-suffering – to West Indies' worst defeat in Test history is anything to go by, it is a false assumption. Cricket in the Caribbean is in severe crisis.

One commentator who recognises the problem is Tony Cozier. His love of West Indies cricket runs deep, but it is not blind and on Thursday evening, as he gave the third Sir Frank Worrell lecture at the London Metropolitan University, he set out a stark message. While interest in the game is still strong, Cozier reckons patience is running thin. If nothing is done soon, he said, 'then there will come a time when the West Indies will find themselves engaged in the ICC's world league, struggling to avoid a loss to Vietnam in some tournament in Outer Mongolia'. Judging by Cozier's pallid complexion in the cold at Headingley, he'd relish reporting from Outer Mongolia about as much as the cricketing oblivion he predicts for West Indies.

The signs of decline are everywhere and they are alarming. On the field, West Indies, a team who went 15 years without losing a Test series before 1995, have not won a single Test match for over two years. The current touring team is the first for generations that does not possess a world-class performer. Observers can relate to a paucity of world-class performers; after all, it is no more than blind luck and chance that England can boast one of their own in Kevin Pietersen, but the absence of basic cricketing skills is harder to understand.

For a team blessed with natural athletes, this must be the worst fielding outfit to visit these shores for an age. Slip fielders standing in each other's pockets (although at Headingley it might have been an attempt to keep warm), ground fielding that has been shoddy in the extreme, and catching in the deep of barely club standard. This lack of basic skill suggests a deeply flawed system; and since many of these players have been around the team for some years now, it also reflects on the slide into amateurism that has accelerated over the past few years. This is a team who have to learn again the meaning of such terms as 'work ethic' and 'professionalism'.

If you don't believe me, then you should read the remarkable report of the physiotherapist, Stephen Partridge, following the 2006 home series (it was released on a website called CaribbeanCricket.

com). In it he outlines how the players held a meeting in St Lucia during which they decided that the training regime was too intense and forced its cancellation. Of Dwayne Bravo, the brightest of the young players around whom you'd think a team might develop, Partridge said this: his 'approach to bowling training is minimalist'; that he has 'largely moved away from adhering to his personalised physical programme'; that 'his diet is of major concern, consisting of sugar and little else', and that any gains in physical conditioning would be 'gradual and directly linked to the support we gain from his fellow countryman and patron [Lara]'.

There are those who believe that, as one West Indies supporter said to me this week, 'there are plenty of young men desperate to play for West Indies, it is when they get into the team that the problems start'. But, surely, the problems run deeper than that and must be linked specifically to an archaic system of first-class cricket, administrative bungling over a period of years, the constant infighting between the players and the administrators and the rising challenge of football (rather than, as is so often reported, other American sports) as the game that really gets the hearts of the urban black youth pumping.

A combination of on- and off-field issues have eroded support so that last year in Jamaica, for instance, there was, for the first time, no first-class cricket broadcast over the airwaves. Simon Crosskill, a Jamaican commentator, said at the time: 'The final nail in the coffin for regional cricket is the poor standard of cricket . . . and the fact that very few listeners under the age of 35 show any interest in cricket, let alone regional games.' There is no doubt that there is a generational gap. For the older generation, success on the cricket field was inextricably linked with the movement to independence in the 1960s and the subsequent nation-building. Cricket meant something way beyond its narrow boundaries. The older generation of cricketers, as Cozier said on Thursday evening, 'needed no reminding of the significance of their performances to the psyche of West Indians everywhere, not least the hundreds of thousands who made their home and eked out a living in England'.

But independence has long been won; third-generation West Indians in England play football and support England, and for the current generation of West Indian cricketers such rhetoric has long lost its meaning. It is difficult not to feel some sympathy for the current players who must constantly stand comparison with the giants of the past. According to Hilary Beckles, the pro vice-chancellor of the University of the West Indies and the leading cricket academic in the region, what is being passed on is not knowledge but 'condemnation'.

For Beckles the way out of decline was meant to be the World Cup. Looking at Caribbean cricket over the past hundred years, he identified two broad phases: the imperialist phase, pre-independence, and the nation-building phase that coincided with on-field domination. He predicted the aftermath of the World Cup would coincide with a so-called 'third paradigm' that would help West Indies cricket develop in the global age. Although it is too soon to say for certain, if anything the miserable World Cup has accentuated the feeling in the Caribbean that cricket has had its day.

What, then, is left to cling on to? A Schofield-type review group, headed by P.J. Patterson, the former Jamaica prime minister, is currently looking into all areas of the governance of West Indies cricket. It is, according to Ken Gordon, the president of the West Indies Cricket Board (WICB), 'perhaps the most important committee the West Indies Board will ever appoint'. Unlike the Schofield Review, its terms of reference are wide-ranging and it is to be hoped that they use the team's current decline and the financial situation the WICB finds itself in, to recommend fundamental change when they report on 30 June.

Elsewhere, brooding like Achilles in his tent, is the Texan billionaire Allen Stanford. So far his largesse has been viewed suspiciously by the WICB, but maybe the Patterson group will find a way to bring him and the WICB together. He recognises the need to re-professionalise West Indies cricket, and to that end he has employed 17 Antiguan cricketers on three-year contracts under the leadership of Eldine Baptiste, the former West Indies cricketer, who for many years has been a highly regarded coach in South Africa. That seems to be the obvious template for other regions to follow, especially if Stanford's generosity embarrasses other West Indian businesses to get involved.

What is clear is things cannot continue as they are. For Beckles, the dominance of the West Indies team over an 18-year period 'will go down in the history of civilisation as one of the greatest achievements of humanity'. Perhaps he overstates his case, but it is surely one of the greatest sports stories ever told, just as the current decline is one of the saddest to behold. Malcolm Speed, the chief executive of the ICC, may last week have deluded himself that world cricket 'has never been stronger', but had he been at Headingley he would have realised that cricket is in danger of losing something precious.

Sunday Telegraph, 3 June 2007

Precious Bond Broken in West Indies Cricket

Michael Holding remembers the first time he realised how important West Indies cricket was to West Indians. It was 1976 at The Oval – a venue he was to grace that summer with one of the most magnificent fast-bowling displays of all time – although this match was simply a warm-up game against Surrey for the Tests to come.

Just a warm-up, but still well supported as any match was at The Oval when West Indies were in town.

There were just three hours left in the game when Alvin Kallicharran and Roy Fredericks began their second innings. The target was an unlikely 239 and Clive Lloyd, the captain, instructed his batsmen to play out time and get some useful batting practice before the internationals. The game finished tamely, but not before the West Indies supporters in the ground had registered their disgust. 'We were booed and heckled out of there, they wanted us to win so much,' says Holding.

Viv Richards remembers the first time he realised how important cricket was to his people. He was 17 and playing for Antigua against St Lucia at the Recreation Ground in St John's. He was given out, caught at short square leg, off a wily leg spinner, a decision he disputed by standing his ground. Richards's displeasure prompted a riot among the Antigua supporters in the ground – a riot that continued until Richards was reinstated – so closely did they associate his fortunes with theirs.

'No other figure in the history of Antigua has enjoyed that symbiotic relationship between individual and community,' Tim Hector, the Antiguan politician, said. Whenever Richards walked to the crease thereafter, he remembered those who walked with him. Richards, Holding and legions of other West Indies cricketers of the pre- and post-independence era could remember countless other examples of how much cricket mattered to West Indians.

A flavour of this relationship between West Indian cricketers and their community can be seen on Sunday 7 June when BBC2 shows the second programme in a four-part series called *Empire of Cricket*. The series, which begins on Sunday [31 May], focusing initially on England, is worth watching for the archive footage alone (and, in the case of the programme on the Caribbean, for the calypso soundtrack). If the present West Indies team are so minded they may find it instructive to tune in and reflect on what they represent. It is all there, the thread running through from the grainy monochrome footage of Learie Constantine to the feline grace of Garry Sobers to the supercharged professionalism of Clive Lloyd's twin blackwash outfits.

West Indies' present tour of England fizzled out at Edgbaston on Tuesday [26 May] and the scenes were far removed from the BBC's archive footage of past England tours. There was no glory to be had and there were not that many West Indies supporters in the ground, although there were a few, given the large numbers of West Indians who live in and around Birmingham. Not many of them voiced their displeasure, though; perhaps they have become immune to failure or maybe they have just taken their cue from the players, whose indifference from the start to the finish of this tour was palpable.

There have been bad early-season series before now, but none, perhaps, in which a touring team seemed so utterly devoid of a sense of duty. Can we talk of duty in this day and age? I think we can – but it is a wholly different kind of duty to the one Holding, Lloyd and Richards talk of in the BBC series, when they say openly that they were motivated to do well on the field so that black men newly arrived in England and struggling could walk around with a greater sense of self-worth. They were, as the programme says, 'political cricketers'.

No, it is a different time now, and the current generation of cricketers cannot necessarily be expected to know of, and understand, past struggles and why, as Holding says in the programme, 'there was a special kind of pride at stake'. But, if today's players are not political cricketers, then they are, without doubt, professional cricketers – at least in the sense that they are well paid. For this tour, the West Indies team received around $1.5 million (about £934,000 – a sevenfold increase on a normal fee because this tour was imposed on them). They also received about $14,000 per scheduled day's play (there were 22 of them) from their sponsor, Digicel. Not an insignificant amount and one – surely – that demands something in return.

It is a strange word, professionalism, implying as it does all kinds of meanings. Professional foul, for example, suggests the worst kind of cynicism. Mostly, though, we understand 'professional' to involve some kind of contract between those paid to perform and those paying to watch. That those paid will do their utmost to be in the best possible shape, technically, mentally and physically, every time they are paid to perform.

If playing for your country, state or club brings added motivation for other reasons, such as national pride, a sense of corporate spirit, mateship or whatever, then that is a bonus. 'Professionalism' for a professional sportsman is a minimum requirement.

To watch West Indies this tour has been to watch a team who have given the impression of going through the motions. Practice sessions have been utterly lethargic. On Tuesday, the fielding practice, if it could be called that, was pathetic. They were merely marking time; it would have done just as much good having a cup of tea in the dressing-room.

Ian Bishop was moved to say that in days gone by, young, aspiring West Indian cricketers would turn up at the Queen's Park Oval in Trinidad just to watch the great West Indies teams practise. This summer, more than one young English cricketer has remarked how shoddy West Indies' practice sessions have been. So in practice, so in the matches: six catches were put down between tea and stumps on the first day at Lord's and things did not improve much thereafter. Only Bangladesh have a worse percentage of dropped catches over the last decade.

But if the captain does not care, why should the players? Chris Gayle deserves some sympathy for the way this tour was foisted upon his team when he and others had prior arrangements, but that is where the sympathy should stop. Captaincy, in no small measure, is about sacrificing yourself for something bigger and leading by example.

How much has Gayle given of himself this tour? When he delivered some half-baked truths two days before the Test at the Riverside, did he stop and think of the effect his indifference to the longer form of the game would have on his team? Reflecting on his team's chances in the World Twenty20 on Tuesday, he quipped that the games would be a bit shorter, so maybe his side would be able to concentrate better. It summed up his attitude.

There are myriad other problems with West Indies cricket. When the West Indies Cricket Board feels obliged to appoint four heavies from industry to deal with the West Indies Players Association's demands during negotiations for a new Memorandum of Understanding, you know things are bad.

But it starts and ends with the captain and the players. Nobody should expect the present lot to measure up to the great players of the past in terms of performance because that level of ability simply does not exist in the current West Indies dressing-room. Everybody, though, should expect basic standards of professionalism. A commitment to excellence in everything you do, as Steve Waugh used to say. Can West Indies look at themselves this week, as they reflect on a truly awful tour, and say that they gave everything of themselves during the past month?

No doubt those who supported their team through the bitter early-season conditions feel let down. But the special bond that used to exist between West Indies players and supporters, one that is clearly expressed in *Empire of Cricket*, no longer exists. West

Indies players play for themselves now more than they ever did, and they let themselves down. Badly.

The Times, 28 May 2009

ICC

Zimbabwe Affair Shows ICC Has Had Its Day

The ICC no longer has the moral authority to run the game. Given one final opportunity to lift decision-making out of the morass of self-interest, deceit and compromise into which it had fallen, it flunked the test. The outcome on Zimbabwe – self-censorship in return for the loot – was in many ways a triumph for Giles Clarke, the ECB's intelligent and forceful chairman, but it should signal the end for the ICC. Like flared trousers, string vests and the Bay City Rollers, what once seemed like a good idea has had its day.

That it took the words of an ageing statesman to bring about a resolution on Zimbabwe was portrayed as a triumph. Here, it was said, was an organisation that can extract its head from the sand, listen to the outside world and see the broader picture.

No matter that Archbishop Desmond Tutu predated Nelson Mandela's belated criticism of Robert Mugabe's regime by months, years even; no matter that the ICC had evidence of financial malpractice and had forced out its previous chief executive, Malcolm Speed, who could no longer keep quiet about the issue. It had plenty of opportunity to act before Mandela's choice words.

In any case, the eventual resolution, described as a 'win-win' situation by Ray Mali, the ICC's outgoing president, was a terrible fudge. It saved the World Twenty20 tournament, but a great deal more was lost in the process. Instead of decision-making in the best interests of the sport, there was shallow vote-counting, posturing and horse-trading. Not so much the longest suicide note in history, as Labour's 1983 manifesto was described, as the messiest.

Michael Holding, one of the good men of the game, has had enough. On hearing of the decision to change the result of the Test match at The Oval in 2006 from a forfeited win for England over Pakistan to a draw, he resigned from the ICC cricket committee. On doing so, he revealed that not one member of the committee had shown any desire to change the result, yet changed it was. England decided to abstain from voting on that issue on the basis that they had been involved in the match, not that it prevented Pakistan from casting their vote. It is not too difficult to work out how these things work, especially because England hoped that Pakistan would side with them had the Zimbabwe issue gone to a vote. I'll scratch your back, if you'll scratch mine. It is no way to run a sport.

Not that this has come as a surprise. When the ICC came into being in its modern guise in 1989, it was an organisation whose time had come. Cricket could no longer be run as an adjunct of MCC in the interests of a minority of white countries; cricket had come too far and the shift in power to the East was too seismic. And there have been some triumphs along the way. The game has spread far and wide, it is on a sound financial footing – on Tuesday, the ICC announced an injection of $300 million, about £152 million, over seven years for the non-Test playing nations – and the standard of umpiring, as a result of the elite panel, has never been better.

But these triumphs have been swamped by the failures. The inability to get to grips with match-fixing before the cancer had spread and the subsequent reluctance to act on information post-Cronje for fear of unleashing some old ghosts. The World Cups in South Africa and the West Indies were no advertisement for a game with global ambitions, both being too long and, frankly, too dull. That the 2007 World Cup was described as a triumph merely highlighted how out of touch the ICC had become.

And so to this crisis of confidence. Speed wrote a confidential report to his board shortly before his enforced 'gardening leave', giving warning that the sport had become dysfunctional. Ehsan Mani, the ICC president between 2003 and 2006, called the handling of Speed's demotion 'disgraceful' and cautioned of a 'loss of credibility' if the organisation did not pull its act together.

Most worryingly, the players have lost faith. Before the annual conference of the Federation of International Cricketers' Associations this year, Ian Smith, the players' legal adviser, said: 'The competence of the administrators is being called into question. It is time to look at whether the players themselves can do a better job. There is no loyalty towards the ICC. They've cocked up on every single policy issue.'

Not much of this failure of leadership is the fault of the executives, who carry a great deal of accountability without the power to change things. For no decision can be made without majority agreement among the constituent nations, who view each other with suspicion, align themselves generally along racial lines and are interested primarily in bolstering their own position.

It makes the job of Haroon Lorgat, the new ICC chief executive, impossible. Some months before Egon Zehnder, the headhunting firm employed by the ICC to find its new chief executive, made its recommendation, it asked Garry Kasparov, the chess grandmaster, for his thoughts on leadership. He said that the most important attribute is intuitive decision-making. When David Morgan, the former ECB chairman, was asked what he thought the most important quality should be, he said an ability to ensure the 'continued unity among our diverse membership'. He was not looking for a leader but a nanny to keep warring factions at bay.

The time has come to disband the ICC as a decision-making body and let the paid executives run the show. Smith had it about right when he said: 'You can't have the ICC board voting on every single issue out of self-interest. We want an independent executive accountable to its shareholders once a year at an AGM.' Any better ideas out there?

The Times, 10 July 2008

Part Two

Glorious Summers

7

True Tests

Watching sport for a living is not quite the glamorous experience imagined. Inevitably, there is much dross strewn among the magic. This, perhaps, is most relevant to Test cricket where the bad days often seem to outnumber the good ones. Usually, though, even the worst days have something to recommend them: a duel between two cricketers, perhaps, or the first glimpse of a potential star.

But when a Test match crackles and sparkles, it provides the ultimate in cricket-watching experience. It is no surprise to me that all the match reports here are from Tests. Many reflect on individual brilliance – Michael Clarke's debut century, for example – or the duel in the sun at Edgbaston between Andrew Flintoff and Jacques Kallis, which, even now, makes my hair stand on end thinking about it.

One-day matches come and go and are quickly forgotten. It is always the Tests that stay long in the memory.

Clarke's Incredible Journey

In sport, the journey from youth to manhood, from promise to fulfilment, can take an awfully long time. Some never make it. For most, a fragile outer shell of confidence protects a softer centre. Even the brashest and most assured possess a nagging kernel of self-doubt: will the years of practice, of training, of graft, of dreaming even, be reduced to nothing when the moment comes?

For Michael Clarke, a young New South Welshman with streaked-blond hair and the now-ubiquitous earring, the moment came on a hazy afternoon in Bangalore with his team tottering on 149 for four. An old blade, Darren Lehmann, had betrayed his nerves the ball before and departed to a dreadful slog. Two of the greatest spinners of the day, Anil Kumble and Harbhajan Singh, were bowling in tandem and four fielders hovered around the bat like vultures over a rotting carcass.

Walking out to bat, it is unlikely that he was thinking of the hours spent on the bowling machine with his father, Les, or the hours spent in the nets of the Western Suburbs Oval, the club side in Sydney where he learnt his cricket. It is unlikely that he was thinking of the first-class cricket for New South Wales that toughened him up, or even the finishing gloss applied by those nice people at Hampshire. But it was all there, part of the package.

Most importantly for him, his family were there. As soon as he knew that he had been given the nod over Brad Hodge he flew his parents and grandparents over, so that there was a very visual reminder of his solid roots in Liverpool, a working-class suburb a dozen miles west of Sydney. It is similar territory – hard-edged but honest – to the one from which the Waugh twins emerged, and it was the No 6 berth so long held down by the elder Waugh that Clarke was now looking to make his own.

What was he thinking as he walked out to join Simon Katich? Probably, he was trying to blank out as much as possible and retreat into what professional sportsmen like to call 'the zone'. Maybe, secretly, he was asking his maker to give him that first run. The noise, the kind of noise that only cricket in India can produce, will have added to his confusion. There were nerves – afterwards he admitted that he woke up at 5.30 in the morning and that he didn't settle down until five overs into his innings – but they were hidden beneath a newly minted baggy green cap, presented to him by Shane Warne, and a cocky stride to the crease.

Expectation is one of the hardest things for a sportsman to cope with. Think of what it did to Graeme Hick. In many ways, Clarke is the Hick of Australian cricket. His eventual selection for Australia has long been regarded as inevitable, but it had been delayed by a combination of a winning, and therefore unchanged, team and a temporary loss of form. A year ago, Clarke signed a deal with Slazenger worth $1.25 million (about £500,000) over four years, reputed to be the biggest kit sponsorship in Australia. And this before he had played a Test match.

He was promoted on the back of a moderate 12 months, which further emphasised the fact that he is the anointed one of Australian cricket. Hampshire received unexceptional returns on their investment. His first-class average is under 40, modest when you think of the likes of Stuart Law and Mike Hussey, who have career averages of over 50 and have largely been ignored. Clearly, the selectors saw gifts beyond the black and white figures. Clarke, himself, took public speaking lessons to prepare for what was to come. The expectation, then, came from within as well as from others.

Unlike Hick, Clarke did not freeze on his debut. He was neatly into his stride, shimmying down the wicket to clip Anil Kumble through the on side. Crisp footwork, fast hands, allied to a touch of unorthodoxy, sums up his play: a hint of Michael Slater. He also has an eye for the moment: as India wilted towards the end of the first day he pressed on, adding 60 in the last ten overs with Adam Gilchrist, tilting Australia's way what had been a hard-fought first day.

Only in the nineties, where he hovered for 45 minutes on the second morning, did his youth betray him. Suddenly, it was as if his feet were stuck in glue and his hands made of stone. He was perilously close to being lbw to Kumble. The crowd, though, were with him for his emotions were plain to see: a glance or two to the heavens, and his parents, a frustrated swish with his bat, scowling then grinning, nervously.

On 98, as fast bowler Zaheer Khan marked out his run, Clarke suddenly turned to the pavilion and called for his baggy green cap to replace his helmet. The trick worked and Khan served up a leg-stump half-volley. Clarke clipped it for two then ran, jumped for joy, thrashed his arms wildly, cried a little and proceeded to kiss everything in sight – his badge, cap and bat – so that we half expected him to plant a smacker on Khan to thank him for his generosity.

After that, his dazzling stroke-play returned and he carved up a tiring Indian attack. By the time he edged Khan to the wicket-keeper for 151 the journey he began as a small boy in the suburbs of West Sydney was complete. It was a glorious debut.

Sunday Telegraph, 10 October 2004

1st Test. At Chinnaswamy Stadium, Bangalore, on 6–10 October. Toss: Australia. Australia won by 217 runs. Australia 474 (M.J. Clarke 151, A.C. Gilchrist 104, S.M. Katich 81, J.L. Langer 52, Harbhajan Singh 5–146) and 228 (Harbhajan Singh 6–78). India 246 (G.D. McGrath 4–55) and 239 (R.S. Dravid 60, I.K. Pathan 55).

Legion of the Damned Prepare to Welcome Ponting

When asked whether England will ever regain the Ashes, Ian Chappell routinely replies, half-mockingly: 'Not in my lifetime.' He usually adds: 'At least not until Shane Warne and Glenn McGrath have gone.' Through an outrageous piece of misfortune for McGrath and a misjudgement at the toss by Ricky Ponting, we had a glimpse of the future on the first day. With McGrath missing and Warne nullified by a plumb pitch, England blasted away merrily at five runs an over.

Ponting's decision to insert England on an old-fashioned Edgbaston featherbed was the more significant of these two happy (from England's perspective) events. McGrath was certainly missed and, in partnership with Warne, would have helped stem the run rate. Not since pre-McGrath days (August 1993) have England taken Australia for more than 350 runs on the opening day of a Test match. But even he would have struggled to recreate the cutting edge he had at Lord's in these benign conditions.

All captains make mistakes but some are bigger than others. This one was a clanger and will probably go down in folklore; the ghosts of Ashes captains past who inserted and were damned are ready to welcome Ponting to their midst. Nasser Hussain has been wandering around the commentary box at Edgbaston with a peculiar grin on his face.

Ponting is no fool. He is an outstanding cricketer of great talent; a brave and honest man and one of the most successful captains in Australia's history. But regardless of what happens in the rest of this match, Australia missed an opportunity to bury England and the series by batting first, making a big score and then unleashing Warne on a wearing pitch. What demons, then, infiltrated his thinking on the first morning?

His decision to bowl first must have been partly based on too much information, too early. From Monday onwards, all the talk at Edgbaston was of the pitch and how wet and unprepared it was because of the tornado the week before. England added to the doubts about the surface by calling up Paul Collingwood. Had Ponting seen the pitch for the first time on Thursday morning there is little doubt that he would have batted first. I made a similar mistake in Melbourne in 1995 when I inserted on the basis of making a decision the day before. After that, I never looked at a pitch closely until the morning of a game – except at Sabina Park before the abandoned Test match of 1998.

The statistics of recent Edgbaston Tests, suggesting an advantage to the team fielding first, would also have been on his mind. Computer analysis and historical reference are tools that every modern captain uses, but they need to be used flexibly. No doubt, too, there was the residue of the mind-set instilled into the Australians by Steve Waugh – when you have a side down, keep them down: Waugh would no doubt have wanted to put England's batsmen straight back under pressure after their twin failures at Lord's. Maybe Ponting felt the same way.

Ponting had probably decided the day before to bowl and may even have told his team of the plan. Once McGrath had been ruled out he was then faced with a dilemma. Does he change his mind on the basis that his pace attack is weakened and his main threat is now Warne? By doing so does that send out a bad signal to McGrath's replacement, Michael Kasprowicz? Ponting decided to show faith in his rejigged pace attack, which has not been rewarded.

A captain must trust his instincts and hope that he gets more right than wrong, which Ponting clearly has over the last couple of years. But the unravelling of events, the complete lack of assistance for his bowlers on the first day, and the increasing help for the spinners as the match wears on, is enough to suggest that on this occasion he was badly wrong. The most damning effect was that it allowed England's batsmen to play Warne in the best possible conditions on day one and so help lift the psychological stranglehold that he had created at Lord's.

It only takes a moment to utter the words 'we'll bowl', but their effect could be far more long-lasting before this series is done.

Sunday Telegraph, 7 August 2005

Warne's Genius Works Wonders

Before the series began, most observers felt that the first Test of this series would be the critical one. If England lost the first, the accepted wisdom was that there would be no way back. Even the Australian players were given to trotting out the old 5–0 predictions after their crushing victory at Lord's. I didn't agree with those premature assertions then and I don't agree now: given the way the schedule has fallen, with the third Test match starting almost before memories of the second will have faded, this game was always going to be the most vital.

Now that victory seems assured for England – although that in itself is a ridiculous statement given the twists and turns that this match has given us – it is they who have the momentum at the most crucial stage of the series. Australia will also be without Glenn McGrath and must be worried about the form of some of their senior players. Matthew Hayden and Jason Gillespie, for example, are surviving in the team on reputation rather than their form.

As the England players awoke to another grey day in Birmingham yesterday, they must have thought to a man that one Australian stood between them and a series-levelling, momentum-inducing victory. For on Friday evening, just as the Australian players' body language started to betray their fears, Shane Warne issued a startling reminder that all things are possible when the ball is nestled in his stubby fingers.

Warne's dismissal of Andrew Strauss on Friday evening from a vicious, spinning leg-break brought comparisons with his 'Gatting' ball of a dozen years ago. The analogy is a poor one: Gatting was bemused by the drift as much as the spin, whereas the 'Strauss' ball didn't drift at all and given the angle from which Warne released the ball – right at the edge of the return crease – it didn't spin as much as might be imagined.

Strauss is not the first batsman to leave the crease befuddled by Warne and he won't be the last, although when he reviews his dismissal dispassionately he will realise that it owed as much to his own misjudgement as to the bowler's brilliance. By moving across his crease, rather than out of it, Strauss allowed the ball to turn past his front pad and crash into the stumps. Then again, muddling a batsman's mind is what Warne is all about, especially an England batsman's mind. Between Gatting and Strauss, Warne has taken 100 Test wickets in this country – the most by any bowler in history in foreign climes.

As Warne walked out yesterday morning, that statistic would have been pushed to the back of his mind. There were conditions to exploit, a match to win and just six more wickets to take to become the first bowler in history to take 600 Test wickets.

He began with the expectation of recreating the previous evening's mayhem, but it was Brett Lee who stole the early limelight, sneaking in on the blind side, with the wickets of Marcus Trescothick, Michael Vaughan and the obdurate Matthew Hoggard during a ferocious opening spell.

Vaughan has now heard the death-rattle three times in this series, which is a worry for a top-order batsman. It could be argued that each dismissal has been the result of a good delivery, but each time Vaughan has been caught on the crease with his bat coming down skewed. He has been telling himself for a long time that he is playing well and that everything is in order, the kind of bluff that all batsmen throw out now and again. At some stage a volume of runs has to back up that assertion. Most faults in batting come from poor footwork and Vaughan needs to work out rapidly why he seems unable to get fully forward once his initial trigger movements are complete.

Once Lee was removed from the fray, the threat of Warne again loomed large. How would England's remaining batsmen – Kevin Pietersen, Ian Bell, Andrew Flintoff and Geraint Jones – have prepared for the battle to come against the great leg spinner in testing conditions? They might have reminded themselves that Warne bowls only two deliveries these days, the leg spinner and the slider. But saying that Warne bowls only two deliveries is a bit like saying Harper Lee wrote only one book. The bare fact is true, but does not alter the majesty of the achievement.

Pietersen, unsurprisingly, was determined to attack, to wrest back the initiative and change the momentum of the morning. He hit two astonishing sixes over mid-wicket and any number of wristy flicks through the leg side: each one against the spin, each one a statement to the great bowler that batsmen, too, can dictate the course of events.

This series has proved to be a steep learning curve for Bell. For a short while, he looked assured: his footwork was precise and his mind clear. And then the end: a leg spinner from around the wicket brushed across the face of his bat into the gloves of the waiting Adam Gilchrist.

Readers of this column will know that I felt that Graham Thorpe should have been preferred, but, despite his modest returns in this series, the selectors now need to show faith in Bell. A tough series like this could be his making. He is at the beginning of a rapid journey, in cricketing terms, from adolescence to manhood and needs to be given time to complete it.

With the end of Bell and Pietersen, the door was ajar for Australia for the first time in the match. It was only the most extraordinary performance from Flintoff that prevented them from barging through. With a mixture of daring, aggression and courage, and riding an emotional wave the like of which this country's cricket grounds have not seen for years, he put in one of the great all-round performances in English cricketing history.

It is not the bare facts that underpin his achievement. But it is enough to say that without Flintoff, England would probably have lost this match. With an array of blistering swipes forged from the village green, he forced Ponting on to the defensive. And then, when England suffered a lacklustre start with the ball, it was Flintoff who rekindled their belief with a double strike against Justin Langer and Ponting. Flintoff has finally proved to be a match-winner against the best of company and his performance was a joy to behold.

Sunday Telegraph, 7 August 2005

2nd Test. At Edgbaston, Birmingham, 4–7 August 2005. Toss: Australia. England won by 2 runs. England 407 (M.E. Trescothick 90, K.P. Pietersen 71, A. Flintoff 68, S.K. Warne 4–116) and 182 (A. Flintoff 73, S.K. Warne 6–46, B.Lee 4–82). Australia 308 (J.L. Langer 82, R.T. Ponting 61) and 279 (A. Flintoff 4–79).

Kumble's Tail Piece

If it was playing on his mind, it didn't show. Anil Kumble awoke yesterday morning with 498 Test wickets to his name. It had taken him 16 years and 32,912 deliveries to get there and so the 500 mile-stone could wait a little while longer. Besides, patience and persistence have been the watchwords of Kumble's career. Others have been gifted with more genius; his two great rivals of the modern era, Shane Warne and Muttiah Muralitharan, spin the ball far more prodigiously, but when it comes to perseverance Kumble bends his knee to no one.

He had bowled well the day before, taking the wickets of Ian Bell and Paul Collingwood, one with a leg spinner and one with a googly. His line had been more consistent than in the first Test and the pitch promised more bounce than the one in Nagpur, which had blunted his effectiveness. Even the rain had disappeared. Surely this was to be his day.

Both Collingwood and Bell had been undone by Kumble's skill and reputation as much as their own failings. The last time England came to these parts, England were tormented by Kumble and so they had given much thought as to how they might play him. Their plan is to play forward, slightly inside the line of the ball, to defend in front of the pad, rather than bat and pad together, and look to score through the on side.

The thinking is sound, and for the most part England have played Kumble comfortably this time around. But Bell, staying inside the line of the ball, lost his bearings and his off stump, and Collingwood, bat in front of his pad, had only one line of defence to a dipping, spinning leg-break. It was one line of defence too few. Great bowlers have a way of defeating even the best-laid plans.

Accordingly, as he walked out at the start of play yesterday, needing just two wickets to join Warne, Muralitharan, Glenn McGrath and Courtney Walsh in the 500 club, Kumble must have been confident that his moment was not far away. Besides, only Andrew Flintoff, his bunny on the last tour, and Geraint Jones stood between him and England's long tail. Unsurprisingly, Rahul Dravid threw the ball to his leg spinner for the second over of morning.

Things did not go well. Flintoff is a much-improved player of spin and he played Kumble beautifully, defending well forward and picking him off through the leg side whenever he strayed in line. Jones was less comfortable, failing to pick Kumble's variations, and he required a healthy dose of luck to survive. At the end of each over, Kumble simply took his cap and strode away to gully, hands on hips. You knew he would be back for more: on a helpful pitch, a long, testing spell from Kumble is as inevitable as death and taxes.

Harbhajan Singh, at the other end, was wearing a white turban instead of his trademark black, hoping the change might bring an end to his wicket-taking drought. He could learn a thing or two from Kumble, whose body language rarely betrays his bowling figures. Harbhajan's spirits visibly rise and fall according to his performance, whereas Kumble juts out his chin and stands erect, an invisible coat-hanger pulling his shoulders back, whatever the situation.

That is Kumble's greatness. This is the man who had his jaw fractured by Merv Dillon in Antigua and went out and bowled 14 overs on the trot against medical advice. This is the man who, as well as taking five wickets in Test cricket 32 times, has also been hit for more than a hundred 39 times. Bowling in unhelpful conditions, and carrying an attack that has often lacked bite, he has always done his bit and he has never given in. If Kenny Barrington was the man who walked out to bat with the Union Jack draped over his shoulders, then Kumble is India's equivalent.

When I first played against Kumble (his debut was at Old Trafford in 1990) I thought of him as a one-trick bowler. He had a non-spinning leg-break and a quicker delivery that skidded on. He later added an easily detectable googly and is currently working on a second. His control is far better than it was 16 years ago, but the essence of his bowling remains the same. It is his strength of mind that sets him apart.

How does he compare to his competitors, Warne and Muralitharan? I still maintain that Warne is the greatest bowler I have seen and Muralitharan the most freakish. But when the conditions are in his favour, Kumble dominates batsmen more than either. He bowls at a pace that pegs a batsman to the crease and, hemmed in by close fielders, it is a claustrophobic experience. In this batsmen-dominated age, Kumble's overall economy rate of 2.6 is astonishing.

After 18 overs of the morning's play it was time for Kumble to give way to his possible successor, Piyush Chawla, who was still looking for his first Test wicket. The way Flintoff treated Chawla like the schoolboy he is, smashing him twice over long-on for six, highlighted the difficulty of the art that Kumble has mastered and how much India will miss him when he moves on.

Kumble's turn came again half an hour after lunch, after the new ball had provided the breakthrough. Finally, the luck that had deserted him all morning arrived. Jones, tethered to the crease by Kumble's pace and aggression, pushed forward only to see the ball dribble through a gap, via bat and pad, and dislodge the bails. Kumble's moment had arrived: 499 wickets and Stephen Harmison walking out to bat.

Has there ever been a spinner who has been better at cleaning up the tail? First ball Harmison groped half forward to a quicker ball that skidded through and rapped him on the knee roll. We all saw it coming. There was really no need to appeal, but five thousand or so spectators did, along with the millions watching, no doubt, and Kumble jumped and punched the air twice in celebration. He was quickly engulfed by his team-mates and lifted up in a bear hug by Wasim Jaffer. Kumble, head above the melee, held the ball aloft and saluted every corner of the ground. It was a marvellous moment and fitting that he reached his milestone with the kind of straight ball that has baffled many down the years.

Matthew Hoggard shook his hand to acknowledge the achievement, which was a nice touch. Two balls later, though, a Kumble googly ended up in the hands of first slip via the edge of Monty

Panesar's bat. As so often in the past, Kumble's patience and perseverance had won the day. Another five-wicket haul.

The ground rose to him and his team-mates applauded him all the way back to the pavilion, all that is except Chawla, who sprinted back to umpire Darrell Hair to retrieve the ball as a memento for his mentor. He could not have a better example of what makes a champion bowler. Kumble is all heart.

Sunday Telegraph, 12 March 2006

2nd Test. At Punjab C.A. Stadium, Mohali, Chandigarh, on 9–13 March 2006. Toss: England. India won by nine wickets. England 300 (A. Flintoff 70, K.P. Pietersen 64, G.O. Jones 52, A. Kumble 5–76) and 181 (I.R. Bell 57, A. Flintoff 51, M.M. Patel 4–25, A. Kumble 4–70). India 338 (R.S. Dravid 95, I.K. Pathan 52, A. Flintoff 4–96) and 144–1 (V. Sehwag 76*).

Woeful Lack of Practice Rebounds on England

Deja vu all over again, as that master of the cricketing malapropism, the former Essex batsman Alan Lilley, once said. England have been horrid in Brisbane just as they were horrid here four years ago. Back then the punishment was self-inflicted by the captain's misjudgement at the toss. For the first two days here, though, England's captain was heroic, utterly heroic – a lone, proud voice rising above the nervy silence of his team-mates. No, Andrew Flintoff has not let himself down, but he has been let down by a team that came into this Test match not so much undercooked as blood-raw.

When cricket historians gnaw on the bones of this tour in years to come, they will marvel at how the defence of a prize so gallantly won could be built on such flimsy foundations. Consider this: that for a full five-Test tour of Australia, the toughest tour of all and for these players probably the biggest tour of their lives, England arranged just one first-class match. One! Admittedly, it is not entirely their fault, due to the scheduling of the Champions Trophy so close to the tour. But even if there had been more time to accommodate a longer run-in of more meaningful matches, it is doubtful that they would have chosen that route if recent history is anything to go by.

This criticism of inadequate preparation time has become a running sore between the England team and the media at the start of every winter tour. Players of the old school, Geoffrey Boycott and Ian Botham among them, believe that the only way to get into any kind of form is to play. The modern player, though, understandably wants to keep touring time (away-from-the-family time) down to a minimum, and Duncan Fletcher has gone on record as saying that he would much rather have his players undercooked than overdone come the big day.

There is no need to turn the clock back to a time when England played every state team in a four-day game, along with irrelevant up-country games, but I believe that one first-class match is completely inadequate preparation. People may argue that Australia's players have been equally short of first-class cricket. However, they know their conditions, unlike England's top six batsmen, none of whom had played a Test match in Australia before. It takes time to adapt to the pace and bounce of the pitches, to the harsh light and the harshness of the conditions. I have not spoken to anybody here who believes that England's preparations have given them the best chance of success.

It is compounded by the squad that the selectors chose. Neither James Anderson nor Ashley Giles, two key components of England's first-day attack, had played any first-class cricket during the English season. Anderson – all the while trying to come to terms with a slightly re-modelled action because of his injured spine – had bowled 24 first-class overs in the eight months prior to his first ball at the Gabba. Giles, because of the bizarre decision not to play him in the final warm-up match, had bowled even fewer.

If you schedule only one first-class match before the Test, it is imperative that everything goes according to plan. But England lost the toss in Adelaide, which gave their batsmen just one hit-out. Andrew Strauss failed and walked out to bat at the Gabba still searching for his first first-class run on Australian soil.

The biggest blow, of course, to England's final preparations was the injury to Stephen Harmison, which caused him to miss the Adelaide game. Even so, it is doubtful that a single match would have put his preparations on track. His malaise goes deeper. It is a long time since he has bowled consistently well for England. Even when he blew away Pakistan at Old Trafford last summer, his radar was wonky.

Standing at the end of his mark on Thursday morning, Harmison's legs would have felt like jelly. Understandably. Any cricketer's legs would have felt the same. What gets you through those moments is a deep, unshakable faith in your talent and in your method and your technique. That belief is honed through good practice and match practice. Harmison has had too little of both. The talent is still there.

When the first ball of the match ended up in Flintoff's hands at second slip, the blood drained out of Harmison's face, and the horrible reality of the situation suddenly dawned. Forty thousand people were in the ground, millions were watching on television and he had no idea where the next ball was going. The cruelty of sport slapped him hard at that moment. Sport does not care a jot for reputation. It doesn't care that you might have been No 1 in the world two years ago. Good form needs to be nourished, cared for and looked after, not neglected, abused and then wantonly thrown away. If you don't treat the game with respect, it will have its revenge.

Harmison is an awful problem for Flintoff to have on his first major tour as captain. He is his leading strike bowler and a player without whom, it is commonly felt, England cannot win. He is also a man who has looked like a liability in this match. More than that, though, he is the captain's best mate. Can Flintoff find it in himself to spell out a few home truths, or does he believe that the gentle approach afforded so far will work? It hasn't yet.

The conditions for the next Test at Adelaide may force Flintoff's hand. Whatever happens, it is clear that Monty Panesar should play. He should have played here, although that is not to say that he would have made much difference. But he is, on current form, one of England's best four bowlers and, in the absence of reverse swing when the ball gets older, England need their best, their most attacking spinner on the park.

After the Ashes swapped hands last September, Cricket Australia asked a few notable former captains, Allan Border and Mark Taylor among them, to look into the failed expedition and make some recommendations. Their deliberations didn't look into the soul of Australian cricket – the system that was apparently struggling to replace some ageing warriors – they simply focused on two areas: inadequate preparation and inadequate support staff. The signing of England's former bowling coach, Troy Cooley, helped rectify the second, and they vowed not to repeat the first.

England have not given the defence of the Ashes due care and attention. In racing terms, they have missed the break and have given their opponents ten lengths' start. You can't afford to give a thoroughbred a ten-length start.

Sunday Telegraph, 26 November 2006

1st Test. At Woolloongabba, Brisbane, 23–7 November. Toss: Australia. Australia won by 277 runs. Australia 602 (R.T. Ponting 196, M.E.K. Hussey 86, J.L. Langer 82, M.J. Clarke 56, A. Flintoff 4–99) and 202–1d (J.L. Langer 100*, R.T. Ponting 60*). England 157 (I.R. Bell 50, G.D. McGrath 6–50) and 370 (P.D. Collingwood 96, K.P. Pietersen 92, S.R. Clark 4–72, S.K. Warne 4–124).

Paul Collingwood and Ian Bell
Conquer Their Demons for England

For most of this match, Old Trafford resembled an Ingmar Bergman film set, all rolling dark clouds and bitter winds. For England the script was pretty bleak too, at least until Monty Panesar, the man of the match for his six second-innings wickets, and Andrew Strauss, with a match-winning innings of 106 yesterday, changed its direction completely. It was as if Hollywood had suddenly got hold of the story and decided to tweak the ending to make it less depressing and more palatable for the audience.

Not that the ending was predictable. The final reckoning featured England easing past the 294 they had been set for victory for the loss of only four wickets, but such bald figures fail to do justice to the tense nature of the afternoon once Strauss had been brilliantly caught by Ross Taylor low down to his left and, three overs later, Kevin Pietersen had run himself out with 46 still required for victory.

Forty-six may not sound a lot, but an England team was once bowled out for that score in the Caribbean and, in Ian Bell and Paul Collingwood, there were two batsmen at the crease for whom runs have been not so much hard to find as invisible. Suddenly, Daniel Vettori started to find the sharp, kicking turn that had evaded him all day and New Zealand began to believe that another twist in the plot was possible.

Collingwood, at the start of his innings, looked like a man playing blindfolded, with a round bat for company, and could have been dismissed at any time. Bell was more assured but was dropped by Iain O'Brien, a catch that was harder to put down than take. That, one sensed, was the moment that the story began to take, finally, a predictable course. Both batsmen fought gamely against their personal demons to be there at the end.

The moment of victory brought hugs in the middle and euphoria on the England balcony. The emotions were mixed; jubilation that something significant had been achieved – this was the fifth-highest successful England run chase of all time, and the highest at this ground – and relief that embarrassment against a significantly weaker team had been avoided.

Victory came at the point of tea, but four sessions earlier it was England who looked the beaten team. Strauss and Panesar will take the bouquets for the turnaround, but honourable mentions should go to Alastair Cook, who helped Strauss set off on the long road to victory, to Michael Vaughan, who began yesterday batting in the kind of assured manner that must have soothed the nerves of the dressing-room, and Pietersen, who rediscovered some belligerence before a moment of madness opened the door to the Kiwis for the final time.

It was Strauss, though, who did most on the final day to ensure that England go to Trent Bridge for the third and final Test in the ascendancy. His was a mature and high-class innings, one of a man who is, once again, at ease with himself and his game after 18 months of searching. There was nothing flashy about his play, at least until he neared his century, when he unfurled some glorious shots. Instead it was the calmness that impressed and the knowledge that he was once again happy to put substance before style, that collecting runs by nudges, glides and flicks, often in the unfashionable areas behind square, can be as valuable as the show-pony smacks down the ground.

There were mysteries aplenty on this concluding day. How, when 16 wickets had fallen the day before, did only three fall now? How, when he had looked near-unplayable with five wickets in the first innings, was Vettori so easily neutered? Why did the pitch, so capricious the day before, appear so easy? The Kiwis did tighten up under pressure and waited for things to happen rather than made them happen, and possibly the heavy roller used by England in the morning had an effect.

But really, when England ponder these questions, they would do well to reflect on their batting on this final day, for there was an urgency about it that was lacking in the first innings and at Lord's, an urgency that they would do well not to misplace in the future. It wasn't necessarily obvious in the big shots, but in the little things such as the running between the wickets at the start of the day which signalled serious intent.

For New Zealand this will be a heavy blow to take, for this is a game they feel they ought to have won, but there were enough signs in the first hour that this was not going to be their day. Vettori set cautious fields at the start, with sweepers either side, allowing England space to breathe by giving them gaps into which to nudge quick singles; there were no-balls, too, fumbles from the fielders and frustrating thick edges that ran down through the untenanted third-man area. The fifty partnership between Strauss and Vaughan came courtesy of five overthrows, a moment of sloppiness that summed up New Zealand's morning and, ultimately, their day.

Old Trafford, then, was left to reflect on another memorable Test match, reward for which will be three years off the Test rota. At a time when administrators should be doing all they can to encourage crowds to Test cricket, Old Trafford's banishment beggars belief. It may not look the prettiest ground, but there is no denying that the conditions, year after year, give us the essence of Test cricket at its best. Sometimes you have to look beyond appearances; Bergman knew a bit about that and, yesterday, so did Strauss.

The Times, 27 May 2008

2nd Test. At Old Trafford, Manchester, on 23–6 May. Toss: New Zealand. England won by six wickets. New Zealand 381 (L.R.P.L. Taylor 154*, J.M. How 64, K.D. Mills 57, J.M. Anderson 4–118) and 114 (M.S. Panesar 6–37). England 202 (A.J. Strauss 60, D.L. Vettori 5–66) and 294–4 (A.J. Strauss 106).

Kevin Pietersen Passes Test of Character

Greatness in sport comes in many guises, but great players rarely fail to deliver when it matters. It mattered yesterday to Kevin Pietersen for a variety of reasons, most of them deeply personal. His response was emphatic and when, after a minute more than three hours of sublime batting, the crowd rose to acclaim his thirteenth Test century, and surely the one that meant most to him, they did so in the knowledge that not only had he provided magnificent entertainment on the day, but that here was an England batsman who belongs in the highest rank.

When Pietersen takes centre stage, as he did throughout yesterday afternoon, there remain only walk-on parts for his team-mates, but honourable mentions should be made of Andrew Strauss and Alastair Cook, whose century opening partnership set England calmly on their way, and especially Ian Bell, who, in an unbeaten stand of 192 with Pietersen, got important runs when they were needed.

For South Africa, this was a chastening day. Graeme Smith, the captain, will take some flak for misreading the conditions and inserting England on a pitch that was neither quick enough to give his pace bowlers comfort nor receptive enough to produce the kind of movement he must have been hoping for. But, given the rain that had fallen for two days, it was an understandable decision and one that Michael Vaughan would also have made.

Moreover, a captain cannot be responsible for his bowlers' performances. Whether because of nerves, inexperience or the pressure that bowlers invariably feel when a captain has put in the opposition, South Africa had a woeful first session. Needing to bowl a full length, they bowled short; needing to make the batsmen play, they bowled wide. Strauss and Cook, who might have been expecting the sternest of examinations, were allowed to breeze through the new ball with barely a question asked.

Things changed after lunch and so came the moment, at 2.50pm – when Pietersen walked out to face South Africa for the first time in Test cricket – that the day and, possibly, the summer had been waiting for. The atmosphere was heightened because England had just lost three wickets in 13 minutes, to Dale Steyn and Morne Morkel. These two smelt panic in England's ranks and they knew that Pietersen lay between them and a peaceful night's sleep.

What was Pietersen thinking? It was hard to know, given that the ECB had wrapped him in protective swaddling in the run-up to this Test. He would not have been human, though, if there were not a few more butterflies than normal and surely he had not forgotten the vicious reception he received against this team during the one-day matches that completed England's last tour of South Africa, in 2004–05. They say that Tiger Woods, the world's finest golfer, never forgets an insult; does Pietersen?

He was certainly pumped up. A quick single to get off the mark has become a trademark start to his innings, but even by his standards his first run off his second ball was of the kamikaze variety. Had Makhaya Ntini's throw from mid-on been on target, Pietersen's innings would have been stillborn. Thank goodness Ntini's radar was awry, for the spectators would have been denied the drama that duly unfolded. Not that South Africa will share such sentiments.

Rather than verbals, this time South Africa gave Pietersen the silent treatment, the cold shoulder. So much so that he was reduced to striking up a conversation with Billy Bowden, the umpire, within his first few minutes at the crease. Not that the silence equated to a softly-softly approach. South Africa's plan for Pietersen clearly involved a liberal sprinkling of bouncers and, er, a few more bouncers. One from Steyn early on crunched into the back of Pietersen's helmet, which necessitated a visit from England's physiotherapist and a time-out while Pietersen gathered his thoughts.

But after that there was precious little evidence of the planning that Smith had spoken about before the match. Mid-wicket, for example, Pietersen's favourite area, was constantly left untenanted. Australia always had a catcher there, often two. Given the short stuff also directed outside Strauss's off stump for most of the morning, it was a day that suggested Smith's increasing maturity has not necessarily been accompanied by any great tactical advance.

Bell has often travelled in Pietersen's slipstream and it was to his advantage yesterday. It was as if South Africa had spent so long plotting and planning how to react to Pietersen that they forgot about the man at the other end. Bell stroked his first ball silkily to the cover boundary for four and was into double figures three balls later. A blazing start subsided into something more sedate, but, having gone in with England under the cosh, these were the tough runs for which everyone has been calling.

As Bell changed down a gear, Pietersen changed up in quick time, the mark of a quality player. The introduction of Paul Harris, the left-arm spinner, was the catalyst. Given that Pietersen has mauled Shane Warne and Muttiah Muralitharan during his career, Harris represented not so much a threat as an opportunity and Pietersen dismantled him with a variety of sweep shots, some hit square and ferociously hard, others played fine with the deftest of touches. Once he took the more direct route, popping him over long-on for six. Child's play.

A hundred was there for the taking now. It came when Morkel, with the second new ball, served up something short and wide that Pietersen crashed to the cover-point boundary. His emotions came pouring out. And while the South Africa players could hardly be said to have bruised their palms, so cursory was the applause, the crowd responded magnificently. As Pietersen left the field undefeated, it felt as if Lord's faithful had finally taken him to their hearts.

The Times, 11 July 2008

1st Test. At Lord's, London, on 10–14 July. Toss: South Africa. Match drawn. England 593–8d (I.R. Bell 199, K.P. Pietersen 152, S.C.J. Broad 76, A.N. Cook 60, M. Morkel 4–121). South Africa 247 (A.G. Prince 101, M.S. Panesar 4–74) and 393–3d (N.D. McKenzie 138, G.C. Smith 107, H.M. Amla 104*).

Andrew Flintoff's Irresistible Force Keeps England Alive

For a long time yesterday the England team resembled a man hanging from a cliff by his fingernails, clawing and scraping the rock-face but slipping ever more gradually into the abyss below. They had scrapped and fought simply to stay in touch, their skill levels never quite matching the sweat produced. Then, in the final hour of the day, Andrew Flintoff summoned up every last ounce of energy and inspiration to produce a magical six overs that brought him the wickets of Jacques Kallis and A.B. de Villiers, with the result that his team will arrive back this morning confident that the series is not beyond them.

This was an hour of cricket the meaning of which stretched way beyond the importance of the match or indeed the series. Here, encapsulated in the heroic bowling of Flintoff, the rediscovered class of Kallis, the calm resistance of Ashwell Prince and the frayed tempers of the rest of the cast was the very reason for watching the damn game. Twenty20 cricket may be the toast of the moment, but when Test cricket provides an hour such as this, its survival as the pinnacle of the game should never be in doubt.

When the umpires finally called a halt to proceedings, as the light closed in and tempers began to flare, South Africa's lead was 25 and, in Prince and Mark Boucher, they had two redoubtable characters who needed all their toughness and skill, and not a little luck, to get through to the end unscathed. Whether Flintoff can recreate the passion and intensity of the second evening, how far Boucher and Prince can stretch South Africa's lead and whether England's under-pressure batsmen can find some form second time around will determine the outcome of the match.

That the result is still in doubt is solely down to Flintoff. At 5.23pm, after a heavy shower and then drizzle had forced the players from the field for an hour, the scoreboard showed that South Africa were 205 for four. The deficit was 26 and, in Kallis (48 not out) and Prince (24 not out), South Africa had two batsmen who were set, as if in concrete, and ready to plunder a sizeable first-innings lead. England needed an inspirational figure to step forward if the series was not to slip away.

Inevitably, that man was Flintoff. He had already bowled 18 overs in the day, a little more than a third of England's total, and initially he might have thought that the gods were against him, since the third umpire had turned down what to this eye looked a good claim for a catch at slip by Andrew Strauss and then Paul Collingwood had spilt a dolly off his bowling at second slip, both chances off Neil McKenzie. But eventually McKenzie had fallen leg-before to give Flintoff his 200th wicket in Tests. He might then have thought that was to be the high point of the day.

He must have been tired, but cricketers such as Flintoff sense the moment and the mood of the game and the needs of their team. England, and Michael Vaughan, needed him now. He called for the ball immediately after the break and began to charge in as if his very life depended upon it. Kallis has often been an immovable object for South Africa and as these two great all-rounders – England's best bowler and South Africa's best batsman, to boot – went toe-to-toe it was immediately obvious that the momentum of the day depended upon its outcome.

Flintoff began by softening up Kallis with a variety of short, nasty bouncers, some which passed over Kallis's shoulder, others in front of his nose. These were rapid missiles, but Kallis never looked anything other than secure, standing firm, staring into space in between balls and doing his utmost to keep his heartbeat down and mind alert. He didn't exactly look as if he was enjoying himself, but here was a man not afraid of a contest; confident in a technique honed through hours of lonely practice.

It was only when Flintoff tested out the other end of the pitch that Kallis began to doubt himself. England believe that Kallis is vulnerable to an early yorker. Now he also had gloomy light and an inadequate sightscreen – over which Flintoff's arm was releasing missile after furious missile – with which to contend.

Flintoff was convinced that he had Kallis leg-before with one such, standing mid-pitch and appealing until the last drop of breath had been squeezed from his body, the veins in his neck standing out like tree roots at the base of a great oak. It was difficult to know what the ball was missing, other than off stump and leg stump, as it crashed into Kallis's toe, and thereafter Flintoff went dangerously close to overstepping the mark with his constant questioning of the sanity of Aleem Dar, the umpire.

He was not to be denied, though. The very next over, still burning with injustice at Dar's denial, he flattened Kallis's off stump with a rip-snorting, late-swinging yorker that Kallis jabbed down on, but missed by a distance. Flintoff stood mid-pitch, arms raised like some conquering Viking while his team-mates mobbed him. The immovable object had come face to face with an irresistible force and, for once, Kallis had to give way.

De Villiers, a bright young thing but not yet battle hardened, fell hooking. Boucher, itching for the fight, survived two yorkers that he plainly did not see and a whole heap of English tongue-wagging. For the second time in the match – the first was when Flintoff was batting – the crowd had come alive. Some cricketers can just do it and Flintoff is one of that rare breed. Since Headingley, his comeback has been a bit of a damp squib, but this was Flintoff-inspired electricity. The man is back.

The Times, 1 August 2008

3rd Test. At Edgbaston, Birmingham, 30 July–2 August. Toss: England. South Africa won by five wickets. England 231 (A.N. Cook 76, I.R. Bell 50) and 363 (P.D. Collingwood 135, K.P. Pietersen 94, M. Morkel 4–97). South Africa 314 (N.D. McKenzie 72, J.H. Kallis 64, A. Flintoff 4–89) and 283–5 (G.C. Smith 154*).

Kevin Pietersen Delivers the Perfect Reply

He could have been auditioning for the Indian Premier League. On a day when *The Times of India* reported that a portion of the Twenty20 competition that has taken India by storm will be played in England in future – something not denied by the ECB – Kevin Pietersen reminded everyone that there is no more entertaining or exciting a player in the world today, scoring a brilliant, instinctive hundred, the first by an England captain in India since Tony Greig 31 years ago.

There are many similarities between Pietersen and Greig, not the least of which is an attitude to cricket, and life in general, that is incurably optimistic. One-nil down in the series, a long way behind in the game, two early wickets having fallen, but what the hell: rather than play in backs-to-the-wall, one might say English, fashion, Pietersen took the attack to India so that for a long time it was not clear which team were in the ascendancy. For most of an absorbing day, England scored at more than four runs an over.

But while it is much better for a captain to be optimistic than pessimistic, occasionally it pays for a batsman to bear in mind the dictum that he should always add, mentally, two wickets to the score, to remind him how quickly situations can change.

Shortly after Pietersen had fallen leg-before to Harbhajan Singh from round the wicket, a fair decision he did not much care for, Andrew Flintoff was snapped up at short leg and what had looked a position of relative security now has danger stamped all over it. After the day's play, the captain admitted that a draw was the best his team could hope for.

Like Pietersen, Flintoff was also unhappy with his dismissal, although he could have no complaints about the inside edge or the catch, a brilliant diving effort by Gautam Gambhir. No, the umpires had already checked their light meters by the time Amit

Mishra came in to bowl the 73rd, and last, over of the day. It was a little before five, the latest that the umpires had allowed play to continue until in this match, and Flintoff clearly thought that he should have already been sitting in the dressing-room, a lager cooling his lips after a good day's work. His dismissal to what turned out to be the last ball of the day would have soured the taste and afterwards Pietersen was moved to wonder how the light could change in such a short space of time.

Flintoff had played beautifully until his downfall. He struck the ball crisply at the start, especially down the ground, which is always a good sign, and he defended easily, bat in front of pad to negate the close catchers. And when the field spread he settled down to play in mature fashion, recognising that there was no need to try to compete with Pietersen for the day's bragging rights.

Heavy fog had delayed the start by 90 minutes and when play did get under way, it seemed that it had been transplanted into the England batsmen's heads. To the third ball of the day, Andrew Strauss moved too far across his crease, his front foot planted on the line of a full, swinging delivery from Zaheer Khan, so that his bat could not get at the ball. Like Virender Sehwag before him, he found that cricket is a capricious companion.

Six balls later, Ian Bell was heading back to the pavilion with the puzzled look of a little boy who was finding life just a little unfair. Playing a loose drive at Ishant Sharma, he did so at a ball that ducked in sharply and late and flattened his middle stump. He may yet have one more opportunity, but this has been a poor tour for him and with the clamour for Owais Shah growing and Michael Vaughan biding his time, he will have a nervous New Year before the tour party for the Caribbean is announced.

Now Mahendra Singh Dhoni played his trump card, a move that highlighted his gambler's instinct. The score was one for two, both new-ball bowlers had taken a wicket, Pietersen had faced only three deliveries and his team were all over England like a cheap suit. So what did Dhoni do? He took Zaheer off after one over and threw the new ball to Yuvraj Singh. This was the decision of the man who enjoys walking the high wire; something that can make you look very clever indeed but is also fraught with danger.

It was clever because Yuvraj has given Pietersen some difficulty with his innocuous left-arm non-spinners and had dismissed him in Chennai. It was an insult that Dhoni knew Pietersen could not ignore. Accordingly, Pietersen, who had fairly sprinted out to the crease on Bell's dismissal, hacked and heaved at Yuvraj's first over and almost lofted him to short extra cover. The manner in which Pietersen, after the day's play, described Yuvraj as a 'pie thrower' who bowled 'left-arm filth', suggested that Dhoni has found the man to get under Pietersen's skin.

It was a dangerous move, though, because insulting players such as Pietersen can come back to haunt you and later in the day, when he had three figures to his name, it was Pietersen who was doing the teasing. From wherever Dhoni moved his fielders, the batsman hit the ball. Like elephants, great players have long memories.

And, once again, Pietersen played strokes that only those blessed with the rarest of talents can play. The quicker bowlers were driven thunderously through an arc between mid-on and mid-wicket, but it was his use of the sweep shot to the spinners that underpinned his dominance. There were orthodox sweeps, fine sweeps, paddle sweeps, reverse sweeps and, glory be, the switch-hit, one of which he smashed long and hard into the crowd for six. At times he stood taunting the bowlers, swishing his bat this way and that, as if to advertise the number of sweeping options at his disposal.

This was magnificent batting to adorn a splendid day: a Pietersen hundred and Australia unable to defend 413 [in their first Test against South Africa in Perth]. What more can a man ask for?

The Times, 22 December 2008

2nd Test. At Punjab C.A. Stadium, Mohali, Chandigarh, on 19–23 December. Toss: India. Match drawn. India 453 (G. Gambhir 179, R.S. Dravid 136) and 251–7d (G. Gambhir 97, Yuvraj Singh 86). England 302 (K.P. Pietersen 144, A. Flintoff 62, A.N. Cook 50, Harbhajan Singh 4–68) and 64–1.

Andrew Flintoff Defies Pain, But England Fall Short

For a long time England huffed and puffed throughout an absorbing final day in Antigua, and looked as if they would blow the house down. But a combination of rain at the start of the day, bad light at the end and stubborn resistance from the foundation stones of the West Indies' edifice, Ramnaresh Sarwan and Shivnarine Chanderpaul, prevented a victory that had looked likely once Andrew Strauss had banished the memories of Sabina Park with a hundred that seemed like an age ago.

So much had happened in the meantime, most of which was not relevant to the essence of the game, like a rich Texan with a dislike for Test cricket accused of massive fraud. But as the five days here reached a worthy climax, it was apparent that many of the best things thrown up by sport were on show: two teams expending every last drop of energy and commitment to a cause that mattered deeply.

As the West Indies resisted stubbornly, how Strauss must have wondered about England's dithering in the second innings. The follow-on decision was fair enough, given the injury situation with

Andrew Flintoff and Stephen Harmison, but sending in the night-watchman in such a dominant position was ridiculous. At times the second innings was a crawl and the declaration on the conservative side. These are good lessons. Once you have your foot on your opponents' throat, it pays to keep it there.

At the end, as the light disappeared, Strauss was forced to bowl his two spinners. The twelfth man ran on and off as the West Indies tried desperately to waste valuable minutes. Nine men were around the bat, one of them Kevin Pietersen, who took a blow and was forced to leave the field. It was almost the final blow of the game.

At 6.03pm local time, with four overs remaining, both umpires checked their light meters for the final time and offered the light to the last two batsmen, Daren Powell and Fidel Edwards, who had survived for ten long overs. West Indies began to celebrate an epic draw, while England were left to reflect on an opportunity missed.

The scenes were extraordinary. This old, tatty ground, reborn amid administrative chaos, had found itself giving birth to an extraordinary Test match. England supporters could not believe that a match their team had dominated had not ended in victory. For the West Indies supporters who gradually filled the popular side as their team's resistance grew, there was more evidence of the renewed spirit that had seemed so palpable in Jamaica.

At tea, England needed five wickets for victory, and such was the importance of the moment that Andrew Strauss was prepared to have Flintoff bowl through an injury that, earlier in the day, was deemed serious enough for replacements to be called for. The day before, Harmison had described Flintoff's three modest overs in terms that made it sound as though he had gone over the top at the Somme, but now, there really was something heroic in the way Flintoff defied a pain barrier that grew with every thunderbolt he sent down. Ball after ball, he charged in against an ever-stronger breeze, and ball after ball he grimaced with pain, sometimes pulling up short as his hip reminded him that fast bowling is most certainly a young man's game.

Flintoff deserved better from his six overs but his performance, so lame up until then, seemed, as so often, to spur his colleagues on. Graeme Swann, at the other end, drifted one into Brendan Nash's pads and Daryl Harper responded to the appeal in the affirmative. Jerome Taylor clipped James Anderson to short mid-wicket, where Ian Bell, on as a substitute for Flintoff, had been placed with expert care by Strauss. Seven wickets down, now, with 28.5 overs remaining, but, more realistically, just over an hour's play. Even the Barmy Army was quiet and absorbed by the play.

The light began to close in now, as did England's fielders around Sulieman Benn and Denesh Ramdin. The wicket-keeper survived any number of close appeals and balls that whistled low past his off stump, but one more grubber from Anderson took his inside edge and cannoned on to his stumps.

Eight down. Powell, a man whose temperament is not exactly suited to cooling a situation, joined Benn. As if absorbing some of Powell's excitability, Benn decided that the best way to save the game was to swipe Anderson for six. It is the West Indian way, apparently. Benn was not far from safety when Swann got the affirmative from Rudi Koertzen after a third raucous leg-before appeal.

Nine down, and the last man in but, unlike in the famous poem, the light was not blinding, more fading. England had 25 minutes at the outside to clinch the deal as Edwards came in. The third umpire brought the light meters to the middle, Flintoff was recalled but had nothing more to give; Harmison could not deliver the killer blow, while Swann probed to no effect.

Earlier West Indies had Sarwan and Chanderpaul to thank for redeeming their 'get out of jail free' card. Sarwan already had one hundred to his name in this series and in the morning he set about adding another. Apart from a leg-before shout from Harmison, he was untroubled. And when he progressed into the nineties, he was not about to make the same mistake. A steer to the third-man boundary, once England had taken the new ball, brought his thirteenth Test hundred.

The second new ball, though, gave England their breakthrough and renewed hope. Stuart Broad, bounding in with energy and eagerness, did the trick, following up a length delivery that bounced a fraction with one that kept a little low and sent Sarwan's off stump cartwheeling. It was the end of a fine innings and as the West Indies batsman left he must have feared the worst. For once, his colleagues proved equal to the task.

The Times, 20 February 2009

3rd Test. At Recreation Ground, St John's, Antigua, on 15–19 February. Toss: West Indies. Match drawn. England 566–9d (A.J. Strauss 169, P.D. Collingwood 113, O.A. Shah 57, A.N. Cook 52, K.P. Pietersen 51) and 221–8d (A.N. Cook 58). West Indies 285 (R.R. Sarwan 94, G.P. Swann 5–57) and 370–9 (R.R. Sarwan 106, S. Chanderpaul 55).

Paul Collingwood's Resistance
Inspires England to a Famous Rearguard

Twice now, within the space of three Test matches, South Africa have laid siege to the fortress without breaching the defences. Led, inevitably, by Paul Collingwood, who is fast becoming the master of the nerve-jangling rearguard action, and by Ian Bell, who responded to the situation as he has not always done in national colours, England held out, just, the last pair surviving the final 17 deliveries of another utterly absorbing Test match.

This was desperate stuff once again, as the England players sat on the balcony chewing their nails to the quick and the supporters cheered every ball that the last pair survived, as they had done in Centurion two matches ago and in Cardiff last summer. Once again it was Graham Onions, 'Bunny' by nickname but not by nature, who was charged with the responsibility of seeing England home, this time with Graeme Swann for company.

It was Morne Morkel this time, rather than Makhaya Ntini, who ran in for the final six balls of the game, his knees pumping as Curtly Ambrose's used to do when the juices were flowing. His third and fourth deliveries were perfectly pitched yorkers, which Onions dug out, his fifth a rip-snorting bouncer, from which Onions just managed to withdraw his gloves, the ball instead flicking the back sleeve of his shirt, as the review, which Graeme Smith called for, showed. It was that close.

The final ball, a powder-puff length one that suggested Morkel's strength had been sapped by his previous effort, was safely negotiated and Swann and Onions embraced in the middle as the rest of the England players celebrated what, by surviving 141 overs, was a significant achievement. They will go to Johannesburg with their hard-earned 1–0 lead intact. South Africa will be hard pressed to prise it from their grasp.

The deflation for South Africa was obvious both in the way that they trooped off the field, heads bowed, and in the low-key manner in which Smith answered the statutory post-match questions. South Africa have had their chances in this series and their captain knows that they may not get another as good as the one they had in the third Test here. England, after losing James Anderson and Jonathan Trott in the morning session, were five wickets down at lunch with the new ball due.

That there is steel hidden in the linings of this England team is not in doubt, but they were helped yesterday by two factors. The pitch played truly throughout, displaying none of the fickle tendencies you expect of a worn, fifth-day strip after four days of hot sun, and, Dale Steyn apart, South Africa's attack lacked bite. Steyn took only one wicket during the day, that of Trott, whose off stump was sent cartwheeling, but this was scant reward for a performance of sustained spirit and high skill.

Friedel de Wet was hampered by a muscle spasm in a buttock, for which he received an overnight injection, and he was noticeably down on pace throughout the day. He bowled only 12 overs in the innings, four on the final day. Morkel did not bowl badly, but his radar was awry with the new ball after lunch when he needed it most. Paul Harris took three wickets but bowled poorly through-out, the large number of full tosses betraying the anxiety he must have felt given the expectation on a spinner on the final day.

The crucial period came not at the end of the day, but just after lunch when Steyn bowled one of the best new-ball spells (6–4–13–0) at Collingwood you could possibly wish to see. Collingwood was camped at Steyn's end, not by intent or design, but because he could not lay a bat on the ball to escape. Seven times, by my count, Steyn passed his outside edge, seven times Collingwood stood and stared impassively, although the final time the bowler beat him, both players acknowledged each other with rueful smiles. Had Steyn broken Collingwood then, there is little doubt that England would have lost.

But Collingwood held firm, as he so often has for England, although he will be thankful for the review system that gave him a reprieve after Tony Hill thought he had edged the first ball of his innings from Harris to slip. It had actually come off Collingwood's back leg.

Bell, too, played beautifully, his 286-minute innings an exercise in self-restraint that goes against the grain for such a gifted player. Bell's talents have never been in doubt, his temperament instead the question mark against him, and this innings has gone a long way to establishing his credentials as a scorer of not just pretty, but important runs.

Others played their part. Trott's innings took up more than two hours and that of Anderson, the nightwatchman, just over an hour. Anderson, indeed, had looked untroubled until he swept a full toss from Harris on to his boot and to leg slip, where Ashwell Prince took an outstanding catch. If South Africa's bowlers lacked the punch to deliver the knockout blow, their close fielding was nothing less than excellent.

Collingwood and Bell stayed together for 235 minutes, until there were only 13.3 overs remaining, by which stage a draw seemed inevitable. But England like to do things the hard way – either that or they really are in the business, as Swann said after the first Test at Centurion Park, of keeping Test cricket alive. Collingwood pushed forward to the part-time off spin of J-P. Duminy and edged to slip, and South Africa, who must have been on the point of calling it quits, steeled themselves for one more effort.

Matt Prior then pushed Duminy into the hands of short leg, by which stage there were 11 overs remaining. It was time for Smith, as he had done at Centurion Park, to captain by gut feeling, and he turned to Steyn with seven overs to go, then to Harris next over, now that the left-handed Stuart Broad was at the crease. Broad took up 22 deliveries before Harris finally located the rough he had sought but not found for much of the day, the ball popping off the left-hander's left glove into the hands of short leg.

There were 20 balls remaining when Swann joined Bell. He hit his first ball nonchalantly through the off side for four, but it was time for Smith to pull the final rabbit from his captain's hat. He replaced Steyn with Morkel from the Kelvin Grove End, and Bell offered half a bat to Morkel's first ball, steering it straight to first slip. Bell will be disappointed with the shot and that he did not see things through to the end, but his was an innings to be proud of.

Onions and Swann combined now to face 11 balls from Morkel and, as it turned out, one more over from Steyn, who replaced Harris. It was little time for recognising that the old game had produced another cracker and that these teams had taken each other to the limits again, but it, and they, had.

South Africa crowded around, like jackals eyeing a kill on the African plain, but not close enough as Onions fended off a bouncer in Morkel's penultimate over to where short gully might have been. It was to be South Africa's final chance.

The Times, 8 January 2010

3rd Test. At Newlands, Cape Town, on 3–7 January. Toss: England. Match drawn. South Africa 291 (J.H. Kallis 108, M.V. Boucher 51, J.M. Anderson 5–63) and 447–7d (G.C. Smith 183, H.M. Amla 95). England 273 (M.J. Prior 76, A.N. Cook 65, M. Morkel 5–75, D.W. Steyn 4–74) and 296–9 (I.R. Bell 78, A.N. Cook 55).

Jonathan Trott Is Solid as a Rock in Face of Amir Audition for Leading Man

At this least jingoistic of cricket grounds, talent and performance, not colour, creed, nationality or reputation, are the only markers by which a cricketer is judged. Yesterday, Lord's stood to three cricketers with little in common except an ability to rise to the grandest of occasions.

Mohammad Amir is an 18-year-old from Lahore who, surely, will be among the most pre-eminent fast bowlers of the coming age and is likely to sprinkle a little stardust wherever he roams. He reduced England to rubble in the first half-hour of the morning session with a magnetic spell of left-arm swing and seam bowling.

Jonathan Trott's Farmer Giles's gait and dogged, self-absorbed style is likely to set far fewer tongues wagging, but he should be a fixture in England's line-up for many years to come. He watched impassively as Amir created havoc before going on to play a really, really good Test-match innings – the best played by an England batsman for some time. Without him, the game might already have gone.

Like Amir, Stuart Broad has been spoken of in leading-man's terms, but in recent months his batting star – and thus his potential as an all-rounder to fill the Flintoff boots – has waned. There were signs of a revival at The Oval in the third Test, built upon here with a dazzling maiden hundred – only the second he has scored in any form of cricket – which confirmed that the promise seen initially in his game had not been misplaced. Without his contribution to a record eighth-wicket partnership against Pakistan, worth an unbeaten 244 by the close, England's revival, from an unpromising 102 for seven when Broad joined Trott, would have been stillborn.

First to Amir, the floppy-haired, white-fanged left-armer who last week became the youngest man in Test history to take five wickets in an innings in England. Yesterday, he became the second youngest and when – having dismissed Matt Prior caught behind just after lunch to take his fifth – he knelt and kissed the Lord's turf before being mobbed by his team-mates, there was little doubt which feat meant more to him.

Not only is there something mystical about the Lord's honours board, but Amir's performance looked as if it had given his team an outstanding chance of squaring the series. At 47 for five, with Kevin Pietersen, Paul Collingwood and Eoin Morgan sitting in the dressing-room after three ducks in a row – the first time England's

Nos 4, 5 and 6 had been dismissed all for nought in Tests – England were a team in need of an injection of self-belief.

It came from Trott, whose calmness under fire and studied concentration were a lesson to others. This was Test batting at its best: watchful early on as the ball darted about like a chased buck; pro-active, though, in the way he sought to nullify Mohammad Asif's length by batting outside his crease; unmoved as Umar Akmal tried to disrupt his concentration with some well-aimed barbs; and then majestically in control in the final session of the day as conditions eased and the bowlers tired.

Trott, of course, has already had his named carved on the honours board thanks to the double hundred he scored against Bangladesh on his previous appearance here. But there is no doubt which of the two innings will have given him more pleasure: Pakistan have a serious attack and, especially in the morning, conditions could not have been more testing. Compact drives, clips off the hip and a clear mind were the hallmarks of an outstanding innings.

And so to Broad, who seems to have benefited from dropping down the order to No 9 – although Graeme Swann, fresh from a second-ball duck, might reflect that his promotion has done him no favours – where the pressure to play like an all-rounder is lessened and his attacking instincts can be indulged.

An aggressive approach was the common thread in Broad's 48 at The Oval last week and his most recent fifty, at Headingley during last year's Ashes, and it was at the heart of his success yesterday – this, note, was properly channelled aggression, not the type to land him in trouble with the match referee.

There was a hooked six to the Mound Stand off Wahab Riaz, and any number of stand-and-deliver drives played with the straightest of bats. When, after tea, he clipped Wahab calmly through mid-wicket for three to bring up his first Test hundred, arms raised and a smile to light up the now-gloomy day, it was the moment a potential all-rounder was reborn.

Pakistan were tiring now, the effects of six Tests in seven weeks perhaps taking its toll on their four-man attack. Yasir Hameed put down Broad on 121 off Imran Farhat's leg spin to further the pain and even the referrals began to go against them as Broad was reprieved to a leg-before off Saeed Ajmal.

With each run scored, there was also the knowledge that the morning position was a distant memory and, more than that, it will be Pakistan's fragile batting for the microscope next. Never had the demoralising effects of a long batting line-up been better illustrated.

And, let's face it, with a top order such as England's right now, a long batting line-up is a necessity rather than a luxury. Alastair Cook went edging to Kamran Akmal, his feet moving into position only after the ball had feathered the edge of his bat. Then Pietersen, poor KP, whose loose drive to his first ball confirmed everything about his troubled state of mind. Then Collingwood, trapped leg-before third ball courtesy of the decision review system, and finally Morgan, edging his third ball into the hands of second slip. Twenty-two minutes of mayhem.

If the collapse at The Oval was in no small part self-inflicted, only Pietersen had reason to curse himself here. The rest were blown away by a bowler at the top of his game.

The Times, 28 August 2010

4th Test. At Lord's, London, on 26–9 August. Toss: Pakistan. England won by an innings and 225 runs. England 446 (I.J.L. Trott 184, S.C.J. Broad 169, Mohammad Amir 6–84). Pakistan 74 (G.P. Swann 4–12) and 147 (Umar Akmal 79*, G.P. Swann 5–62).

8

From a Foreign Field

Some players are easier to write about than others. Of the greats, Shane Warne is the easiest, his bowling being a pure reflection of his character, and Sachin Tendulkar the hardest, his batting giving nothing away beyond the narrowest of aims – to score as many runs as possible. If his cricket tells us about the man, then I have been blind to it.

Nevertheless, it would have been strange not to have written at all about the greatest of modern players and there are a couple of Tendulkar pieces here, one talking with his schoolboy prodigy chum, Vinod Kambli, and the other on the occasion of Tendulkar becoming the highest scorer in Tests of all time.

Elsewhere, there are profiles of the curious, Ajantha Mendis, and the forgotten, Richard Austin (one of my favourite pieces in the collection), as well as some of the other great players – Brian Lara, Curtly Ambrose and Allan Donald, for example – who I have had the privilege to both play against and watch at close quarters.

Curtly Ambrose

A cricketer's retirement, in both its timing and manner, can often tell you as much as you need to know about that player's career. In Curtly Ambrose's case, the timing, like his approach to the crease, was near perfect. He was still at the top of his game, as the 2000 series in England showed. Yet, some of his trademark pace and fire was beginning to wane, and in his final spell the ageing legs seemed to be sending him a message. Rather than risk a trip too far to Australia, which with its unremitting heat, big grounds and flat wickets is no place for old bones, he decided enough was enough and left us with memories of how great he is, rather than was.

The manner of his retirement, too, was typically Ambrose-like. He announced at the beginning of the summer, with no histrionics, that the series against England would be his last, and, with little or no fuss from the big man himself, he was true to his word. There were precious few titbits for the media to scrap over, although he did give his old pal Michael Holding one interview to ruin that oft-quoted phrase, 'Curtly talks to no one'.

In this modern age of image and spin, with the accent on style rather than substance, he has been a refreshing change. He went, as he came and then conquered, with little to say. And yet, despite the low-key approach to retirement from Ambrose himself, rarely can a crowd or an opposition team have acknowledged a cricketer's leaving in such a fashion. An indication, if one were needed, of the high esteem in which he is held. It was one of the most touching moments I have seen on a field, when The Oval crowd rose to Ambrose and his great mate, Courtney Walsh, to applaud them off the field for an assumed last time. They left, arm-in-arm, one sensed close to tears, and halfway up the pavilion steps Ambrose symbolically removed his famous white armbands, safe in the knowledge that his legs would have to do no more pounding.

The next day, as he walked to the crease with West Indies on the brink of a famous defeat, the England team lined up and applauded him all the way to the wicket. It was a fitting mark of respect and, no doubt, a private thank you that their tormentor was finally on his way. (A few of us had remembered his wave to The Oval crowd five years before, hoping we wouldn't see him again.) In the middle of the salute he mumbled, 'Thanks, lads,' which is about as much as I've heard him say. In cricket, even when you are losing, you can sometimes be a winner.

In statistical terms, Ambrose's career ranks among the very best the modern game has to offer. He took 405 Test wickets at a shade under 21, with a strike-rate of a wicket every 54 balls. Testimony to his parsimony is the 1,000th maiden in Test cricket that he notched up during last summer's series. As someone he dismissed more times than anybody else, I think I am reasonably well qualified to comment and compare him with the other fast bowlers from the last decade of the last millennium.

At his best, there is no doubt he moved beyond the fine line that separates the great from the very good. Quality bowlers essentially need two of three things: pace, movement and accuracy. Ambrose had all three. He was certainly quick, especially in the mid-1990s, and the extra bounce he generated from his beanpole frame made life even more awkward for the batsman. More than anything, though, he was a mean bowler: he hated giving away runs. Twice during last summer's series it took me half an hour to get off the mark, and then it was only a nudge off the inside edge through square leg for one. But each time Ambrose was livid with himself for offering even this measly morsel.

His best spell against England was undoubtedly at Trinidad's Queen's Park Oval in 1994. On a wearing fourth-innings pitch, we needed 194 to win. But from the very first ball, which he nipped back to trap me leg-before, it looked a distant target. For the final frenetic hour on the fourth evening Ambrose steamed in, reducing the England innings to tatters (40 for eight) with as good a display of hostile and aggressive fast bowling as you will see. One look at Graham Thorpe's eyes as he walked off that evening told you everything. Ambrose's performance prompted Lord Kitchener to pen a calypso about him and about that extraordinary hour, and for the remainder of the tour the whole of the West Indies could be seen dancing to its beat.

Lest you think it was only the English he harassed, his spell at Perth in 1993, when on the first day he took seven wickets for one run in 32 balls on a trampoline of a pitch, was apparently even more devastating. One can only be glad not to have been 22 yards away at the time.

As West Indies became more fragile during the second half of the 1990s, they came to rely on their fast bowlers more and more. So often defeat seemed inevitable, and yet somehow Ambrose and Walsh responded to the call. They always had. Their classic come-back was probably in the inaugural post-apartheid Test against South Africa at Bridgetown, where West Indies, outplayed for four days, roused themselves through Walsh and Ambrose to an aston-ishing victory on the last day in front of a deserted Kensington Oval. With South Africa, eight wickets in hand, requiring another 79 runs, Ambrose took four for 16 and Walsh four for eight.

In spite, or maybe because, of the hostility of his bowling, there was never a battle of words with Ambrose. There was no need. In the truest sense, he let his cricket do the talking. The most I ever heard him say was 'Morning, skipper,' and there were never any verbals during our frequent battles in the middle. Over time, however, there was a little more animation, to add spice to the contest. Before the first ball of the innings, he came to have a habit of walking down the wicket, yards from the batsman, and looking at that area of the pitch he deemed to be the 'business area'. He would rub his hands with anticipation, and invariably at the end of the day there would be a cluster of ball marks worrying the patch.

This discipline and professionalism typified his bowling throughout his career. With his going, and the imminent departure of Courtney Walsh, West Indies have lost the last link with their great teams of the 1980s and early 1990s. Thankfully, for batsmen, there will no longer be the sight of Ambrose stood in mid-pitch after another wicket, pumping his arms skywards. He has been a magnificent servant to West Indies cricket, playing his part fully in carrying forward the famous fast-bowling legacy. He leaves an enormous hole to fill.

This article originally appeared in the
2001 edition of *Wisden Cricketers' Almanack*

Farewell to a Near-perfect Fast Bowler

He might have imagined the final over to be in Johannesburg with the World Cup in his grasp. Instead, Allan Donald's career ended [in the World Cup game against Sri Lanka on 3 March] with him ferrying drinks out as twelfth man, dropped for Monde Zondeki, a bowler who would not have been mentioned in the same breath a year or two ago. The lure of the fairytale ending proved too strong. Yesterday lunchtime reality hit home and Donald announced the end of a wonderful international career.

He will still play for Free State for a couple of seasons yet, and he chose his home ground in Bloemfontein to make the announcement. His press conference was shown outside on the big screen and a small crowd gathered around to watch. The majority seemed unconcerned and continued to enjoy their picnics on the grass verges that surround the playing arena here.

It was almost as if, silently, they were agreeing with Donald's decision; that they knew the fast bowler had gone on slightly too long and that when a sportsman was past his best he must collect his cards and go. In truth, Donald did slightly overstay his welcome. Unlike Curtly Ambrose, for example, Donald's trajectory was too flat, had no 'loop' and so he could not so easily survive a loss of pace. Batsmen who had suffered in the past were keen for retribution.

Donald, himself, acknowledged that the time was right to step aside. 'I have simply reached the end of the road,' he said, flanked by Gerald Majola, the chief executive of the United Cricket Board of South Africa. 'I have no more personal goals and I feel it is now time to move on. I have had a wonderful career playing for South Africa and I have no regrets.' It was a dignified, if low-key, retirement.

It was interesting to note, too, how quickly the UCB have welcomed him into the fold. They have fast-tracked him so that he will travel to England with South Africa's Under-19s and the senior team next year to work as their technical adviser. 'He will continue to play a vital role in developing and training our fast bowlers,' Majola said. The contrast with England is stark.

But rather than remember Donald's end, we should recall a young, paper-thin Afrikaner, of rare pace, who emerged from Bloemfontein Technical College nearly 20 years ago. From the Free State it was on to England, and to Warwickshire, where I saw him bowl for the first time: he put five Lancashire batsmen in hospital that day and as many stitches in Wasim Akram's chin.

I was not to know then that I would develop a kind of 'special' relationship with him, for I was not yet an England player and South Africa had not yet been readmitted into international cricket. 'Special' in the sense that the two performances I am remembered for were against Donald. Two days of defiance at Johannesburg in 1995 and the gut-wrenching 40 minutes at Trent Bridge in 1998. 'Special' also for the reason that he dismissed me 11 times, more than any other batsman. Both of us always anticipated the contest; I think we brought out the best in each other, a fact he kindly alluded to in his press conference.

For a while he was the quickest bowler in world cricket. He was a fearsome sight for opposition batsmen – the long, loping run, the athletic follow-through and always a touch of war-paint thrown into the mix. His pace came not from brute strength, but from the long limbs and wiry frame that he inherited from his mother.

His mental strength probably came from his upbringing in Bloemfontein, an Afrikaner heartland, and from the national service that he was forced to attend. I needed only one look at his battered and bloodied feet after two days in the field at Old Trafford to know that this was a cricketer of great heart. The physical and mental combined to produce a near-perfect fast bowler who took 602 wickets in internationals at a combined average of 22.

Not many of those wickets came in this tournament, and his own performance mirrored that of the host nation. Since then it has been amusing to see South Africa undergoing the same kind of self-analysis and self-doubt that we usually reserve for ourselves; too many players, too many clubs and too little strong competition is the general gist. Heard that before somewhere. Amusing, too, to see the giant sponsors' billboards being gradually taken down. 'Polly – we'll fly them here, you send them home,' said South African Airways. Well, it is South Africa who have departed first, amid plenty of criticism.

Donald was one of two players – the other being Jonty Rhodes – who astonished the cricketing world by dedicating this World Cup to Hansie Cronje. It showed that this team have yet to escape their former captain's shadow. That is the main reason why there are so few tears shed by cricket lovers here over South Africa's poor showing. Ironically, Rhodes, like Donald, failed to shine in this tournament.

But yesterday at Bloemfontein [during the Super Six game between New Zealand and Zimbabwe] there were no recriminations for South Africa or Donald. Those of us who thought the majority of the crowd were cocking a deaf 'un to Donald's statement were wrong. He finished by saying, rightly, that he could walk out of the room with his head held high and that he would like to be remembered as someone who played for his country with great pride. At that moment the whole crowd burst out into spontaneous applause. They had been listening and they appreciated the man and the moment.

Sunday Telegraph, 9 March 2003

Kambli's Bit Part in Sachin's Surge to Stardom

The story of Sachin Tendulkar and Vinod Kambli, contemporary schoolboy champions who became international team-mates, is one of lifelong friendship. It is also a story of middle-class comfort and working-class poverty, of fulfilment and disappointment, of discipline and distraction, of acquiescence and rebellion, and, ultimately, of what is and what might have been. As Tendulkar passed Kapil Dev's record for the number of Test matches played by an Indian yesterday, Kambli watched from the stands, in the middle of finalising a divorce and dreaming of his next Bollywood film.

Kambli looks different now from the player who smashed 224 (still the highest by an Indian batsman against England) in Mumbai 13 years ago – my only Test on Indian soil. His waistline is thicker, what remains of his hair is braided back, a grey-flecked beard covers his face and, when he opens his mouth, attention is drawn to a diamond-encrusted molar.

He certainly looks more Bollywood than batsman, although these days, as the likes of Kevin Pietersen and Mahendra Singh Dhoni suggest, the two are not mutually exclusive. In any case,

Kambli, out of Test cricket for more than a decade, has not given up on a recall to the Indian team.

Kambli's story begins in Bhendibazar, a poor and violent mainly Muslim suburb of Mumbai, and in the single-room *chawl* (slum dwelling) that was home to anything up to 24 members of his extended family. The small patch of land that served as his first cricket pitch was surrounded on all sides by high-rise buildings. The scoring system was dictated by the lack of space, and the higher a batsman hit the ball into the buildings the more runs he scored. It explains why Kambli was one of the best over-the-top hitters of spin I have seen.

His talent was recognised early on, and with his school fees and travel money paid for, he was sent to Shardashram School and placed under the tutelage of a coach called Ramakant Achrekar. He would rise at five, take the hour-long train journey to school, often sitting among the fish and the vegetables at the back of the train so that by the time he got to school he stank. In the afternoons and early evenings he would practise for five hours, often not returning home until after midnight, when his mother would feed him before he grabbed the five hours or so of sleep that nourished this cycle of sacrifice.

Tendulkar also travelled an hour by train to Shardashram School, but at least he came from East Bandra, which, despite being looked down upon by the inhabitants of West Bandra, was a relatively comfortable middle-class suburb. It was at Shardashram where the two first met, when Kambli was eleven and Tendulkar was ten.

According to Kambli, Tendulkar was frozen by nerves on the day Achrekar came to select 50 youngsters for summer camp. 'He was so tense that he was getting beaten each and every ball. Initially, he was told he wasn't good enough and he started crying and begged for another chance. He came back with his brother, Ajit, the next day and his talent was there for all to see.'

The two became the most famous schoolboy cricketers in the land in February 1988 when, in a three-day semi-final match against St Xavier's College, they put on a world-record 664 for the third wicket. Tendulkar made 326 not out and Kambli 349 not out, innings that extended to over three pages of the scorer's book. A mutual friend from those days says that Kambli is the only real competition Tendulkar has ever had.

Kambli remembers the carnage on the Azad maidan that day; that bowlers were crying and didn't want to come back for the second day. Neither did the fielders, who were leg-weary from continually having to fetch the ball from miles away. Kambli says that Achrekar had demanded that they declare overnight, a dictat that Tendulkar, the captain, ignored. It was only when Achrekar returned at lunch the following day that Tendulkar declared at 748 for two. But it was to be Kambli, not Tendulkar, who became the rebellious one.

Tendulkar made his debut for India in 1990, 'taking,' Kambli says, 'the elevator to the top while I took the stairs.' When Kambli's chance came to join his friend in the team three years later, he made the most of it.

After a quiet start in his first two Tests against England, he scored that 224 in his third (putting on 194 with Tendulkar), followed by scores of 227, 125, 4, 120, 5, 82 and 57. Sixty-four runs in six knocks followed in the West Indies and after two more Tests against New Zealand he was dropped from the Test team. Despite averaging 63 for Mumbai, 59 in first-class cricket and 54 in Tests, Kambli never played Test cricket again. Finished at 23.

He did have a problem against the short ball, often fending it off to gully, but it was his attitude as much as his batting that cost him his career. While Tendulkar played straight, Kambli swaggered to the crease in an earring and with experimental haircuts long before it was fashionable to do so, wore enough bling to make David Beckham blush, and drank openly when Westernisation was still frowned upon in certain quarters.

If he started playing now it is likely that he, not Tendulkar, would receive the biggest cheers (as Dhoni does) from crowds who find the combination of consumerism, cricket, celebrity and soap opera impossible to resist. Instead, it is Tendulkar who is the megastar of Indian cricket, while Kambli is recovering from a shin operation and hoping for another season or two as part of the Mumbai team before he calls time on his career. After that, Bollywood beckons. He has already starred in one film called *Anaart*.

'Anaart' translates into 'disaster' which, in box office terms, it was. He is lined up to star in another, a romance called *Pal Pal K K Saath* ('Along With the Heart'). As we walk through the Cricket Club of India during our evening together, the waiters implore him to make a comeback rather than go into Bollywood. I'm not sure whether that is a reflection on his batting or his acting.

He is still close to Tendulkar. When they meet they do so alone, even though Kambli must be frisked first by the security staff who guard Tendulkar's apartment. Kambli, like the England bowlers, thinks that his friend's reactions have slowed a little, that he is hitting the ball squarer than he used to, that he is playing a little too conservatively and needs to try to dominate more, just as he did on the Azad maidan all those years ago.

Does he tell him? 'You must be joking. We never talk cricket when we get together.' He also thinks Tendulkar will get a hundred in Mumbai.

Recently, Kambli was an honoured guest at the party to celebrate Tendulkar's record-breaking 35th Test century. Since their schoolboy days together, Kambli has always given Tendulkar a *vada pav* (a delicacy of fried potatoes in bread) for every hundred Tendulkar scored. This time, Kambli offered up 35 *vada pavs*.

Despite my promptings, Kambli shows no trace of envy towards his old friend. After all, he says, it took Tendulkar six years longer to get a Test match double hundred.

Sunday Telegraph, 19 March 2006

Exit Warne – Saint, Sinner and Spinner

'Dad' – do all children elongate that one syllable word into a whiny two? – 'Why is Shane Warne retiring?' 'Well, son, he said that he felt it was just the right time. He said that an old cricketer once told him that he'd know when the time was right, but that he wasn't sure at first what that old cricketer meant. Now he does. He just feels that he hasn't got anything left to prove, and like all champions he wants to go out on top, under his own terms, while the crowd are asking why rather than why not.'

'Dad?' 'Yes, son.' 'Who is Shane Warne?'

Over the past few days, in Melbourne, children have been more interested in Warne's departure than Santa Claus's arrival – even if, as in the case of my five-year-old, they have no idea who he, Warne, is. He has been everywhere – front page, back page, editorial, leading news item and closing – his exit from the stage calculated to echo as closely as possible his domination of it, that is in the fullest glare of publicity with a dash of theatre thrown in.

No wonder Glenn McGrath wasn't keen on announcing his impending retirement simultaneously: the fast bowler wouldn't have been given a second look.

When Ian Thorpe, the great Australian swimmer, retired some weeks ago he shared the stage with officials from the Australian Swimming Federation. For Warne, there was only one chair on the podium and no one was going to be allowed to share the stage. James Sutherland, the chief executive officer of Cricket Australia, sat anonymously in the front row, while their media manager hovered anxiously in the wings trying to co-ordinate affairs. All the focus was on Warne, which is how he likes it. Whereas Thorpe's announcement was carefully choreographed, with an eye on his future, Warne was Warne. He said he'd have a couple of beers and smokes and think about his future after that. He was without artifice, completely natural.

Had my son watched the press conference, I would have said simply, in answer to his question, 'Look: that's who Shane Warne is.' All that he is, or was, as a cricketer was in evidence on that stage: the ego, the confidence, the sense of theatre, the modesty, the intelligence, the competitor, the team-man, the mate and the physical strength. And the one thing that was not always in evidence during his playing career was finally added to the mix: maturity. This was a mature decision made in mature fashion: the Peter Pan of cricket has at last grown up. Only the technical mastery of his art was invisible from his press conference, but with his hands, strong and compact, clasped in front of him on the table top, it was obvious that he had the tools to spin the ball as hard as anyone else.

The first surprise for those who have not met Warne, or heard him speak, but know him only by reputation would have been how well he spoke. He is the best and most interesting talker of any contemporary cricketer. If he repeated himself a little, it was because of the crassness of some of the questions. He used no notes, and had none of the verbal tics ('you know', 'obviously', 'to be honest', 'kind of' and 'take the positives' are the present favourites of the England team) associated with professional sportsmen. He didn't resort to cliché and was bright and respectful enough to answer the question put to him, rather than trotting out some prefabricated thoughts.

He has got a voice, too, (the lucky bastard's going to make a great commentator), even if it betrays his dual existence as both a saint and a sinner. It is the voice – slightly grainy and harsh – of a thousand late nights, much booze and many fags but it is also one of conviction and honesty.

Unrealistically, we like our heroes to be infallible and there is no hiding away from Warne's human failings, but I tend to agree with the sports editor, in Ring Lardner's famous short story 'Champion', who insists that one of his reporters does not mention in the champion's obituary that he knocked down his mother and his disabled brother. Why? Because he was the champion. Warne, too, is a champion. He can answer for the dodgy morals elsewhere.

Gone was the bluff, bluster and bravado of his recent press conferences. In its stead was a deep confidence of his place in cricket's grand scheme of things, and a conviction that he was doing the right thing at the right time. He didn't have to, as they say in the Caribbean, 'pomp scene'; he has 699 Test wickets to do that for him. He knows his legacy is secure. Nor was there any hint of sadness or regret in his voice. This is the perfect script: the Ashes already regained and therefore a chance to let his people make merry on his behalf at his ground – the ground where he first dreamt of playing Aussie rules, where he gave notice that his talent had come to full maturity with a flipper in 1992 that flummoxed Richie Richardson, and where he achieved his only Test-match hat-trick, against England three years later. It should be some party.

Throughout, Warne gave no hint that he regarded himself as bigger than the game or the team whose presence he graced. He emphasised that he would not have made the announcement if the series was still alive. He stressed how lucky he was to have played in a great era of Australian cricket; how he hoped he might have contributed a little to that; how proud he was to leave Cricket Australia with the full set of trophies – the Ashes, World Cup, Champions' Trophy, Border–Gavaskar Trophy, Chappell–Hadlee Trophy and the Frank Worrell Trophy – in their safekeeping, and, no, he didn't think he was irreplaceable since Australia has the best first-class system in the world and the wheel, after all, continues to turn. He paid full compliment to those who had helped him through: Richie Benaud, Ian Chappell, Terry Jenner and Allan Border.

Throughout his whole press conference, it was the honest-to-goodness cricketer, rather than the performer, that shone through. As an opponent on the field, I always felt it to be so. For sure, the performance, the ego and the theatre were essential characteristics of his art and his act, but the showman never superseded the cricketer and the show never got in the way of the substance. Some England cricketers would do well to take notice. This is a man, as much as Ricky Ponting or Steve Waugh before him, who knows what it means to be an Australian cricketer. He never shied away from hard work, or from confrontation or a challenge (except when he drew up the white flag at Adelaide to Kevin Pietersen – and even then it was to put the team's needs first). He was that rare breed: the willing workhorse with the touch of genius.

He even made himself into a capable batsman and excellent slipper. He was a cricketer first and foremost.

His appearance on stage at the MCG on Thursday was not his final public appearance, of course. No doubt he will be as confident and foot-sure in his final two Test matches as he was on stage, and cricket lovers should take the opportunity while they can to marvel at the most brilliant cricketer of the modern era. He will play on for Hampshire, but by then the fire will have gone out.

Enjoy him while you can, for there is little chance of his like coming again any time soon. The combination of the slow, calculating, taunting run-up, the fierce spin and wicked drift, the fast bowler's mentality, the animal cunning, the exploitation of the umpire (each delivery is accompanied by more oohs and aahs than ever escaped the lips of John Inman) and the stage presence is unique – and has proved to be irresistible to a generation of batsmen.

You know that Warne will be the one player that your children and grandchildren will ask you about. 'Was he the best you played against, Dad?' Oh yes, he was the best, all right.

All that can reasonably be said of Warne in answer to my son's question is that he is an ordinary human being with an extraordinary gift. Ordinary in the sense that he suffers from the same flaws as the rest of us; extraordinary in that he can bowl leg spin better than anyone who ever lived. Is he the greatest slow bowler that ever drew breath, to paraphrase Fred Trueman? Undoubtedly.

Sunday Telegraph, 24 December 2006

The Mighty Craftsman

In the moments after the Ashes were won at Perth in December 2006, only one of the victors managed the moment with due dignity. As the Australians hugged each other and celebrated with the crowd, England's players, who had emerged to shake their conquerors' hands, were ignored. Only Shane Warne broke away from the pack to acknowledge the vanquished.

At the end of the next Test, at the MCG, I was waiting near the podium to interview Warne, chivvying him along because we were about to go off air. He started to walk over to me, then stopped. Andrew Flintoff was in the process of answering the usual post-match questions. Warne took off his cap, listened to Flintoff, applauded when Flintoff had finished, and then continued on his way towards me.

If anyone had an excuse to be self-obsessed at the MCG it was Warne, but his respect for the game, and for the people who play it, was an essential and often overlooked part of his greatness. Michael Vaughan touched on this point in his book *A Year in the Sun*. He said that Warne was 'great to face because he gives you respect. If you do well against him he is not one to give you abuse. He will just say "shot" and, after the game or your innings, he will come in and say "well played".'

It is true that such respect has not always been in evidence (contrast his behaviour at the end of the 2006–07 series with his loutish celebrations from the Trent Bridge balcony in 1997), but they are the reasons why Warne the showman and Warne the celebrity never quite consumed Warne the cricketer. He never forgot that he was but one link in an Australian leg-spinning chain that goes back generations. He never forgot that he was a craftsman as well as an entertainer.

The link with the great Australian leg spinners of the past is enough to explain why nothing that Warne did was revolutionary. Despite his claims before each and every series, there were no new deliveries. The googly, of course, had been invented by the Englishman B.J.T. Bosanquet while experimenting with a tennis ball during a game called twisti-twosti; Clarrie Grimmett perfected the flipper and passed on the secret to Bruce Dooland and Cec Pepper; after the Lord's Test of 1953, Doug Ring picked up an apple on a train journey and showed a young Richie Benaud how he bowled the slider, pushed out of the front of the hand between the second and third fingers. And there, in essence, was Warne's armoury: the original leg spinner and top spinner, the googly, the flipper and the slider.

During his apprenticeship, and in an interesting echo of Bosanquet's experiments with his tennis ball, Warne used to entertain fellow inmates at the Australian Academy with his ability – from his strong forearm, wrist and fingers – to spin balls in all directions on a billiard table. At the Academy he learnt how to perfect the variations on offer to a leggie, and at various stages throughout his career he revealed each delivery to perfection: the curving, dipping, viciously spinning leg-break that bowled Mike Gatting in 1993; the flipper that befuddled Alec Stewart at Brisbane in 1994; the top spinner to bring him the only hat-trick of his career against a groping Devon Malcolm at Melbourne later that series; the googly that crept through Matthew Hoggard's defences towards the crushing denouement at Adelaide in 2006; and the sliders that put Ian Bell into a near-permanent state of confusion throughout 2005.

Within each variation, there were variations. Before the Ashes series of 1997, David Lloyd, aware that Warne's trade was a mystery to many of his players, invited the former New South Wales leggie, Peter Philpott, to talk to the England team. Philpott explained how leg spinners would, to use his phrase, 'go through the loop', varying the amounts of side spin and over spin.

They could start with a leg-break that had just side spin (the seam rotating at 90 degrees towards extra cover, imparting maximum turn), gradually increasing the amount of over spin (seam now rotating towards third man, with less turn but more dip and bounce) until reaching the top spinner (seam rotating towards the batsman) and then the googly, which is simply an extension of that (seam now rotating towards fine leg). The flipper is the opposite of the top spinner, being released from under the hand, imparting back spin (seam now rotating back towards the bowler).

Later on that summer, during the one-day series that preceded the Ashes, I was watching from the commentary box, and saw

Warne do exactly that – go through the loop – in the first over of a spell. He began with a side-spinning leg spinner, then bowled a leggie with more over spin, then a top spinner, then a googly, then a slider and ended up with a flipper. Each delivery landed perfectly.

After his shoulder operation the following year, he gradually began to bowl fewer and fewer wrong'uns and flippers, relying instead on the leggie, in all its variations, and the slider. He even lost the ability to bowl a flipper for a while. His dismissal of Saj Mahmood in his last match at the MCG demonstrated both that he had rediscovered it, and that he had never stopped working at his craft.

Once he had perfected his stock ball and variations, he needed to learn where to bowl them. With help from Bobby Simpson and Allan Border, he devised tactics that would keep most right-handed batsmen in check for the next decade. Because he was such a big spinner of the ball, the traditional middle-and-off-stump line would be a waste, because most deliveries would not threaten the stumps. Instead, they devised a line – middle-and-leg if the pitch wasn't taking a great deal of spin, more leg stump and outside if it was – that meant he would always be attacking.

Again this was not revolutionary. On an unresponsive pitch, Grimmett apparently bowled more round-arm at leg stump. Benaud, of course, out-thought England at Old Trafford in 1961 by bowling outside leg stump from round the wicket. For Warne, though, this was his default line, rather than a variation. And, as his mentor Terry Jenner once explained, it was not so much where the ball ended up that caused such problems for a right-hander, but how it got there.

It got there, as The Ball (to Mike Gatting at Old Trafford in 1993) revealed, with a great deal of curve and drift. This presented serious problems for all but the very best players. Most right-handers moved forward down the initial line, only to find themselves in the wrong position by the time the ball arrived. As a result, most found themselves playing across their front pads and against the spin. This was exacerbated by the prevalent technique of the time – the forward press – whereby batsmen pushed their weight forward slightly before the ball had been bowled. Advancing down the pitch to Warne was difficult; the drift in the air often meant a batsman would end up too far to the off side of the ball, again resulting in him playing across the line.

So, as with all great bowlers, Warne demanded that batsmen think carefully about their technique and, in order to succeed, alter it. Salim Malik, for example, had the courage to bat outside leg, showing Warne all three stumps, so that he was still able to score through the off side. No right-hander, in my view, played him better than Kevin Pietersen, who had such exquisite balance that he was able to change direction – with the drift – while still advancing down the pitch. He battered Warne into submission at Adelaide in 2006, causing him to run up the white flag by bowling so wide of leg stump that a stalemate ensued. It was a rare admission of failure.

Has any slow bowler ever bowled his overs so slowly? Grimmett was once told by his captain to slow down so that the bowler at the other end could be given more of a breather. Warne didn't need to be told to slow down, because it was an essential part of his act. Occasionally during the last series, I timed his overs and, even when wickets were not falling, they could take up to four and a half minutes to complete. The long pause at the end of his run-up, the slow walk to the crease, the oohs and aahs after every delivery, the cold stare down the pitch at a batsman, a word or two in his ear, often a slight field change and a chat with the captain. All were designed not only to give him time to think, but to give the

257

batsman time to think. What did he bowl me there? More to the point, what's coming next?

The thinking time he gave himself was put to good use. No bowler was more cunning. One example, from personal experience, will suffice. At Lord's in 2001, after miraculously surviving Glenn McGrath's opening spell, I was bowled round my legs by Warne. It wasn't a particularly great ball, nor a good shot but, since I'd felt a bit tangled up around leg stump, I decided to shift my guard towards leg stump during the next Test, at Trent Bridge, to open up the off side. In the second innings (I didn't face him in the first), he noticed the difference within three balls, and altered his line more towards off stump, so that I found myself defending with half a bat towards extra cover. I was soon caught behind.

In that same match, towards the end of the second day, Mark Ramprakash was a victim not so much of Warne's cricket craft but of his understanding of the game situation, and of his opponent's mind. Ramprakash had been batting well in a low-scoring affair and was torn between the desire to be positive against Warne and the need to bat out the day. Warne goaded him continually, urging him to come down the pitch: 'Come on, Ramps, you know you want to.' Ramps did want to, and eventually had a mad charge to be stumped by a distance. England ended the day six wickets down.

Umpires were there to be exploited and, in Warne's view, existed only to offer suitable judgement on appeal. No slow bowler ever worked an umpire so well. No slow bowler, in my time, ever got more lbws. Appeals were followed by the ritual 'I-can't-believe-you-didn't-give-that-one-out' look, and maybe a little chat to let him know that was the straight-on-er: 'What, you can't pick me either, Rudi?'

He might go too far with a batsman, but not with an umpire. When, in his last Test at Sydney, he told Aleem Dar not to worry about where his feet were landing, and 'just take care of what's happening at the other end, mate', those were the words of a man who had already mentally retired. After all, Aleem Dar could be of no further use.

Days before the first Ashes Test of 1993, when Warne announced himself with the Gatting ball, Old Trafford was awash with rain. Warne had been belted around Worcester by Graeme Hick in the run-up to that Test and was by no means, in our estimation at least, a certain starter. The pitch was sticky – you could shove your thumb in it – and all the older players, those who had played on uncovered pitches, were certain that Australia should play their finger spinner, Tim May. I can well recall David Lloyd saying that a leg spinner would be of no use in the conditions.

Over the coming years, Warne would show everyone that leg spin was not a luxury but an essential if a team were to have an attack for all conditions. In that sense, Warne has been the greatest advocate for his craft that there has ever been. Australia only ever left him out once when he was available: Antigua, 1998–99, and even then they still had a leg spinner, Stuart MacGill.

He was at once aggressive and defensive, a wicket-taker and a sponge (to dry up runs), a captain's dream. Here was no revolutionary but an amalgam, the perfect amalgam, of all that had gone before: Arthur Mailey's carefree big spinners, Grimmett's miserliness, O'Reilly's competitiveness and Benaud's cunning, all combined in a showman from the television age.

In that sense, Warne might not have done his craft any favours at all. Every leg spinner will be compared to Warne; every leg spinner will be expected to be at once accurate and incisive, and to have all the tools at their disposal, at a moment's notice, to be dropped on a length. We will never see anything closer to perfection.

This article originally appeared in the
2007 edition of *Wisden Cricketers' Almanack*

The Entertainer Departs

You don't really want to remember great players like this: Brian Lara filling his boots, not with runs but dollars, in the fledgling Indian Cricket League at a far-flung cricketing outpost on the outskirts of Chandigarh, the surroundings of Panchkula more scrub than stadium.

Puffy-cheeked and short of inspiration is no way to remember the most instinctive, attractive batsman of his era, so it was slightly appropriate that he made a match-winning century for Trinidad & Tobago in an attempted comeback a few weeks later. In any event, he was denied the grand farewell to his international career that two other modern-day greats, Shane Warne and Glenn McGrath, were accorded last year in Sydney, with the Ashes in the bag and the public paying full homage. At the magnificently revamped Kensington Oval, Lara had the setting all right, but not the script to match.

Responding in turns to Marlon Samuels's confused calls for a single, Lara shuffled forwards, backwards and then finally towards the pavilion for the last time. For once, he was at the mercy of events, rather than controlling them. Even now, at the end of his career, Lara could not escape the intrigue and controversy that accompanied his cricket from the moment in Antigua in 1994 that he broke Sir Garfield Sobers's world record for the highest score in Tests. For some said Samuels had been disillusioned about the way Lara as captain had treated him, and this was the ultimate payback. Others said the cock-up confirmed the deep malaise within the West Indies team, that not even the basics could be executed competently – a malaise, moreover, in which Lara was deeply complicit. All this was a pity.

Quite how Lara could have come to evoke such visceral and conflicting opinions, at a time when West Indies were not exactly flush with talent, is one for West Indian cricket historians. For some in the Caribbean, those two developments – Lara's ascent to greatness and the decline of the West Indies team – are interwoven; for others, he was simply unlucky with his timing, and the fact that he was a great player in an undeniably shabby side merely added lustre to his reputation. Some day, someone from inside the West Indies dressing-room will write the definitive tale. It should be quite a read, failure being more interesting than success.

Lara's quixotic impact within the four walls of the West Indies dressing-room is, anyhow, beyond the scope of this appreciation. Lara the batsman can be assessed objectively on what we saw, rather than what we did not see. And any fair-minded assessment could only conclude that he must be one of the finest entertainers to have played in this or any other era.

For entertainment was the creed by which he lived as a batsman. Many talk the talk but Lara, undeniably, walked the walk. Records and statistics must have been important to him – how else does a batsman galvanise himself to score 501 in a county match against Durham? – but the means were never sacrificed to the ends. 'Did I entertain you?' he bellowed to the spectators in the newly minted Kensington stand at the end of his last match. They cheered, but not loudly enough. 'Did I entertain you?' he asked again. And even those in the anti-Lara camp could not deny it.

It is the West Indian way, of course. If, broadly, batsmanship can be split into two schools – the roundheads and the cavaliers – then West Indies have always specialised in the latter. It is the main reason why West Indies cricket is so cherished beyond narrow international boundaries and why the current decline is felt so deeply and so widely. Cricket, put simply, is more fun played the West Indian way. It is to Lara's great credit that, whatever the circumstances, he stayed faithful to that particular creed.

Lara was in the tradition of great batsmen for whom the fundamentals were essentially self-taught, for whom technique was always the servant and not the master. His eye for the ball and his co-ordination were granted by nature, and nurture in Trinidad did the rest. With his brothers and the community of Cantaro in the Santa Cruz valley to sustain him, Lara's upbringing may not have been as solitary as Don Bradman's, but his early methods bring the Don to mind: for a stump and a golf ball substitute a broomstick and a lime or a marble. Such was his subsequent impact as a schoolboy batsman that Tony Cozier would write in these pages of his record-breaking spree in 1994 that 'there was no real surprise among his countrymen – simply the feeling that his inevitable date with destiny had arrived rather more suddenly than expected'.

This schoolboy brilliance did not, it must be said, extend to the Youth World Cup in Australia in 1988, when I first came across Lara as an opposing captain. Word certainly had it that he was special, but a combination of poor outback pitches and fierce heat (appropriately, James Boiling had a good tournament for England) made batting far from easy. With just one half-century in the tournament, Lara flopped. But within three years he was captaining Trinidad and had become the owner of a maroon cap. Two years later, he played his great innings of 277 at Sydney, described by Rohan Kanhai, no stranger to instinct and individuality at the crease, as 'one of the greatest innings I have ever seen'.

There was no looking back after that – only a question of how far he would go and how many records he would break. What, then, made him stand out? Four things, I think. Barry Richards once said of Garry Sobers that he was the only 360-degree player in the game. He was referring, I think, to his back-lift and follow-through, which routinely travelled through a full arc. Lara might well be described so, too, not just for his back-lift, which reached the perpendicular when he was 'on the go', but also for where he could hit the ball – if not quite 360 degrees, then as near as dammit. No other contemporary player, save perhaps Mohammad Azharuddin, could deflect the ball so finely and so powerfully with a turn of the blade and flick of the wrists. Lara had subtlety in an age of power and brute force.

This unrestricted repertoire, the widest of arcs being open to him, and the ability to hit good balls to the boundary made him uniquely feared by opposing captains. You might worry about Adam Gilchrist, say, butchering an attack and smashing a bowler to smithereens, but Lara made captains, not bowlers, look silly. If you knew you were going to die, you'd prefer a single bludgeoning blow to the head, or a quick bullet to the brain, rather than death by a thousand ever-so-precise cuts. Eleven fielders were never enough; there were always gaps to plug. When he scored his 375 against my England team, I remember moving first slip out when Lara had scored 291. He edged the very next ball right where first slip had been. I'd love to know whether it was deliberate; I always doubted it, simply on the basis that such a level of genius was beyond my comprehension.

Thirdly, Lara was undoubtedly the best player of spin in his era, an era that did not lack for world-class spinners. There might not have been such abundance of quality as before, but in Anil Kumble, Muttiah Muralitharan and Shane Warne, he came up against three of the greatest ever. No one has played Murali better than Lara in Sri Lanka in 2001–02. He hit 688 runs at 114 and reduced the maestro to impotency (against everyone else Murali was omnipotent, bowling Sri Lanka to a 3–0 win). It was no coincidence, perhaps, that it was against Lara's West Indies in 1999 that Warne was dropped for the first and last time in his Test career.

That series saw Lara at the peak of his powers, and his unbeaten 153 to win the Barbados Test is the fourth reason he stood out. Great batsmen play great innings, and on that day Lara created, I believe, the best innings I have seen either as player or observer of the game. England were watching in Lahore, where we were preparing for the 1999 World Cup, and no other contemporary batsman would have had the effect of keeping a bunch of professional cricketers glued to the screen until the small hours of the morning. It was a stunning innings. 'Christ,' one of the team said to me, 'I wish you'd get as excited by some of our players.' Well, honesty always was my downfall.

Only one reason prevents this observer from placing Lara at the apex of modern West Indian batsmen. Against extreme pace he got hit too often, and he could seem extraordinarily jumpy at the crease. I've often wondered what kind of effect removing helmets would have on modern-day players, a hypothetical that doesn't apply to Vivian Richards.

Still, to hold both Test and first-class records for the highest innings, and thrill a generation of watchers in the process, is something Lara can look back on with a great deal of pride. Warne, assessing the cricketers he played against, was once heard to say that Sachin Tendulkar came first, daylight second and Lara third. That may be so. But who would you rather watch? The answer is not in doubt: a Lara innings was always a thing of beauty, no matter who the beholder.

This article originally appeared in the
2008 edition of *Wisden Cricketers' Almanack*

Cronje and D'Oliveira: Same Country, Different Planet

Two documentaries on Monday evening [2 June], one about Hansie Cronje and one about Basil D'Oliveira, proved conclusively that sport remains the finest polygraph test known to man. You can tell the world who you think you are, you can write about who you think you are, and agents and PR schmoozers can erect around you screens of puff and nonsense, but the playing of sport – and especially international sport with all its intrusiveness – will reveal you in the end exactly as you are.

Few modern cricketers were born with more sense of entitlement than Cronje. Not just white and Afrikaner, in a country where those twin classifications automatically conferred a sense of superiority, but white, Afrikaner and privileged, too, because he attended Grey College, that bastion of sporting and educational excellence in the heart of the Free State.

Few modern cricketers were as image-conscious as Cronje. There were television adverts in which he, woodenly and without irony, encouraged his fellow citizens to 'be fair in sport; be fair in life and don't do crime'. There were statesmanlike public speeches, during which he portrayed himself as a leader of the new and improved Rainbow Nation. And there was, of course, the wristband on which he had inscribed WWJD (What Would Jesus Do), which told the world that he was on 'the right side'.

By the time Cronje left the witness stand at the end of the King Commission on match-fixing in June 2000, in tears and physically broken, able to walk only with the support of two helpers, we knew that he was also a liar and a match-fixer and manipulative beyond measure. Self-revelation had come to him at last, too, as he told the commission he was 'driven by greed and stupidity'.

D'Oliveira was born in Bo-Kaap, the Malay quarter in Cape Town, at a place called Signal Hill. The beautiful surroundings, in the shadow of the majestic Table Mountain, were not matched by the opportunities on offer. At 17, when most cricketers are just beginning to spread their wings, D'Oliveira was told that, because of his colour, he was not recognised as part of the 'official' sporting landscape and, in time, he was forced to leave his homeland to fulfil his ambitions.

The D'Oliveira documentary was based on Peter Oborne's award-winning book, some of the details of which have stayed with me long after its reading. Such as the 'pencil test', the measure by which non-white cricketers were classified according to colour. Once placed in the hair, if a pencil stayed there you were classified as 'black'; if it fell out you were 'coloured'. Or the bruises on D'Oliveira's arm caused by his wife's frightened grip as they sat in a cinema in England alongside whites for the first time. Or the look of confusion on D'Oliveira's face as, on his arrival in this country, he looked around the immigration area in vain for the queue marked 'non-whites'.

But whereas Cronje was unable to live up to the expectations of birth and his own image-building, D'Oliveira beat the system and the low expectations of others. Forty-three years after he left his homeland, D'Oliveira returned to lead the parade of South Africa's greatest living sportsmen at the start of the 2003 World Cup at Newlands, a ground where, as a young man, he had been forbidden to play.

The Cronje documentary was important because there has been, and is, a concerted effort in South Africa to rehabilitate him as a role model and icon. In a poll to find the greatest South Africans conducted by SABC, the broadcaster, in 2004, Cronje came in at No 11. (He was just ahead of Hendrik Verwoerd, the founder of apartheid, which gives some idea of the type of person who voted.)

Now Frans Cronje is to release a film about his brother. Commenting on its scheduled release this September, Frans had this to say: 'It looks at Hansie the captain and the hero for his team and his country, Hansie the fallen angel and Hansie the man of strength who could, after overcoming depression, find the strength to come back and remake his life.' Given that the blurb recounts how, within four years, Cronje had moulded South Africa into the world's best Test and one-day team, despite winning very little of substance, the film is likely to be more fiction than fact.

It was, ultimately, the playing of sport that revealed the truth about Cronje and D'Oliveira. Modern international captains come into contact with all kinds and Cronje was unable to resist the charms of sycophants and money men. The most horrific example was his manipulation of two of the most vulnerable players on his team, Herschelle Gibbs and Henry Williams. Both were offered $15,000 (about £10,000) to underperform in a one-day international in India, not knowing that their captain had taken a cut of $10,000 for himself.

Then there was also the team meeting in India in 1996 during which Cronje tried to persuade his players to accept an offer of $200,000 (about £130,000) to throw a one-day international. It took four team meetings for the offer to be rejected, meetings at which (I have been reliably informed by those who were in it) the essential distinction between right and wrong became blurred. One player asked, in all seriousness, whether the money would be taxed. Bob Woolmer, the coach at the time, was quoted as saying he thought it was a sign that his team had finally 'come of age' on the world stage, now that they were receiving the same kind of offers as other top teams. Thank God England were crap.

D'Oliveira faced similar temptations in 1968. Rothmans (acting, Oborne says, at the behest of the South African government) offered D'Oliveira £4,000 and considerable perks to coach in South Africa during that winter. The snag was that he had to make himself unavailable for the England tour that year. It was, in effect, a bribe to prevent him from touring and so prevent the kind of problems that ultimately led to that tour's postponement.

The money was huge for the time (four times more than a county contract) and when the offer was made D'Oliveira was out of the Test team. It must have been tempting. But the sacrifices made by his friends at St Augustine's Cricket Club in Cape Town, who partly funded his initial trip to Britain, mattered more. It was their dream that D'Oliveira would one day walk out at Newlands as a Test player, the most visible way of ridiculing apartheid. D'Oliveira turned down the money.

The documentaries intended to show the changing face of South African sport and society, pre- and post-apartheid. For me, they simply shone a light on humanity and how sport reveals the essence of it. South Africa arrive in Britain this month for a four-Test series that is played for a trophy named after one of these two players; not the man from the Free State who enjoyed every advantage, but the man from Signal Hill who enjoyed none.

The Times, 5 June 2008

Let's Enjoy Mystery Man Ajantha Mendis While We Can

What is at the heart of a great story? Narrative and character are usually a good place to start. A storyline, perhaps, that weaves through unpromising beginnings to a triumphant end with a little-known character possessed of a touch of mystery? If that is what you want, read on because a great narrative is unfolding right now in Sri Lanka, where Ajantha Mendis is the latest to join an exclusive club whose members have included Bernard Bosanquet, Sonny Ramadhin, Johnny Gleeson and Jack Iverson. Mendis, who starts his second Test match today, is the latest incarnation of the Mystery Spinner.

He is certainly a mystery to India's batsmen, who were bamboozled, flummoxed, befuddled and bewildered by him first in the Asia Cup final earlier this month, when he took six for 13, and then in last week's Test match, in which he took eight for 132, the best match figures by a Sri Lankan bowler on debut. The week after Monty Panesar and Paul Harris wheeled away for England and South Africa, stock ball after stock ball, unimaginative over after unimaginative over, Mendis and Muttiah Muralitharan flicked their fingers and rotated their wrists to such effect that they took 19 of the 20 wickets to fall. And this against batsmen who were breastfed on spin.

For those who have not seen Mendis in action, he stands at the end of his run, twirling the ball in his fingers just as any common-as-muck off spinner would. That is where the similarity ends. He then grips the ball like a seamer in the tips of his fingers, as if he is holding a precious relic, runs in quickly and bowls at a quickish pace. As his non-bowling hand reaches upwards just before delivery, the index finger on that hand points skywards as if in premonition that the umpire is about to give the batsman out. So far, the umpires have responded with bewildering regularity.

On release, the mystery unfolds. He lays claim to more deliveries than an NHS midwife, a mixture of off spinners, leg spinners, googlies, flippers and a ball that is flicked out somewhere between the thumb and second finger. None of India's batsmen could pick him. Mendis, 23, says he has five variations and is working on a sixth. This may be true, or may reflect that he has learnt a trick or two from Shane Warne, who began every Ashes series with the claim that he had developed a 'new' delivery when, in fact, the older he got the fewer he had at his command.

This variety is accompanied by unerring accuracy. Basically, whatever ball Mendis bowls, he bowls at the stumps. This might sound like a Pythonesque statement of the obvious, but it is an important factor in his success. Today's umpires are much more likely to give batsmen out leg-before on the front foot, which forces them to play with bat rather than pad. As a result of the batsman being unable to play with his pad on the line of the ball, a spinner does not have to spin the ball hugely to take either edge. And Mendis, for all his variations, is not as big a spinner of the ball as, say, Muralitharan.

Every time Mendis fools a batsman – which is often – he does so with the ghosts of Bosanquet, Iverson, Gleeson and Ramadhin looking on proudly. Are there common themes that bind these strange creatures together? Mystery is an obvious prerequisite.

Bosanquet, of course, was the man who invented the googly after years of playing a game called twisti-twosti, in which he would spin a tennis ball across a table in such a way as to fool his opponents. Iverson, Gleeson and Ramadhin all flicked the ball, one way or another, from the finger much as Mendis does now. This flicked ball has recently been christened the 'carrom ball' because it resembles the way carrom players flick their disks on to a carrom board.

Such finger-flicking ability requires enormously strong digits, something Mendis seems to share especially with Iverson, whose fingers and hands were so big and strong, according to his biographer, Gideon Haigh, that the ball settled into his grip 'like a marble for squirting'. Gleeson attributed his finger strength to his upbringing in the Australian outback, where he spent much of his time milking cows. Did Ramadhin's finger strength come from his enthusiasm for motor mechanics?

These men of mystery often started bowling late in life, were self-taught and had little formal coaching. Ramadhin did not bowl at school and only began to at all because, at 5ft 4in, he was not big enough to get a regular go as a batsman at his club.

Gleeson has been quoted as saying that he learnt his bag of tricks playing 'backyard cricket with a jacaranda tree as the wicket'. Iverson bowled fast at school and then did not bowl for 12 years, until he began experimenting with a ball during army service in Papua New Guinea.

Mendis shares an army background with Iverson, having been trained as a gunner (let's hope his finger strength doesn't come from constantly pulling the trigger) in the artillery. He began bowling early enough, but, crucially, was left to develop without the interference of coaches. Sri Lankan cricket has often looked chaotic from the outside, but chaos can be a good thing in cricket, especially if unorthodoxy rather than rigid conformity is encouraged. Would Lasith Malinga, he of the low, slingy action, have been left alone had he been English? Would Mendis have been allowed to develop in such a free-spirited way in England? I doubt it.

Instant success is another common theme: Bosanquet took 16 wickets in his first three Tests against Australia; Ramadhin came to England in 1950 and took 135 wickets at 14.88, and Iverson played five Tests against England in 1950–51 taking 21 wickets at 15.23. Mendis's own first-class career to date has been startling: in his first two years in first-class cricket he has taken 119 wickets at 14.68. But then this success is often short-lived.

This is unsurprising, perhaps. Word gets around, tactics are discussed (unless, as the story goes with Gleeson, you are Geoff Boycott and refuse to share the secret with your team-mates) and the mystery is gradually unravelled. Gleeson eventually took on a more defensive, stock bowler's role. Iverson did not play much after 1951 and ended up committing suicide. Peter May and Colin Cowdrey administered their own form of death to Ramadhin in 1957 by using their pads, something that could not happen today.

But now, of course, the mystery men are even more disadvantaged by television and the use of slow-motion replays making that which is mysterious seem mundane. Either that, or batsmen come to realise what Gleeson admitted in typical Aussie fashion when asked about his five types of ball. 'That's bullshit,' he said. 'You can only do three things: spin it from the leg, spin it from the off or go on straight.'

After Mendis's startling success against India, he has been twice promoted in the army, first to sergeant and then to second lieutenant. The question is where will he end up: as commander-in-chief or back in the ranks? Watching Panesar and Harris take all the mystery out of spin, let us hope his mystery is not unravelled and his success is long-lasting. But if the historical antecedents are anything to go by, we should enjoy him while we can.

The Times, 31 July 2008

Sachin Tendulkar on Top of World

Significant milestones in cricket often come absent of drama. When Shoaib Akhtar clocked up cricket's first recorded 100mph delivery in Cape Town five years ago, Nick Knight turned it off his hip as if he was facing a trundler on the village green. Statistics, after all, are among the least interesting things the game has to offer. So it was yesterday [in the second Test at Mohali] when Sachin Tendulkar overtook Brian Lara to become the highest run-scorer in Test cricket.

The bowler, [debutant] Peter Siddle, was an unknown and will probably remain so – a footnote of history, a name for future pub quiz nights. The crowd was minuscule, rows of empty seats passing silent judgement on Indian cricket's changing priorities. The game was in limbo, as if nothing of import could happen until Tendulkar, 35, had passed this most pressing of personal milestones.

Needing 15 runs at the start of his innings to pass Lara's 11,953 runs, it was, in truth, a painful process. It was a grind, nothing to suggest that we were watching one of the greats. There were nerves, too: an attempted paddle-sweep on the stroke of tea miscued off the bottom of the bat, after which Tendulkar tried to scamper a single only to be sent back in undignified fashion by Sourav Ganguly.

The record came innocuously enough. Tendulkar simply let the first ball after tea from Australia come, turned his wrists a fraction, opened the face of the blade and ran the ball down to third man for three. He looked to the heavens, raised both arms in triumph and accepted the congratulations of his partner and the Australians who, to a man, shook his hand, as if in acknowledgement that while they might have steamrollered the rest of the cricket world over the past two decades, they had never quite found a way to subjugate Tendulkar's talent. He has averaged 56 against the world's best team.

Numbers, statistics and records matter more in India than anywhere else. Accordingly, the firecrackers were lit and play stopped as smoke filled the ground. A pause ensued as if to give everyone the chance to reflect, if not on the undramatic nature of the moment when the record was passed to its rightful owner, then certainly on the achievement itself. Two decades of consistent run-scoring against the very best that the game has to offer, having made his debut at 16, a time of life when growing up presents enough challenges in itself, and achieved in a country that has refused to allow him the possibility of failure.

Tendulkar's genius is how lightly he has carried this last burden. Since his teenage years he has been public property: every innings, every statement, every movement scrutinised. It was both his good fortune and his curse to play at a time when India emerged as an economic powerhouse, looking for heroes on the world stage.

Rupees have flowed into his bank account but he has not been able to enjoy the fruits of his labours. He must drive his Ferrari at night to avoid attention, lives in a security compound and enjoys the relative anonymity that spending time in London and America brings.

Despite this scrutiny, he has carried himself as well as any sportsman on the planet. The archives recall not one single incriminating incident, not one drunken escapade, not one reported affair, not one spat with a team-mate or reporter. Throughout, he has maintained his professional integrity, tailoring his game to the demands of the situation and the team, always giving the game and his craft due care and attention. As Matthew Parris wondered of Barack Obama in these pages recently, is he human?

His gifts were natural, although never neglected. I listened to him once giving a masterclass on batting at the Rose Bowl in Southampton and he talked with such intimacy and knowledge about his art that it was as if he was born to bat. Why, he was asked, did he grip the bat as he did – as opposed to how the textbooks instruct? Well, that was how he first gripped it as a toddler and he had not seen the need to change. He talked of his 'floating technique' – a kind of dream-like state where he responded intuitively to the conditions and the bowlers' tactics.

This was his take on batting that day: 'For a batsman, each day is different. The mental set-up, the way the feet move, the bat swing, all of it. You have to adjust, to play according to mood and moment.' Above all, he said, the hands need to remain supple to manoeuvre the ball at will. And that was that: have faith in your talent, keep coaching to a minimum and trust your instincts.

But, of course, there was more to it than that. Witness his preparation for Shane Warne's first coming to India, when he took a number of young spinners into the nets, made them bowl into the rough, as he knew Warne would, and swept and swept until his arms and back became sore. After that, he swept Warne some more.

A story is told of an MCC portrait painter who went to sketch Tendulkar at a sitting. The artist was granted an hour and on his return was asked about the 'Little Master'. What was he like? Unbelievably dull was the reply. It is true that Tendulkar's circle of competence – run-getting in international cricket – is a narrow one; but, as of yesterday, nobody in the history of the game has done it better.

The Times, 18 October 2008

Richard Austin: The Fallen West Indies Star

The last time I saw Richard Austin, he was living in a bush. Location, location, location, the estate agents say, and this was a well-positioned bush, to be sure, in the car park opposite the Hilton hotel in New Kingston. The Hilton hotel, you see, is where international cricket teams stay when they are in Jamaica – England are staying there right now – and Austin had located on the principle that someone might just remember him and give him some money to feed his habit.

He's moved now – at least when you do not own a home, selling up is not a problem – and he inhabits the Cross Roads area of Kingston in a triangle between Tastee, the patty store, the Texaco garage and Union Square, sleeping rough, begging and, when he is flush, getting high. He is high a lot of the time, says the man who runs the garage where Austin hangs out, but people are still fond of him and enjoy his company, unless he's so high that he starts talking crazy.

Austin was not a great cricketer, but people in Kingston remember him as a magnificent all-round sportsman. He played two Test

275

matches for West Indies against the Australia team captained by Bobby Simpson in 1978 and then played three 'Tests' during Kerry Packer's World Series Cricket, bowling off spin and hitting the ball hard. He was a dual international, representing Jamaica at cricket and football, and was, by all accounts, a brilliant table tennis player.

Things began to go wrong when he signed to play for the West Indian rebels in South Africa in 1983. Whereas English cricketers who took the apartheid rand were banned for a brief period of time, then quickly rehabilitated and often rewarded with high office, the West Indian cricketers were banned for life and ostracised from their communities. Many, such as Lawrence Rowe and Everton Mattis, the Jamaicans, left their country, fleeing shadows, but those who stayed had it hard.

Austin, 54, stayed, as did Herbert Chang, another Jamaican rebel, who is also living rough in an area of Kingston called Greenwich Town. Elsewhere, David Murray, the Barbadian wicketkeeper, and Bernard Julien, the all-rounder from Trinidad, both of whom toured South Africa, have also struggled through some tough times.

It was an emotive issue and the memory of the choices made then rankles with some. Last week Rowe, one of the greatest stylists that the West Indies has produced, celebrated his 60th birthday in Miami, Florida, and while the Jamaican Minister of Sport sent congratulations, a prominent lawyer here was moved to say: 'There are certain choices in life that define you and even predestine you to a certain future. You can't powder people when their behaviour prolonged our agony. Sometimes life doesn't give you a second chance.'

It has not given Austin much of a second chance. Everyone calls him by his street name now, 'Danny Germs' or simply 'Germs'. It is as if he is a different person, which he is.

It costs about a hundred Jamaican dollars (less than a pound) to buy a lump of crack about the size of a small piece of road grit and it is readily available in Kingston. Smoking it – the usual way is to put the crack and a piece of copper wire down a syringe, heat it up and inhale – produces the strongest hit, but it is also one of the most addictive drugs known to man. 'Germs' has been addicted to it, and homeless, for the best part of two decades.

The last time he was clean was for a short time about ten years ago and he began playing again for Kensington and coaching the youngsters. He had the help of a local businessman to get clean then and the manager of the garage says that there is no end of people willing to help now, but 'Germs' has to want to help himself first. The drug rehabilitation programme Teen Challenge, originally a charity for Jamaican teenagers but which has expanded because of the size of the problem, will take only addicts who walk through the front door by themselves.

Dinanath Ramnarine is the president and chief executive of the West Indies Players Association and he regrets not being able to do more to help former players who have fallen on hard times. 'We're committed to helping former players, but we are constrained by a lack of funding,' he told me this week. 'We started a benevolent fund a while back and we've educated a number of our younger players as to the dangers of drug abuse, but these things cost money and we are not a wealthy organisation.'

While accepting that individuals must take responsibility for their actions, that Austin has made poor choices and that a number of people have tried to help him, it is strange that a sport that can pay a player a million bucks for three hours' work cannot do more to help to look after its own. This week, as the Test match involving West Indies and England takes place at Sabina Park, 'Germs' will be on the street less than a mile away looking for handouts.

'Germs' was not high when Michael Holding and I met him this week and he laughed readily. He spoke warmly of his time in England, playing club cricket for Enfield and Church in the Lancashire League. 'Give my regards to the Queen when you see her,' he said in a moment of high comedy. 'Yeah, give my best to the good lady.' And he raised back his head and blew a kiss to the sky. Those in the forecourt of the garage fell about laughing.

He is still remembered with affection. As we were talking, a middle-aged man pushed his young daughter over to us to get our autographs. She asked Holding for his and then she asked me and was about to go when her father ushered her in the direction of 'Germs'. She held out her piece of paper and he signed his autograph in fine, spidery handwriting: Richard Austin.

The Times, 5 February 2009

Shivnarine Chanderpaul's Bat Always a Precision Tool

Scarcely commented upon, it was. No doubt throwing garlands around a West Indies player was felt to be inappropriate during another supine performance from the touring team, but when Shivnarine Chanderpaul flicked Graham Onions for four in the final over of the fourth day, he went past Vivian Richards as the second-highest run-scorer in Tests for West Indies.

It was something he achieved, remarkably, in exactly the same number of matches as Richards. Only Brian Lara awaits now, although Shiv needs a pair of binoculars to sight him, so far ahead is Lara with 11,953 runs.

Whether he will get there – at present he has amassed 8,576 Test runs – depends on his body, which has always seemed a trifle fragile, rather than his mind, which must be one of the strongest in sport. Chanderpaul did not have the greatest of series, but as

West Indies subsided on the final day at the Riverside with barely a whimper, it was left to him again, as so often, to display some fight, integrity and pride in performance.

The evident pleasure Paul Collingwood took on taking Chanderpaul's edge in the second innings was not only because it was his first as stand-in wicket-keeper; the left-hander's dismissal is always a signal that the end of West Indian resistance is nigh.

No matter what the state of West Indies cricket, no matter how bitter the quarrel between players and administrators, or sometimes between the players themselves, no matter how heavy the defeats, Chanderpaul has simply put his head down and batted oblivious to the chaos around him. To have averaged more than 100 in Tests in each of the past two years in an ordinary team is staggering and something that Andy Flower, the England team director, would appreciate.

And yet when the greatest names of cricket are routinely thrown around, Chanderpaul's is usually absent. His name was missing from C.M.J.'s [Christopher Martin-Jenkins'] list of his top 100 players this week and yet the man he went past in exactly the same number of games – albeit Richards had fewer innings – was ranked No 6 in C.M.J.'s greatest players of all time. No cricketer in history had more presence than Richards, who walked to the crease as if he, and he alone, were carrying the hopes of his countrymen. Chanderpaul, in contrast, walks out to bat as if he is walking to the gallows, but sometimes you have to look beyond the obvious.

When Chanderpaul arrived on the scene for the first time on England's 1994 tour he was something of a curiosity and we were, initially, blind to his talent. We had never seen somebody bang the bail into the ground to take his guard and he looked so slight, fragile and bony that we reckoned he might struggle to hit the ball off the square. During Chanderpaul's first Test, Phil Tufnell did a regular skit in the dressing-room, to great amusement, mimicking Chanderpaul's stance and his lack of authority at the crease. Thereafter, Tufnell spent enough time bowling at the left-hander to perfect his imitation.

Chanderpaul is now a reassuring presence in a game dominated by biceps and bats as wide as tree trunks. He is a butterfly among elephants. The stroke with which he went past Richards was fitting, crabbing across his stumps and deftly turning his wrists where others would have powered their forearms through the ball and looked to smash it down the ground.

He relies on his eyesight, his instincts and touch, manoeuvring the ball with supple wrists and, by modern standards, a wafer blade. In a power-obsessed game, Chanderpaul reminds us that there is room for precision.

But, noting that he stands with his right shoulder pointing due east as the bowler runs in from the north, it would be wrong to dismiss Chanderpaul as a curio. He does enough things right to realise that there are certain basics that cannot be ignored. He watches the ball more carefully on to the bat than any current batsman, plays it later than most and you could balance an egg on his head as the bowler releases the ball.

And he likes to bat. Four times he has gone more than 1,000 minutes in Tests without being dismissed and no one has gone longer than his 1,513 minutes undefeated in India in 2002. A sense of calmness at the crease is the key, something that has developed alongside his spirituality; he once described his phenomenal concentration as a 'gift bestowed by Lord Shiva'. Not that he is unable to raise his tempo when the situation demands – a 69-ball hundred against Australia is testament to that.

It has taken a boy from Unity, a remote fishing village in Guyana, to demonstrate that cricket is poorer when it is straitjacketed according to demands of modern coaching and coaches. Chanderpaul's game is largely self-taught, honed during many hours of practice with his father, Kemraj, at the village ground and on the shores of the Atlantic, and talking to elders who learnt about cricket not by reading the MCC coaching manual but by listening on the radio about heroes like Rohan Kanhai.

He knows his own game, even if others are blind to it. This is the man who had to wait until 2007 to be given an opportunity in county cricket and who was unwanted this year by Indian Premier League owners who overlook substance for style. Whether scoring runs for his club side in Guyana as a ten-year old, or ignored alongside Sachin, Ricky, Rahul and Kevin when lists of the great players of the day are drawn up, Chanderpaul has always been looked upon as a boy among men. It is time he was given his due.

The Times, 21 May 2009

Makhaya Ntini a Champion for South Africa's Lost Generations

Although he was scarcely seen after the warm-ups, this was Makhaya Ntini's day. On a different continent it is not a good time to be a black sporting icon, but here in South Africa millions were with Ntini yesterday as he joined that exclusive club of cricketers who have represented their country 100 times. Not just yesterday, either: the silent majority have been with him every step of his long walk to freedom.

It was a batting day and so Ntini spent the day in the dressing-room. The only sight of him on the pitch was a sprayed-on image on the outfield, finger raised, grinning, with the phrase 'Inqaba Makhaya' underneath. It translates from the Xhosa as 'Champion Makhaya' and a champion, if a slightly underrated one, he has surely been. Today he will lead the team out with his son, Thando, receive his hundredth cap, put emotion aside and set about England's batsmen with gusto.

Inevitably, the colour of Ntini's skin has been a blessing and a curse. A blessing because he has been afforded the kind of international opportunities and patience that might – only might – not have come his way had he not been black; a curse because that knowledge has sometimes camouflaged his achievements as a cricketer, rather than as a black cricketer. It is time he was given his due.

To have played 100 Test matches as a quick bowler – white, brown, black or yellow – in the modern game is a magnificent achievement. Just ask, say, Andrew Flintoff, Darren Gough or Jason Gillespie, fast bowlers with as much talent as Ntini but without the hardness of body to enable them to cope with the problems thrown up by a sport that is increasingly batsman-friendly. The treadmill, the training, Twenty20, the requirement to dive around the outfield, all take their toll, weakening bones and dulling the mind. For sure, Ntini, 32, is not as quick as he was – but he is still going.

Nature and nurture blessed Ntini with a body for all tasks: copious fast-twitch muscle fibres gave him pace to and through the crease, a cruiserweight's build; powerful thighs and glutes protect his back against an unorthodox action; a boyhood spent on his feet, herding cattle and sheep and running with the wild horses in the hills of his native Eastern Cape, gave him stamina in abundance. 'I once thought he was made of titanium and carbon fibre,' Richard Pybus, a former coach of Ntini, said this week. 'He's such a phenomenal athlete.'

Heart and spirit, without which no fast bowler can flourish, have accompanied these natural gifts. He was picked for four series before he had his first taste of Test cricket in March 1998 and the gibes and slurs that accompanied his early selection cannot have been easy to live with, nor the rape charge that came later and of which he was acquitted. There have been other black fast bowlers who promised to share the load, but Monde Zondeki was not quite good enough and Mfuneko Ngam's body was not strong enough. Ntini was left to carry the torch alone.

While the South African authorities were desperate for a black cricketer to act as the role model and to be a champion of transformation, there is no doubt that the embarrassment of obvious over-promotion would have been far worse than not having a role model at all. Most international players have enough on their plates dealing with their own expectations and those of their friends and families, never mind a nation. Ntini has carried the load magnificently.

If there were doubts early on as to the merits of his inclusion, these were swiftly dealt with. His slippery pace and unorthodox style – jumping wide of the crease, a legacy of his spiked boots not agreeing with the concrete pitches of his youth – have caused problems for a generation of Test batsmen, so that before the start of yesterday's match only seven fast bowlers in the history of the game had taken more than his 388 Test wickets. His *coup de théâtre* came at Lord's in 2003, when he took ten wickets in the match and, in an image high on resonance, knelt and kissed the turf.

It is important to celebrate Ntini's achievements in their own right, but it is unquestionably more important still to place them in context. He was not the first black cricketer of note in South Africa as historians have recently shattered the myth that cricket played no role in the non-white community pre-apartheid: in the Western and Eastern Capes and Natal, cricket was strong within the black communities – but not strong enough to resist those who used sport to build rather than break down barriers.

A little over a century ago the Ntini of his day was called 'Krom' Hendricks, a loose-limbed, extremely fast bowler who, those of an unprejudiced mentality agreed, ought to have represented South Africa on merit. It was his misfortune to be playing in the Cape about the time that colonial policy, dictated by Cecil Rhodes, was shifting from integration to segregation, by virtue of the Glen Grey Act, which reduced the amount of land owned by blacks, so giving a stimulus to the numbers of black labourers available for the mines.

Hendricks, scandalously, was not selected for the 1894 tour to England, even after agreeing under duress to accept the role of baggage handler to appease those who were uncomfortable with the thought of a black man being a *bona fide* member of the team. After that disgrace, he was then drummed out of provincial and league cricket. From that point South Africa travelled down the long, dark cul-de-sac of all-white selection, until the promotion of Omar Henry, the left-arm spinner, in 1992.

Like it or not, then (and in this regard, Ntini is more Tiger Woods than Muhammad Ali), Ntini has been playing for the generations who were denied the opportunity to shine. Alongside him yesterday were Ashwell Prince and Hashim Amla, a Coloured and a Muslim, at the heart of this increasingly representative team. Still, there are too few black cricketers, and no black batsman of note yet. But there is no going back.

On Ntini's first tour to England, I remember him telling me how, as a young herder on the winter mornings, he used to walk behind his cows so that he could stand in the cowpats to keep his feet warm. Yesterday, he became a member of a rare club. From cowpats to a hundred caps: a long journey for him, and for his country.

The Times, 17 December 2009

Hail Muttiah Muralitharan,
the Humble Hero who Changed the Game

There are those who will tell you that Muttiah Muralitharan's gains have been ill-gotten. You know the types: the sneerers, the cynics, those who see a dark lining in every silver cloud. Do not listen to such people.

Today, Muralitharan becomes a former Test cricketer. He finished his penultimate day in Test cricket yesterday with 798 wickets as India closed on 181 for five in Galle, 63 away from making Sri Lanka bat again.

He has been a great player; by any estimation he has been one of the greatest players ever. You don't agree? You think he's chucked his way to nearly 800 Test wickets? Well, here's a challenge: next time you are down at the nets, run up and chuck an off spinner – bend that arm as much as you like – and see what happens. It spun, did it? More than normal? OK, now run up and do it for four hours at a stretch, preferably in 40C (104F) heat, landing it time and again on a sixpence; now throw in half an hour of 'doosras', again landing each ball on a sixpence, and then imagine Sachin Tendulkar at the other end.

That bit is not so easy, is it? I know, because I watched an England off spinner try it. In a one-day international a few years ago, this off spinner was miffed that Muralitharan was turning the ball yards while his straight-arm off spinners could barely impart any turn. 'Right,' he said to me as I stood at mid-off, 'I'm going to chuck this next ball. Just watch it go.'

I did watch and it sailed down the leg side, didn't spin an inch and was signalled a wide. He didn't try it again.

Muralitharan has bowled thousands of balls in Test matches. I cannot remember one that ignominiously floated down the leg side without turning on the way. He was at it again yesterday, inducing an India collapse. Having added the world's most expensive cricketer, Mahendra Singh Dhoni, and the world's sulkiest, Yuvraj Singh, to his dismissal the day before of the world's best, Tendulkar, he walked back to the pavilion at teatime in that familiar bow-legged way, his smile radiant. Two more later gave him his – wait for it – 67th five-fer in Tests.

So even if you think he is a chucker, you must admit he has been a bloody great chucker. If you still think he's a chucker, your complaint should be with MCC and the ICC, not Muralitharan, for it is they, between them, who altered the law, and redefined the regulations, to allow for a liberal interpretation of what is legal. You might say they have allowed Muralitharan to keep on playing; more power to *their* elbow, I say.

In 2000, MCC added an extra sentence to Law 24.3, the definition of a fair ball. It reads: 'This definition shall not debar a bowler from flexing or rotating the wrist in the delivery swing.' Muralitharan is the only bowler I can think of who does that, so it is fair to say that the change was designed to accommodate one man.

Next, it was Muralitharan's good or bad fortune, depending on your point of view, to play at a time of great technological advance. The use of super-slow-motion cameras revealed that every bowler straightened their arm to varying degrees on delivery, which meant that every international bowler and, by extension, every bowler in the game broke Law 24.3.

What was the ICC to do? If it supported umpires such as the Australians – and it has always been the Australians who have been most anti-Muralitharan – Darrell Hair and Ross Emerson, who called Muralitharan for throwing, and if it then kicked Muralitharan out of the game, it surely faced legal action on the basis of discrimination. It found a sensible way out, bringing in a playing regulation that allowed for a certain degree of latitude in the straightening of the arm. It also should have silenced, at a stroke, the naysayers. Not that it did.

Muralitharan has had to live with the ongoing jibes and doubts and criticisms before and since. The way he has reacted without bitterness has been extraordinary. How many great players would have subjected themselves to the indignity of bowling in a cast to prove his 'innocence' on television? Muralitharan did, and Channel 4 viewers might have been surprised that he managed to bowl both his off spinner and his doosra in that cast, albeit not at the pace he often did in a match. It was said before this experiment that nobody could bowl a doosra without straightening their arm. Muralitharan did.

It was because of his super-rotation of the wrist that he was able to do it, and it was this that was at the heart of his greatness. Before Muralitharan, most off spinners adhered to the MCC coaching manual: a sideways position in delivery with the standard off spinner bowled off the index finger, with an arm ball as the variation. As a result, off spin, as a match-winning threat, was a dying art before Muralitharan came along, rendered so by covered pitches and a leg-before law that discriminated against them if a batsman was canny enough to use his pad as a second line of defence.

Then came Muralitharan. He bowled off spinners from the wrist rather than the finger and from a front-on position, which was the precursor to his discovery of the doosra – effectively the off spinner's googly. As a result he has been a game-changing bowler, and one who has done it over a long period, unlike other 'mystery' bowlers who flickered briefly and were extinguished.

If that was not enough, he has done it for an emerging country rather than an established one. There have been other fine cricketers from Sri Lanka in the past two decades, but without Muralitharan they would not have become a genuine Test threat, would not have won a World Cup and would not have won abroad. When Arjuna Ranatunga won the toss and bowled on a plumb pitch at The Oval in 1998, he was widely thought to have lost his marbles. He later explained that his strategy was based around giving Muralitharan a breather: if he had batted first, Muralitharan would have had no rest when, not if, England followed on, he said.

A game-changer, then, and the architect of a country's emergence as a cricketing power. More than that, he played his part in rebalancing the game after the excesses of pace in the eighties. With Shane Warne and Anil Kumble, he reminded us you didn't have to bowl quickly and at the head to induce paralysed terror among batsmen.

The battle for leading wicket-taker in Tests see-sawed between Muralitharan and Warne until the leg spinner took his leave of serious cricket for the Indian Premier League, poker and other attractions. The argument as to who was better is often framed by parochialism: to this disinterested observer, Warne's cricketing brain put him a notch above Muralitharan, one reason, perhaps, why some batsmen dominated the off spinner (left-handers such as Stephen Fleming and Brian Lara spring to mind) as few did Warne.

Against that, Muralitharan had to overcome barriers that Warne and most cricketers could not imagine. A Tamil in a country where Tamils were persecuted; an up-country boy in a cricket team dominated by the elite from Colombo and born with a congenital defect of his arm that, initially, might have persuaded him that a career following his father as a biscuit maker was more likely than one in international cricket.

Humble and sweet-natured, Muralitharan is revered in his country as much for his humanitarian efforts as his off spin. In an era when great sportsmen have used a charitable foundation as a fashion accessory, Muralitharan has gone about his charitable work without fuss. It is fitting that his final Test match should be in Galle, on a ground that was devastated by the tsunami – which Muralitharan fortuitously avoided by 20 minutes – and was rebuilt in no small measure thanks to his efforts.

Galle will stand to him today when the curtain descends on his Test career. He has been a remarkable cricketer: an opponent to fear; a team-mate to treasure, and a man who, time and again, has not been found wanting.

The Times, 22 July 2010

9

In Search of the Three Lions

England has not produced a genuinely great cricketer since Sir Ian Botham. Kevin Pietersen has a chance to gain that status, but needs to turn the second half of his career around to do so. Both are profiled here, Botham on receiving his knighthood and Pietersen on the idiosyncrasies of his batting.

In between, there have been many fine cricketers who have worn the three lions and the crown, others who will be remembered as characters, some who will be but a footnote in English cricket history and some for whom the question 'what if . . .' will always accompany their name.

A curious assortment here then, from the greats such as Botham, to the one-cap wonders like Darren Pattinson; from the workhorses such as Angus Fraser, to those who didn't quite fulfil their dreams like Mark Ramprakash or the unique, such as Phil Tufnell. And, of course, there is Ben Hollioake, whose death almost a decade ago affected us all.

A Young Life Cruelly Curtailed

Those of us who tuned in late on Friday evening in the hope of following England's serene progress [in the second Test] in New Zealand's green and pleasant land were confronted instead by images of a black Porsche, literally wrenched in two and cruelly smashed to pieces, and the knowledge of a young life curtailed. It was a profoundly shocking image. As Ben Hollioake's family are left to cope with their tragic loss, so the rest of us, colleagues and friends, are left to our memories.

As captain of England, I recall handing a first one-day international cap to Ben on a glorious day at Lord's in 1997. The series against Australia had already been won and it was a chance to let this precocious young cricketer, straight out of the Under-19s, show off his talent. I asked him if he fancied going in at No 3, and he shrugged and said, in his laconic way, he'd give it a go.

Give it a go! Against Shane Warne and Glenn McGrath, he scored a breathtaking 63 off 48 balls to justify the selectors' judgement; it sounds violent but the drive for four off his third ball and the swept six into the Tavern Stand off Warne were launched with a languid ease and grace and it earned him the man-of-the-match award in his first game.

His brother Adam had already shot to prominence earlier in the summer, and in the spirit of fraternal competition he scored the winning runs in that game, as he had in the first two matches of the series. The Hollioakes were suddenly the talk of the town, part of a brighter future for English cricket, and Ben the new *wunderkind* of our game.

Ben's initial success, and the manner of it, propelled him into the nation's consciousness and brought immediate adulation, and all its attendant problems. Like others before and after him, he was labelled 'The New Botham' – that king of all albatrosses. And when you are young and lacking in knowledge and guidance, the rise to fame can be so difficult to handle.

The media's voracious appetite for all things black and white, with no room for any shade of grey, creates personalities instead of people and caricatures instead of character. Suddenly expectation is upon you, a cloak that is so difficult to remove and a cup so difficult to fill.

There was the odd glimpse of brilliance afterwards. Two man-of-the-match awards in one-day finals for Surrey reinforced the initial belief that he had the temperament to match the big occasion, and he did become the youngest player since Brian Close in 1949 to win a Test cap for England. Mostly, though, after the initial burst, the limelight and success evaded him: he was ill-suited to the backwaters and daily grind of county cricket and the expectation went largely unfulfilled. We are left wondering only what might have been.

For there is no doubting the talent was there. His batting looked casual, and occasionally was casual, but he had a grace and ease of movement and time to play, visited upon only the lucky few. His loose, long limbs enabled him to bowl without apparent effort – quickish with a hint of away swing.

His athleticism was ready-made for the modern game; a captain would always send him to patrol the most important parts of the outfield. He had got back into the one-day international team, and was pushing hard for a place in the World Cup squad. There was still plenty of time.

Yesterday Nasser Hussain was right to emphasise the futility of the game at such a time. Understandably, in the aftermath of Ben's death, there will be those who will overplay his talent and achievements, but what does that, or the reality, matter? What is undeniable, and ultimately more important, is the affection with which he was held by everyone who shared the Surrey and England dressing-rooms with him. Remarkably, only five years after Graham Kersey's death in a road accident, Surrey have lost another.

It is difficult to imagine that he and Adam were brothers, so different were they in character, build and temperament. Adam, short and pugnacious, very physical and fiercely committed – every inch the street fighter. Ben, tall and languid, seemingly at ease with the world and his place in it – not cerebral but quick to smile and easy to laugh. He really was a player you wanted to see succeed, and I cannot imagine that he would have inspired jealousy anywhere within the game. He could be infuriating on the field, but it was quickly forgiven.

Along with his brother, he was part of the influx of Australian-born cricketers who came to England throughout the 1990s. With Ben it was easy to see the influence of both his English roots and the land of his birth; most at home in the outdoors and on the beaches of Perth, but without the abrasiveness that characterises so many of his countrymen. Both Australia, where his family is, and England, his adopted home, will feel his loss keenly.

It is in the dazzling light of youth, rather than the decay of old age, that we'll always remember Ben – but that does not make it any easier to bear.

Daily Telegraph, 23 March 2002

End of the Track for 'Steam Train' Fraser

Some time tomorrow, at Hampshire's spanking new ground, Angus Fraser will remove his Middlesex cap, now frayed at the edges, and a couple of sweaters, and mark out a run that has not changed for 15 years. He will then stoke up his engine for one last time and choo-choo in to bowl like a steam locomotive of a bygone age. At the end of the day he will reflect on a journey completed, and he will go and fill his pen with ink and retire to issue forth from the press box.

He will be missed, but his retirement is well timed. Once, he bowled a heavy ball – the type to cause a batsman serious jarring between the thumb and forefinger of his bottom hand. Now, with the passing of time, his first ball lands as gently as a fly on a trout stream – invariably near a length, however, just like the thousands of other deliveries he has sent down in his long and illustrious career.

When I watched him bowl to Mark Butcher this week, the ball arced down, its trajectory more of a spinner than a seamer – not quite above the batsman's eyeline, but nearly. Thankfully, at Hampshire, there will be no speedometer to record the lack of pace of his last spell for Middlesex. If there is, no doubt old Gussie will invoke the spirit of the ICC and declare its findings invalid and unofficial.

While there will always be room for a line-and-lengther, the game seems to be moving on. It is now a crash, bang, wallop affair, ill-suited to patient probing and a Fraser-like spell of 9–2–15–1. Nor will he miss the 20-over slogathon. When he was asked last week what he thought the new competition should be called, he paused for a moment and then grunted: 'A bowler's nightmare.'

No, he is firmly in the departure lounge of his playing days. Beneath the blue cap his hair is thinning markedly, and his gait is ever more stooped. The legs take just a little longer to get going now, and the next morning the stiffness a little longer to overcome.

It wasn't always so, of course. In the summer of 1989 he burst into the England team, a bright young thing. In the midst of an Ashes thrashing, he was the promise of better times to come. Ted Dexter, then chairman of selectors, had scoured the country for a bowler to dismiss Steve Waugh. What the rest of England couldn't do, Fraser did in his first Test at Edgbaston and Waugh became the first of 177 Test victims.

The next Test was at Old Trafford and I was there as twelfth man. I didn't know anybody in the England team so I sat next to Gus in the boot room at the back of the pavilion for no other reason than I knew his brother Alastair. It was the start of an enduring friendship. We watched together as England tamely surrendered the Ashes and we watched in disbelief as the South African rebel touring party was announced mid-match. Three of them (Neil Foster, John Emburey and Tim Robinson) were playing in that Test and Fraser sat there, constantly shaking his head and muttering darkly.

The best of Fraser was in those years before 1991, when a hip injury threatened his career. Before the injury, his body action had a little more snap, was less stiff, and his right arm followed through past his left not his right side. His six wickets in Melbourne on a 'flattie' in 1990–91 was his best performance, though it contributed to his presence in the same surgeon's room as mine six months later. He doesn't agree, but he wasn't quite the same bowler afterwards. He needed a little something in the pitch, and his 'nip' could occasionally go AWOL for a while.

Because of our shared injury problems I was delighted, as captain, to be able to recall him to the team against Australia in 1993. He led the attack that game and took us to victory, our first over Australia for seven years. My new-ball pairing of Fraser and Devon Malcolm began to take shape in my mind and after that there were many match-winning performances, notably in Trinidad in 1998. Each one was a testament to how good he might have been but for injury.

Most of all he was an absolutely wholehearted team player. He enjoyed bowling on a helpful pitch, but you sensed he really loved the challenge of rolling up his sleeves and bowling when conditions were less friendly, and others had cried 'enough'. And he relished proving the doubters, such as Ray Illingworth, wrong. In attitude, temperament and style, I liked to tell him that he was a modern-day Alec Bedser. 'Bedser,' he snorted. 'The keeper used to stand up to Bedser!' Precisely Gus.

But that was then and this is now. He has nearly bowled his last ball in anger; his work is almost done. It has been a long and, you sense, thoroughly enjoyable journey.

He leaves with his cup full to the brim with respect, from team-mates and opposition alike. He can rest safe in the knowledge that his presence over the last 15 years has enriched the game, not diminished it. And that, at the end, is all a man can hope for.

I hope at the Rose Bowl tomorrow that a Hampshire batsman inside-edges a Fraser delivery past leg stump for a streaky four. Just to see Gussie standing mid-pitch, hands on hips, kicking a sod and giving the batsman a baleful stare, and even a word or two. I wish I could be there to see it.

Sunday Telegraph, 4 May 2002

Tuffers Retiring But Not Ever Shy

Phil Tufnell arrived at the home of cricket wearing a leopard-skin G-string, baggy pants and winkle-pickers. He left, after 18 years, suddenly and no less surprisingly.

During that time he smoked and drank himself through 42 Tests, 1,057 first-class wickets and brushes with authority that must number somewhere in between. The reality TV show *Survivor*, the rigours of which Tufnell has now chosen instead of pre-season training, doesn't know what it has let itself in for.

Neither did I when I toured with Tufnell for the first time in Australia in 1990–91. At the start of the tour, Graham Gooch, the captain, asked me if I minded people smoking. Nonplussed, naïve and eager to please, I said I did not. As a result, I roomed with Tufnell and Wayne Larkins throughout the whole smoke-filled trip. What a pair! Larkins, who did his tour fee before Christmas in phone calls home, and Tufnell, whose socialising hours didn't quite mesh with my own.

Even then, the neuroses that afflicted Tufnell throughout his career were in ample evidence. At the end of a day's play, whether he had taken five wickets or none, he would need constant reassurance: 'How's it comin' out, Ath?', 'I am spinnin' it, aren't I?' In those days, of course, before the years of plenty had taken their toll, the ball always came out well and he really did give it a tweak.

And, after he had batted (briefly) against some fearsome Aussie quick, who spat and snarled but really only needed to say 'boo!', Tufnell would have to ask the inevitable – even though he knew the answer: 'I didn't back away too much, did I?' Or: 'It didn't look that bad, did it?' Of course, he always backed away and it always looked terrible, but he simply had no control over his right foot sliding away to square leg as the bowler bore down upon him.

I knew what to expect, then, when I was appointed England captain in 1993 and I decided that Tufnell was too good to leave out of my first touring party to the West Indies later that year. I gave a lot of thought to how to handle him. With fresh memories of him kicking his cap all around the outfield at Vishikhapatnam, I felt a change from Gooch's disciplinarian approach was necessary. I went to the other extreme, offering him more latitude than any other England player I can recall. The result was much the same; Tufnell kept up his record of being fined on every tour he'd been on.

Having played with Tufnell and having captained him and having seen countless others captain him, I now think that trying to 'manage' him was pointless all along. I asked Stephen Fleming during the World Cup how he went about captaining Tufnell at Middlesex. He rolled his eyes and shook his head: 'Couldn't do it, mate. Gave up trying.' It didn't matter, actually, who captained him and what the approach was because the end product, how he actually performed, was always the same.

No matter whether he had just emerged from a psychiatric unit (as he did in Perth in 1995), whether he was in the middle of a messy divorce (which he was at various times down the years), whether he was being pursued by angry in-laws (at least once), whether he was hungover (often) or whether everything was on an even keel (rarely), he was always able to bowl a length. I think he felt that with the ball in his hand, he was, at least for a short time, in control. It was best just to let him bowl and judge him on that.

So how do we judge him? Certainly, at his best and in favourable conditions, he was very good. Two match-winning performances at The Oval, against the West Indies in 1991 and Australia in 1997, stand out. Viv Richards, Ricky Ponting and Mark Waugh were all, in turn, deceived by his flight and sharp turn. Against Australia the dusty pitch, and therefore the expectation upon him, made him irritable and tense but nevertheless his performance that day was a near-perfect display of finger-spin bowling.

His final analysis of 121 Test wickets at 37.68 apiece suggests that those performances were a long way from the norm, which, in truth, they were. Two things, both out of his control, conspired against him.

The pitches in England in the nineties became ever more seamer-friendly and, when they did start dry, they tended to crack rather than crumble and were more suited to wrist rather than orthodox spin. In a different era, Tufnell would have played far more than the 11 Tests he played at home.

The second thing was the emergence of Shane Warne. All of a sudden it wasn't trendy to bowl a nice line and length, to not get cut too often, and occasionally to get one past the outside edge. Now, you had to rip it alarmingly from leg to off, with a bit of drift as well, if you please. Every time Warne spun one yards, you could see Tufnell cringe. 'This bloke's making me look crap,' he would complain. 'He's ruining my career!'

But Philip Tufnell's career is not really about comparisons. Or statistics. The scorer's ink will dry and fade and the laughter remains. I'm thinking now about my final moments as an England player: the retirement had been announced and I had taken the good wishes of the coach and my team-mates. Then, Tufnell sauntered over with a fag in his mouth and a sad look on his face. I took his limp, outstretched hand and awaited his eulogy.

'Jesus, Athers,' he said, 'I bowled OK, didn't I? I've just gone for 170 on a "bunsen" but I bowled well, didn't I?' I roared with laughter, but Tuffers turned away, shaking his head and muttering, too self-absorbed to notice.

Sunday Telegraph, 13 April 2003

Now Is the Time, Freddie

Every once in a while a sportsman comes along who changes the perception of his sport and, by doing so, changes his own life forever. Jonny Wilkinson's drop-goal in Sydney and David Beckham's last-minute free-kick against Greece were two such moments. Rugby and football blossomed in the afterglow, much as cricket is doing now, but Wilkinson and Beckham have been in slow decline ever since. Wilkinson because his body cannot cope; Beckham because he cannot cope.

Regardless of the result at The Oval, Andrew Flintoff now walks in such company. Maybe he is not earning the dollars (yet) of the other two, but in terms of profile and popularity he bends his knee to no one at present. Edgbaston, where Flintoff starred with bat and ball and then, damn it, showed grace and humility at the moment of victory, was his drop-goal and free-kick rolled into one.

From that moment on, the Ashes series of 2005 seemed destined to become known as 'Freddie's Ashes', just as the 1981 series has gone down in legend as 'Botham's Ashes'. It is worth recalling Flintoff's performance in that match. But first it is worth recalling his performance in the match prior to that match. Lord's was Flintoff's first Ashes Test match in seven years of playing international cricket.

A combination of injury and poor form had prevented him from playing in the previous three Ashes series. Lord's was his moment. He scored nought and three, took four wickets for 173 expensive runs and dropped a dolly at slip. England were hammered.

He retreated to Bovey Castle in Devon for a few days with his family. Not exactly purgatory, I grant you, but whatever he did there – and I'm led to believe not much other than thinking – it worked. He was a man transformed at Edgbaston. What he did at Edgbaston is what all-rounders are supposed to do, but very rarely manage to do – that is score runs and take wickets at crucial times in the same game. He scored 68 and 73 and took seven for 131 in the match as England sneaked home in one of the greatest Test matches of all time.

When England wobbled with the bat, Freddie smashed a few boundaries to ease their nerves. When they wobbled with the ball, he answered his captain's call time and again with vital wickets. And after a tense, gripping final morning, Flintoff bent down to console the vanquished Brett Lee at the moment of victory, in what may become the series' defining image, to show that our sporting heroes don't have to be egotistical maniacs.

Freddie's impact from Edgbaston onwards has been to turn upside down the perception of Test cricket, himself, the English team and, crucially, the Australian team. Even before this summer, Flintoff's star had been rising fast. But there was still a doubt, at least in my mind, whether his batting would stand the scrutiny of high-class bowlers (I've thought he has been England's best bowler now for a couple of years). Not only has he led the attack with gusto, destroying the confidence of Australia's most dangerous match-winner, Adam Gilchrist, he has played a swashbuckling innings (Edgbaston) and a great innings (Trent Bridge). Flintoff has become only the fourth England all-rounder in history to score more than 300 runs and take 15 wickets in an Ashes series.

Before this summer, Test cricket appealed to a minority. Like an English beach holiday, it was the preserve of an older generation. The games were invariably sold out, but viewing figures for Test cricket hovered around the one to two million mark. Twenty20 was the new destination for the sun, sex and sangria seekers. No amount of lobbying on Test cricket's behalf, by those of us who love it, mattered a damn. All that crap about Test cricket revealing character and the advantages of the subplots and twists and turns of the five-day game over the one-day game. Where was the tension? Where was the excitement? We aficionados knew it could be so, but spectators had become used to watching mismatches of titanic proportions. England versus Bangladesh? About as exciting as creosoting the garden fence.

This summer has seen the rebirth of Test cricket in this country. Old Trafford's officials recalled the glory days of cricket, when people had little else to do, as between 10,000 and 20,000 people were turned away on the final day. Over seven million tuned in to watch that epic draw on television, a figure that was dwarfed as England inched towards victory at Nottingham. Women – I'll say that again – women have been captivated. Kids are demanding the latest Freddie DVD and an England replica shirt. It's been an expensive summer holiday for parents.

Before this summer, England were seen as a decent outfit, one that had turned over some moderately good teams. But everyone knew that at the first sight of Glenn McGrath and Shane Warne their batsmen would buckle; at the first sight of Matthew Hayden advancing down the pitch their bowlers would run for cover, and crucial catches would be spilt. Lord's gave us the confirmation. Same old story.

Now, the talk is not just of the Ashes. The way we're carrying on, you'd think they were already safely nestled in Michael Vaughan's hands (now's not the time for those famous butter-fingers of yours, skipper). The talk is of greatness, of eras, of empires – one crumbling, the other about to be born.

Before this summer, Australia were the supermen of cricket. This was the team who were faster, fitter, stronger than and tactically superior to anyone else; a team who attacked at every opportunity; who refused to use nightwatchmen; who caught flies; who scored quicker than everyone else; who abhorred the draw; and a team whose blueprint (six batsmen, wicket-keeper, four bowlers) was the one that everyone else copied.

Suddenly, old bones are creaking; catches have been put down; the nightwatchman has been pushed out of the dressing-room door at every opportunity; the Old Trafford draw was greeted with exultation, and at Nottingham Ricky Ponting set some decidedly Vaughan-like, defensive (defensive!) fields. At The Oval, Australia are thinking of bringing in Shane Watson, the all-rounder, and copying England by playing five bowlers. If you cut their veins, the Australians might even spill red blood.

Of course, all this is more than can be achieved by the feats of one man. And no doubt Freddie would be the first to shower praise on his team-mates. Equally, I am quite sure that without Flintoff's performance at Edgbaston none of it would have happened. England would have gone 2–0 down and we might have all lost interest.

So what is the likely denouement of this saga? The Oval's most famous cricketing moment came 52 years ago and the symmetry to the here and now is marked. In 1953 England had not held the Ashes for 19 years; a resolute Yorkshireman was their captain, and the golden boy of the day, Denis Compton, hit the winning runs. Who would bet against Vaughan emulating Leonard Hutton and recovering the urn after a hiatus of 18 years? Who would bet against Freddie Flintoff, the Compton of the day, administering the full stop to this most magnificent of sporting dramas?

If he does, we will bask in his reflected glory and wallow in his moment. But if he does, spare a thought for Freddie, too, for he will be a man who has climbed his Everest with a whole lifetime ahead of him. His life will have changed forever and forever is a long time.

Sunday Telegraph, 4 September 2005

Loyalty Ultimately Proved Fletcher's Undoing

After a winter when most things he touched turned not to gold but dust, Duncan Fletcher got one thing spot-on last week. Given that Fletcher had manoeuvred himself into an all-powerful position within English cricket, it is only right that a large dollop of accountability has been laid at his door for a winter gone disastrously wrong. The manner of his departure – resignation or sacking – was irrelevant. It was time for a change.

It has been a harrowing six months following the England cricket team. During the Champions Trophy they played with their minds elsewhere, eyeing a greater prize on the horizon, as if the tournament at hand was beneath them. The fug of self-delusion that enveloped them following the Ashes triumph of 2005 was subsequently blown away by an Australia team who were demonstrably better prepared, more focused and more determined (and, it must be said, more talented).

The fag end of the Commonwealth Bank series provided blessed relief, but even that proved to be a curse, encouraging Fletcher and the selectors, as it did, to keep faith with a bunch of players who were clearly out of their depth in one-day cricket. The result was a World Cup in which England appeared as bemused and grumpy onlookers, unable to comprehend a game that had moved on without them. After such a winter, the position of the man responsible had become untenable.

And Fletcher was responsible. He was given more authority than any other figure in recent English cricket history, save for Raymond Illingworth, who enjoyed a brief period of megalomania. The chairman of selectors, David Graveney, was sidelined. To say the relationship between Graveney and Fletcher had broken down would be wrong; there was never much of a relationship in the first place. Dissenters departed (Rod Marsh) or were sent to Siberia (the press). Lieutenants were hand-picked – some on the basis of familiarity and friendship rather than expertise – outsiders were shunned.

Although he often described himself as a consultant to the captain, this was very much Fletcher's ship. When things went well, as they did for much of his first five years in charge, it was right that the skipper of the vessel received much of the praise. And he did. For a long time, he was accorded a fair passage by Fleet Street, the Ashes triumph widely reported as the culmination of years of Fletcher's hard work and meticulous planning. A gong, a handsome publishing contract, a rolling ECB contract (from which Fletcher will now benefit with a large pay-off) and public affection were the rewards.

In the aftermath of 2005, a great outcry went up to give Fletcher a British passport; those same newspapers last week called for his deportation. Such is the nature of the job. The winds were bound to turn less favourable – they always do – and so the passage was always going to turn rough in the end. Fletcher had the good grace to accept that after the hosannas comes the cross. Once his mind was made up, as we have seen with his cricketing decisions over a period of time, he was not for turning.

Given Fletcher's overriding influence on selection, strategy and the make-up of the back-room staff, it is certain that his departure will have a destabilising effect. For the England team have lost more than a coach. They have lost a mentor. There is not one survivor from the pre-Fletcher era (apart from Graveney, and his future might be short-lived if certain members of the Schofield Review have their way). All the players have bought in to Fletcher's habits. The good – such as the discipline, the hard work, the forward press, the sweep and reverse sweep – and the bad – such as the insularity, narrow-mindedness and suspicion of those with a broader-minded, more generous view of life.

In that sense, as well as having a destabilising effect, it might also have a liberating one for players who are good enough to force themselves into a new era. It became increasingly evident to outsiders, and this process accelerated as the criticism of Fletcher grew, that players were discouraged from seeking out a fresh view or a different take on things. It did not say much for the strength of mind of the majority of players that they acquiesced, and it said much about the insecurity of the management group. The relationship between the players and the coach should never be servile.

It is inconceivable that there will not be further changes. One such should be announced with immediate effect. The blame for England's woeful one-day performances over the last four years should be shared equally with Michael Vaughan. Graveney, last week, announced that Vaughan is likely to lead England into the first Test against the West Indies in three weeks' time. Fair enough, but it is inconceivable that Vaughan can carry on as one-day captain. At some stage the figures cannot be ignored: England do not win many one-day games under his leadership, and he does not score enough runs to warrant a place in the side. You can have as many good nets as you like, but ultimately you have to score some runs in the middle. For the best part of 90 matches, Vaughan has been accorded due deference. His time as a one-day player has run out.

At some stage England will have to come to grips with one-day cricket. It is not true to say that England have not produced any decent one-day cricket in the last 15 years. When they were intermittently successful, though, it was by playing a brand of cricket – gradually increasing the impetus when batting because of the absence of field restrictions and defensive bowling – that is no longer relevant in the modern game. England need to discover some power players of their own, and a wicket-taking bowler or two. The first will be easier to find than the second.

I believe that not only should England have split captains now that Vaughan no longer warrants a place in the team, but split coaches too. The job is too demanding, physically and technically, for one man to do well. There could be problems if two coaches are telling the same set of players different things, but I would envisage two coaches working in tandem for the benefit of each other, able to keep players fresher and more motivated by dint of the fact that they themselves would be fresher and more motivated.

Much of the analysis last week of Fletcher's mistakes in the past 18 months has focused on the coach's misplaced loyalty. Loyalty was one of Fletcher's greatest virtues, and it also proved to be his undoing at the start of this winter's Ashes series, but I also think that many of the mistakes can be put down to mental weariness. Think of the amount of time a coach spends away from home with the same set of players. It becomes difficult to step back and view things with detachment. Fletcher looked increasingly burdened and tired this winter. Two coaches would result in greater periods of rest and recuperation (important in itself for men who are normally older and less fit than the players) and would allow them a chance to step back from the melee and organise their thoughts.

That will not happen now that the ECB have rushed to replace Fletcher with Peter Moores. It is a missed opportunity. Although the Davids, Morgan and Collier, have repeatedly said this week that Moores's name has been inked in for a while, two members of the Schofield Review group told me last week that Fletcher sounded like a man who wanted to carry on for some time yet. So how much thought have the ECB given to how the England teams of the future should be coached? In any case, wasn't this supposed to be part of Schofield's brief? It is messy.

I have no idea whether Moores is the best man for the job. The ECB do not know either. How can they when they have not talked to any other candidates? Sometimes the inside replacement is not necessarily the best thing, as the Football Association are finding out with Steve McClaren. Besides, Moores is linked to an Academy that is failing English cricket right now, producing decent cricketers but human beings who are so one-dimensional and so narrow-minded, unable to do little more than grunt in public, that they became an object of derision this winter among Australian cricket reporters.

Had the ECB appointed cosily from within, instead of going through a thorough process designed to get the best man for the job, they would never have appointed Fletcher in the first place. And although inevitably recent weeks have homed in on Fletcher's failings in the last 18 months, and in one-day cricket, it should be stressed that Fletcher was the best appointment the ECB ever made.

Unwilling to face his tormentors, Fletcher issued a statement that indicated he had much to be proud of during his time as England's coach. He is right. Stability in selection, clear-sighted planning, inspired selections of some under-performing cricketers from county cricket, victories on the sub-continent and, of course, against Australia, were all accomplishments of which Fletcher can be justifiably proud.

Ironically, things had come full circle by the end. Fletcher arrived just after an England captain had been booed, and he leaves with the same sound ringing in Vaughan's ears. But, and it is a big but, Fletcher leaves the England cricket team in a far healthier state than he found it. In between the jeers there was plenty of joy.

Sunday Telegraph, 22 April 2007

Incomparable Botham – a Knight to Remember

It was fitting in a way that Durham [hosting the fourth Test against West Indies] should be the scene of the confirmation of the worst kept secret in cricket – that Ian Botham is to be the first English cricketing knight since Colin Cowdrey was so honoured in 1992. Durham, briefly, was home to the court of King Beefy, as they took their first tentative steps as a first-class county. In truth, he was way past his best then, but in these surroundings he found much to like, not least the salty humour of the locals and the wild, windswept countryside in which he has always felt most at home.

Eventually he put down his family's roots not far from here. He gets to shoot and fish and we get to quaff from his wine cellar (if you watched Gordon Ramsay's programme midweek, you'll appreciate that his palate does not quite match the majesty of his cellar) on the third day of every Durham Test match. Tonight will be quite a celebration. For weeks now he has done his best to conceal what every newspaper seemed to know, but those who know him best have remarked how chuffed he is at this ultimate recognition. It is the culmination of his life's work, and, as such, we are all chuffed for him.

The knighthood, apparently, is for services to charity as well as cricket, which is a bit like remembering Winston Churchill as a good writer as well as a half-decent prime minister. That is not to denigrate Botham's immense charitable contribution, which has raised more than £10 million for leukaemia alone (an amount the charity says has been worth nearly £100 million in publicity), but none of it would have happened without his greatness as a cricketer. People came to see him walking the road for who he was, and what he had done, not for what he was doing.

And what a cricketer he was. Our paths crossed only briefly, although long enough for me to put him out with a torn hamstring after calling him for one sharp single too many, and his skills had faded somewhat by the time I joined him in the England dressing-room. But it was enough to witness at first hand the enormous vitality and unquenchable self-belief that underpinned his talent, the combination of which was enough to scatter the Australians to the wind throughout the 1980s.

We all have our favourite memories of that particular time. My own is returning through Manchester in the summer of 1981 and witnessing a remarkable sight outside an electrical store where hundreds of people gathered, peering through the shop window looking at the televisions for sale, all of which were showing the denouement of the Edgbaston Test of that year. I stood there in the crowd cheering and shouting with the rest as Botham ripped through the Australian tail taking five for one in 28 balls.

Technology means that you can revisit that with a flick of a switch these days. And if you want to remind yourselves what a magnificent competitor he was, bring up that spell on YouTube. This was Botham in his prime (although Vic Marks, who played with him at Somerset, reckoned him to be at his best with the ball in the late 1970s), pre-mullet, pre-back injury and pre the ridiculous flirtation with Tim Hudson, who promised that together they might crack America. All told there were 14 Test hundreds and 27 five-fers. Contrast those figures to the modern-day cricketer who is most often compared to him – Andrew Flintoff has five hundreds and two five-fers. Truly, England have not had an all-rounder like him.

The vitality and self-belief still run through his veins and allow him to pack more into a single day than most people pack into a week. He is not prone to introspection or quiet contemplation. Yesterday, he breezed into Chester-le-Street in his Bentley – a suitable vehicle for one so celebrated, even if it is second-hand (but do not tell him I told you) – knocked off dozens of interviews, received hundreds of congratulatory texts, from 'Mick' (Jagger), 'EC' (Clapton) and other such luminaries, spoke to mates, booked flights for his next adventure, told everyone who will win the US Open, gave Dwayne Bravo some advice all-rounder to all-rounder, passed time with his old chum and fellow knight Sir Viv Richards, pontificated on the pitch, set about organising his wine and food for the evening and settled down to do a little commentary.

Think what you like about the honours system in this country, but at least they are an antidote to vacuous celebrity. Honours, by and large, celebrate achievement and nobody in English cricket and few in charity have achieved more than Botham. During a couple of damp and miserable days in Durham it is a story that has brought a smile to our faces.

Sunday Telegraph, 17 June 2007

Why We're Right to Put Kevin Pietersen on a Pedestal

At dinner with friends during the Lord's Test, I was mocked gently for bestowing greatness on Kevin Pietersen after his first-day hundred. They were right, of course: greatness comes with the perspective of time. Bernard Levin called the process the 'sieve of history'; only when the sieve has stopped shaking and all the dross has been removed, can what is left behind justly be called great.

Fair enough. Suffice to say that, for me, Pietersen is the most fascinating of the current crop of international batsmen. Given a choice, he is the one I would choose to watch and, given that he is a length or two ahead of the field in the narcissism stakes, I suspect that he would say the same. Here are a few reasons why he is such a special player.

Balance
'Footwork and balance and their co-ordination will always remain the cornerstones of batting' – Don Bradman, *The Art of Cricket*.

It is no coincidence that many of the great batsmen (Bradman, Sachin Tendulkar, Sunil Gavaskar, Brian Lara) have been relatively short men. A short, compact physique, with a low centre of gravity, helps balance. Pietersen is 6ft 4in, but in his stance, with his knees bent and his bottom sticking out as if he is flashing a moonie on the back of the school bus, he makes himself into a much smaller man without – because his back-lift and hands are so high – losing the advantage of height.

Most tall batsmen struggle with their head position. That is why Tony Greig, for example, stood with his bat off the ground. Alastair Cook spoke yesterday of a technical glitch that is infecting his game, where his head falls over to the off side, unbalancing him at the crease. Pietersen's balance is superb. You do not think so? Next time you are facing a spinner, try going down the pitch along the line of off stump and, while the ball is in the air, change direction so that you hit the ball on the line of leg stump.

Facing Shane Warne's drift in the 2006–07 Ashes series, that is what Pietersen was doing all the time. Always on the balls of his feet, he is amazingly nimble for a big man. Like a ballet dancer.

Athleticism

'The greatest of players can improve by means of concentration and practice, but the natural athlete must start with a great advantage' – Bradman.

If you were born in Pietermaritzburg in the first half of the 20th century, you had drawn a bad ticket in the lottery of life. Especially if you were Boer (the British built a concentration camp there to house Boer women and children during the Second Boer War) or, later, if you were not white (Gandhi was thrown off a train in Pietermaritzburg for refusing to sit in a third-class carriage while holding a first-class ticket).

If you were a young (white) sportsman, though, Pietermaritzburg at the end of the 20th century was a winning ticket. Pietersen led an outdoor life from an early age, swimming competitively with his brothers in the family's large swimming pool and enjoying sport all year round. 'I went to school to play sport,' he says in his autobiography. Blessed with this start, Pietersen added a strict training regime when he became a professional cricketer, taking creatine, the muscle-building supplement, to increase his power.

Now, Pietersen is a magnificent physical specimen. Sam Bradley, the England strength and physical conditioning coach, has said Pietersen is a role model to the rest of the team in this regard. Bradley says that recent tests show Pietersen to be heavier but leaner (i.e. stronger with less fat) than a year ago. Compare that with members of the South Africa team, who look out of condition.

For all Pietersen's occasional negative publicity, when was the last time he was involved in a drunken escapade? He drinks, but in moderation and at the right time. When you travel with the team, you see all kinds of shenanigans, but I have never seen Pietersen behave irresponsibly. Discipline and athleticism combined.

Intelligence
'My movements at the crease depended to some extent on the type of bowler who was operating' – Bradman.

Intelligence and Pietersen are not obvious bedfellows, especially to snobs who think only of intelligence in terms of schooling. Pietersen may not have a university degree (in his autobiography he admits to three A levels) and he may not be able to translate Homer, but he is England's most cricket-savvy batsman.

Instinct – the ability to not think and simply react – is critical, but just as important is the thought given to his approach to each bowler. Some of it is premeditated: watch, for example, how far across his stumps he goes to Makhaya Ntini to open up the leg side against a bowler who bowls from near the return crease.

Equally, Pietersen is adept at changing his approach according to circumstance. This is how he described his thinking behind the switch-hit for six off Muttiah Muralitharan at Edgbaston two years ago: 'To understand that shot you need to know that I had just come down the wicket to Murali three times; I had hit him over mid-off for four, through mid-off for four and then I had cut the doosra for four. Murali moved his mid-off and mid-on back and put men at deep square leg and cow corner. All my options had been blocked.' Cue the switch-hit, which he had practised assiduously for just that situation.

Yogi Berra, the baseball great, is reputed to have said: 'Think? How can you hit and think at the same time?' Pietersen does.

Big-match Temperament

'A tremendous premium must be placed on this peculiar characteristic, which is probably more essential for a batsman in cricket than any other sport' – Bradman.

When is an international batsman most nervous? At the start, of course. Pietersen's impact at the beginning of his international career was immediate. The beginning was in Zimbabwe, but because we are talking big-match temperament, let us fast-forward to South Africa in 2005. Pietersen had many things to cope with, not least the start of his international one-day career proper and sustained abuse from those who thought that an Afrikaans-speaking boy from Pietermaritzburg ought to be playing for the home team. Pietersen scored three hundreds and averaged 151.

His Test debut was against Australia at Lord's the following summer. Pietersen came to the crease with England 18 for three and Glenn McGrath dominant. He scored 57, was the ninth man out and by the end of the innings McGrath was bowling to him with six men on the boundary. Since then the two biggest games that Pietersen has played have been at The Oval against Australia, with the Ashes at stake, and his first Test against the country of his birth. He scored big hundreds in both matches. English cricket has been littered with talented players who have frozen on the big stage. Pietersen is not one.

Desire must be at the heart of it. He has not forgotten his tough cricketing apprenticeship, moving from home, living in a one-bedroom studio in Cannock and playing as an overseas player there. That the club owed him some money at the end of his stay is a running sore through his autobiography. It is a cliché to say that a tough upbringing produces better sportsmen, but I do not think Pietersen has forgotten his time at Cannock.

Attacking Flair

'It is a batsman's duty to take the initiative and play shots' – Bradman.

'Know your limitations' is a fair motto for the less talented, but the best players attack. Only once, in the early stages of the series against New Zealand last winter, did Pietersen seem to want to blunt his flair and attacking instincts. For a while he looked, in practice and in the match, as though he was trying to become more regimented, hitting the ball straight in the 'V' between mid-off and mid-on.

Pietersen is at his best when he uses his wrists to hit the ball where bowlers do not expect him to. It is time to worry when he stops playing the 'flamingo' shot (the one-legged whip through mid-wicket). At their best, Ian Bell and Michael Vaughan are more pleasing on the eye, but Pietersen extends the boundaries of the possible. There is not a more dangerous player in the England team.

Greatness comes with the judgement of time. How much time do you need?

The Times, 17 July 2008

Row Rumbles On over Darren Pattinson's Cap

'As a rule they will refuse even to sample a foreign dish, they regard such things as garlic and olive oil with disgust, life is unliveable to them unless they have tea and puddings' – George Orwell.

There is a story told about Fred Trueman, who turned up to a Test match at Headingley and cast a mordant eye over a debutant who was opening the bowling for England from the Kirkstall Lane End. It did not take long for the first splutter (and here you will have to do your own best Trueman impression): 'There have been many fine bowlers run down that hill for England,' said Trueman, who then paused with the comic timing for which he was justly famous. 'And he is not one of them.'

The bowler referred to was Neil Mallender, the classic horse for an idiosyncratic course. It was an anecdote that sprang to mind when Darren Pattinson took the new ball for England from the same end [against South Africa in the second Test] that Mallender did, with great success, some 16 years ago. Trueman, of course, is not around to pass judgement now, although there were plenty of people last Friday morning, in full-on Trueman mode, who just could not fathom what was going off out there. I do not think I have ever heard a selection provoke more comment, most of it adverse.

Jonathan Agnew, the BBC's cricket correspondent, was incandescent. Trying to gather some last-minute information on the internet about Pattinson, he was redirected to the Cricket Australia website. Then, interviewing Pattinson shortly after he received his cap, Agnew was taken aback when, in response to a question that asked of Pattinson whether this was a moment he had dreamt of all his life, he simply said, with disarming honesty: 'No.'

It has been a popular baton to run with since then. Matthew Hoggard was annoyed to hear that Pattinson talked with an Aussie twang. I know Hoggy has not been in the England dressing-room for a while, but has he forgotten how Tim Ambrose talks, or Kevin Pietersen? It did not stop him celebrating every time Geraint Jones took a catch off him. Graham Gooch, in yesterday's *Times*, wondered how Pattinson could have played with the requisite passion and pride, given that he has not been brought up in England.

For Gooch, it is where you are brought up that counts. In 1989, he was England captain when a punt was taken on a raw fast bowler called Ricardo Ellcock. Ellcock was born in Barbados and attended Combermere Secondary School there, before winning a scholarship to Malvern College in Worcestershire at 15. He was picked for the 1989–90 tour to the Caribbean, but the story had an unhappy ending. Well, cricket-wise it did, in that Ellcock suffered horrendous back problems and rarely played thereafter. He became the first black captain on Virgin Atlantic Airways, so things worked out fine. But he was raw and rapid back then and, even though he still talked like a Barbadian, Gooch obviously thought it was a risk worth taking, regardless of where he was brought up.

And surely this is the point about the Pattinson selection, that it made no sense cricket-wise. Plucking someone from obscurity after just a handful of games is usually a sign of special talent, the kind of talent gifted to the few, whether that is raw pace or mystery spin. Pattinson, 29 on 2 August, looked a worthy seam bowler, in a classical English way, but he was neither young and on the start of a potentially great journey, nor experienced enough to justify the kind of upheaval it caused. If there are not other more suitable candidates of a younger age who can do that job, all the anger would be better directed at the 18 first-class counties.

That the award and acceptance of an England cap should

provoke such outrage is a welcome thing in a cricketing age increasingly dominated by dollars rather than dreams. The idea of what it means to play for England matters. Thankfully, we have not yet been affected by the faux mawkishness and sentimentality associated with Australia's 'Baggy Green', but the idea of the England cap is important. And for most, it did not sit well on Pattinson's head.

The criticism of Pattinson was at its fiercest before the match and before most people had seen him bowl in the flesh. Understandably he looked nervy at first – wouldn't you be with the Western Terrace bellowing 'who are ya?' as you marked out your run? – but after that I thought he bowled well, at least as well as England's other bowlers. With his strong, repeatable action he did not look out of place and if he was trying any less hard than the others, it was not apparent to me. But for most this was irrelevant. Because he had not spent his formative years drinking warm beer in a village pub, somehow he was not as worthy.

That background, rather than personal and professional pride, is at the heart of performance is an old argument and one that has been levelled at any number of supposedly 'non-English' players. In its most extreme form, the question of national pride, performance and being 'unequivocal Englishmen' was asked by Robert Henderson years ago in an article in *Wisden Cricket Monthly* titled 'Is it in the blood?' Devon Malcolm and Phillip DeFreitas sued, successfully.

The idea that an English upbringing makes for greater commitment out in the middle has never struck me as having one grain of truth in it. It certainly did not strike me as particularly relevant when Robin Smith, who was brought up in South Africa, was being carried down the stairs on a stretcher at Old Trafford in 1995, his cheekbone bloodied and smashed to bits by a bouncer from Ian Bishop, the West Indies fast bowler. England were subsiding at the time – from memory, we were four down chasing a smallish target – and Smith refused to be taken to hospital until it was clear that victory had been won and that he would not be needed to bat again. That was commitment of the deepest, most desperate kind.

It is true that there have been some, whose right to play for England has been questioned, who have performed poorly. Remember Martin McCague, born in Ulster, raised in Australia, the 'rat that joined the sinking ship'? But McCague was a timid, weak cricketer, rather than someone torn by loyalty, and there have been plenty of blue-blooded Englishmen like that. Remember Mark Lathwell? His idea of sporting nirvana was not opening the batting for England against Australia but playing darts in his local in Devon. What could be more English than that?

The question is not one of upbringing but commitment. If Pattinson stays for a short time with Nottinghamshire, returns to Australia with his England cap, never to be seen again, then his selection will leave a sour taste. But opportunity and choice should never be frowned upon. If he makes a commitment here, he should be welcomed.

On the basis that it is where you are brought up that counts, England have assimilated South Africans (Allan Lamb, Smith, Pietersen), Zimbabweans (Graeme Hick), Australians (Ambrose, the Hollioake brothers, Geraint Jones) and any number of West Indians (Gladstone Small, Ellcock, Roland Butcher) over the last two decades. That is not a roll call of shame, but a list of which to be proud.

Cricket-wise, the England selectors misplaced their marbles momentarily at Headingley last week, but on another level Pattinson's selection was to be celebrated. Notwithstanding that Pattinson, English-born and with a British passport, had every right to play, the day when the lottery of where you are born and where your parents take you can be overridden by a positive choice of where you live, where you work and where you bring up your family must be a good thing. It is one more step towards a more humane, civilised and enlightened world.

The Times, 24 July 2008

Art and Craft of Mark Ramprakash's Hard Graft

It was entirely fitting that Mark Ramprakash scored his hundredth hundred at Headingley on Saturday [2 August]. It was there that he scored his first, some 19 seasons ago, and coming when it did, it was and has been completely overshadowed by events elsewhere [with South Africa beating England at Edgbaston to win the series]. After all, this is how it has been for him these past few years – honing his craft, if not quite in the cricketing wilderness, then certainly out of the limelight. He has been playing repertory, while the West End, an increasingly glitzier and well-funded West End, has been flourishing without him.

It is a quite staggering and magnificent achievement. It is worth thinking about the statistic for a moment, because a hundred is a magical figure and one that every cricketer can comprehend. Good or bad, every batsman knows how difficult it is, at times, to score one run, never mind a hundred. Good or bad, every batsman knows how hard it is to score that first century; some never do. Ramprakash, now, has passed that milestone a hundred times. He will probably be the last to do so.

He joins an elite group of 25, including some of the greatest batsmen to have played the game. Don Bradman is there, of course, as is Viv Richards and maybe the granddaddy of them all, W.G. Grace. Because of the amount of first-class cricket played in England it is an Anglo-centric list and so Ramprakash joins some of the great names of English batsmanship, names that roll off the tongue almost in homage to a glorious past: Hobbs, Hammond, Compton, Hutton and Cowdrey.

Stepping out of the area of his expertise somewhat, Paul Sheldon, the Surrey chief executive, reacted to the moment by describing Ramprakash as the 'greatest batsman of his generation'. Had Sheldon limited his horizons to the English county game then there would have been only one person, Graeme Hick, who could have possibly quibbled with his assessment. In the past two decades they have milked county attacks to the tune of about 55,000 runs and have been more feared on the circuit than any other players.

County cricket is a glorious thing in many ways: the comradeship, the variety of surroundings and the sheer fun if you are lucky enough, as I was, to play in a team that puts enjoyment at the heart of everything it does. It is also a grind: the cold days in April, when the ball nips around into unpadded parts of the body, and the grim days in September when the trophies have been hoovered up by other teams and there is nothing other than personal pride and professionalism to play for.

It is easy, and God knows I did it too often myself, to persuade yourself on such days that it does not really matter and that it is all right to coast along. For a long time, I reckoned that scoring runs when it really 'mattered' was a sign of mental strength. I now realise that not scoring runs when it did not 'matter' was a sign of mental weakness – and of not being good enough to do it without the necessary amount of application.

For a long time I was suspicious of cricketers who gorged themselves in county cricket while wilting when put under scrutiny of a more intense pressure, or indeed batsmen who scored what I might have termed soft rather than tough runs. Me, I thought the whole point of playing professional cricket was to play and perform in front of a crowd, and to perform when it was most difficult. Otherwise what was the point?

I can now see that this was a fundamentally flawed (self-deluding?) notion. Craftsmanship for its own sake is to be admired no matter where and when it is seen. It was reading a passage in a brilliant essay by John Updike about Ted Williams, the baseball player, that made me change my mind. I think it is worth quoting because it touches on the qualities that have enabled Ramprakash to go on, year after year, scoring runs in the most mundane circumstances and surroundings and why it is this particular feature of his achievement that should be celebrated the most.

'Baseball,' Updike wrote, and here he might have been referring to county cricket as well, 'is a game of the long season . . . Irrelevance always threatens its interest, which can be maintained not by the occasional heroics that sportswriters feed upon but by players who always care; who care, that is to say, about themselves and their art. In so far as the clutch hitter is not a sportswriter's myth, he is a vulgarity, like the writer who only writes for money.'

It is hard to get away from Ramprakash's relative lack of success in Test cricket and as much as I understand the sentiments, I cannot agree with my predecessor on these pages when he said that Ramprakash's Test record was 'unjust'. It is what it is. Sport is neither just nor unjust; it simply reflects time and again an absolute truth. Ramprakash was tried and tested many times in international cricket and more often than not he was found wanting.

But that is not relevant to the achievement at hand: the tears at Test level should not diminish the triumph at county level. Ramprakash's great glory is the way he has put the disappointments of his Test career to one side – the scale and frequency of which would have finished less dedicated craftsmen – and the way that he has been able to emerge notably happier (at least until the weeks before the final hurdle had been overcome), more relaxed, still wanting to hone his craft and still able to give of his best every time he has walked to the crease.

Sport, and life, is not so much about the days when the glittering prize is in your grasp, the crowd cheering, but about the days in between. Ramprakash has endured. He is not the greatest player of his generation – does not even come close – but he is one of the game's finest craftsmen. That is enough.

The Times, 7 August 2008

Andrew Flintoff Has Whole of England's Gratitude

There was a lot going on yesterday, what with the County Championship reaching a dramatic climax, Mervyn Westfield being charged by Essex police with spot-fixing and the Pope taking time out to bless these atheistic shores. There was still the appetite for Fred, though.

In itself, this is remarkable since Flintoff's last appearance as a cricketer, rather than as a by-standing celebrity, was just over a year ago at The Oval. Then, in a glorious scene-stealing moment to rival any played by Marlon Brando, he threw down Ricky Ponting's stumps to help England regain the Ashes. Given yesterday's announcement of his retirement from all forms of the game, it was to be his last act. What a way to go.

That is not what Flintoff wanted, of course, hence the 'sadness' he referred to in the press release. Flintoff wanted, more than anything else, to continue to hear the crowds chant his name, if not as a Test cricketer any more, than as a travelling Twenty20 entertainer. 'Freelance Fred' they called him and he saw himself charting a new course, independent and free from control of cricket's governing bodies. A contract here, a contract there.

That may yet come to pass for some, but not for Flintoff whose body finally gave up on him before he was ready to give up on the game. For anyone, whether you have played a hundred Tests or one, whether you have played for ten years or for two, that is a hard thing to cope with. Despite all the baubles won and the accolades rightfully due, Flintoff will have been a sad man yesterday. That locker at Old Trafford now belongs to someone else.

But rather more quickly than most, because of the fortunate position he finds himself in – not many can afford to simply take time out as Flintoff said he will do – and because of the enormous fund of goodwill he has built up, that sadness will be replaced by relief. No more injections, no more operations, no more rehab and no more uncertainty. He can get on with the rest of his life now that his period in limbo is over.

It was the English public that Flintoff was quick to thank yesterday, along with his family and his team-mates from Lancashire and England. 'I am indebted to the encouragement and support I have always received from England's magnificent supporters,' he said. And that may well be the link that endures most strongly for him. After all, he has been little more than an intermittent presence for Lancashire throughout his career and England have moved on seamlessly without him.

There has always been a special bond between those supporters and the man they saw as the heart and soul of English cricket throughout the first decade of this century. Partly, this was because they saw in Flintoff something of their best selves: a down-to-earth Northern lad, unchanged by success, popular with all, quick to smile, slow to anger and quick to enjoy the fruits of his labours. No matter there was as much myth as reality.

What cannot be doubted was that Flintoff, more than anyone, helped English cricket learn to love itself again after a period in the doldrums. In that brief time, either side of 2005 and especially during the Ashes series of that summer, Flintoff was the best face of English cricket, harrying the Australians to defeat after years of kowtowing and doing so in a manner that forced Ricky Ponting into admitting that, yes, he would not have minded having Flintoff in his team.

When supporters take a little bit of Flintoff with them, it is that series they will take; the thundering all-round performance at Edgbaston and the way he consoled Brett Lee at the end, in particular. By any standards, they are special memories. That people have a selective memory is one of the most pleasant things I have found out about retirement: so they won't remember the injuries, the drunken episodes and the whitewash in Australia under his captaincy. They will remember the good bits and that will sustain him.

Yesterday, in a warm tribute, Andrew Strauss, the England captain, hailed Flintoff as 'the ultimate impact' cricketer. That is about right. It is hard to argue, over the length of his whole career, that Flintoff belongs to the elite. But there were moments and matches, when he sniffed the air, sensed the mood, dragged his team-mates and the crowd with him, when he could change the course of a game, when he belonged in exalted company. They were brief moments, but undeniable.

In a rather less generous tribute, Graeme Swann indicated that England had moved on and would not be troubled by his absence. 'Our team last year was very confident,' he said. 'We didn't need people going round and geeing up little quivering leaves in the corner. If he can't come back, it's sad, but so be it. No individual is bigger than the team.'

That, too, is true. But somewhere between the words of Strauss and Swann there is a link and Flintoff was part of that link. England are confident and successful now and they will not miss Flintoff. But they were not always so bold and brave and Flintoff played his part in that renaissance. For that, and for the memories, he has our gratitude.

The Times, 17 September 2010

10

Cricket Is Not the Only Game

Deciding what to leave out of this collection was the hardest thing of all. There have been interviews with other sportsmen and the occasional travel and politics pieces. They all went the way of the dustbin in the end, but I thought I would put one or two pieces written about other sports and sportsmen (and, here also, one about a horse, Best Mate), because I enjoyed writing them and because there is always something to be gleaned from other sports and the people who play/coach it.

John Wooden's philosophies, for example, would benefit any sports-man from any sport; the way baseball coped with an erroneous call because it lacked technology was a lesson for all sports; and the two (non) events I experienced with two greats from boxing and football – Mike Tyson and Wayne Rooney – impressed upon me the general decency of cricketers compared to some in other sports. Sent to do a profile of Rooney some years ago, he didn't even turn up. Leopards and spots spring to mind . . .

Best Mate and the Odd Couple

I have been to training yards before but none quite like this one. At first sight it is more Old MacDonald's Farm than an elite equine operation: ducks flapping and quack-quacking around the pond in front of the main house; hens laying eggs in nooks and crannies; dogs running loose, and horses, seemingly, appearing from everywhere.

The yard is Henrietta Knight's and the horse I've come to see is Best Mate. Both trainer and horse have left an indelible mark on the nation after their exploits at the past two Cheltenham Festivals – Best Mate, powering up the hill to become the first horse since L'Escargot in 1971 to win consecutive Gold Cups, closely followed by Knight's uninhibited, if less stylish, gallop of joy around the winner's enclosure into the arms of a tearful Terry Biddlecombe.

It is the face of the former champion jockey, now husband and assistant trainer to Knight, whom I see first. And what a face it is too – memorably described as one that could 'double up as a relief map of Wessex'. It is ruddy and round and obviously lived in. It is smiling now, though, and I am offered an outstretched, misshapen hand – the result of a fall too many.

'I'm glad you're early. We've got to go all the way to Newton Abbot. The chase track at Kempton's like a fucking road!' The only person that Biddlecombe, apparently, toned down his language for was the late Queen Mother, but getting through two sentences before the first F-word is a respect of sorts.

Knight appears looking rather prim and school-mistressy (appearances can be deceptive) and the two of us set off on a tour of the yard. First, we head off to the new £200,000 ecotrack gallop – a gentle right-handed pull uphill for about a mile where we might see a horse or two working out. What we see first is a bright yellow Dobson's double-decker bus stranded in the middle of an arid field. 'It's my sighting post,' explains Knight. 'I can see the dip from the top of the bus.'

Her phone is ringing constantly. First it's Attheraces for a bulletin on Best Mate. Then it's Biddlecombe who is reporting from another gallop. All horsey talk and trainer speak:

'Is he fresh?' 'Is he sound or lame?' 'Did he hang?' We are still sitting in the double-decker and haven't seen a horse yet. And then, 'No, I don't see a horse at all. I wonder where he's gone?' Boldly, I venture that things seem a little chaotic. She shoots me a sharp look.

'Organised chaos, I like to think.' Sure enough, as we drive around the estate passing horses walking in pairs, in the golden light of an autumn morning, Knight points every one out, along with their quirks and temperaments, strengths and weaknesses, without recourse to the notes in her lap.

It strikes me that the chaos is central to her success as a trainer. The horses enjoy the natural farmyard atmosphere. They enjoy the fact that this is no regimented training establishment. They settle in, they are given time to mature and they relish the wonderful surrounds of the West Lockinge estate. This is a place where horses are trained, and winners produced, but also where they are looked after. 'Best Mate thrives here,' she says, 'in a way he might not elsewhere.' Later, as if to confirm the theory, Biddlecombe points to Edredon Bleu, who the previous day had hacked up in the Haldon Chase. 'At some other yards, he wouldn't be racing now,' he says.

I suggest to Knight, with some understatement, that she and Biddlecombe are an odd couple. 'You're not the first person to say that, you know. But you're absolutely right, we are complete opposites and I think that's why it works.' Opposites, but with a shared problem in their past: the bottle.

'Terry hit rock bottom for a while after leaving the saddle. I was training on my own, with no help, and without really noticing I was getting through three bottles of wine a day, often with champagne on top. When we got together, Terry had already dried out with the help of the Injured Jockeys' Fund and he gave me a choice between him and the bottle. Neither of us has had a drop since.'

Here, suddenly, is why the Best Mate story, so well told by Knight in her book *Best Mate: Chasing Gold*, is an important one. His second Cheltenham triumph may not be the final chapter – Best Mate chases a record-equalling third Gold Cup in March – but it is certainly the climax of what is, in racing and human terms, a genuinely happy and heart-warming tale – without any of the Hollywood schmaltz that accompanies Seabiscuit.

Finally, we come to the part of the yard where the older and better horses are stabled.

Best Mate and Edredon Bleu live next to each other, although the pecking order is clear since Best Mate's box has more creature comforts – the soft lining on the walls is to prevent him banging his head badly as he did just over a year ago. Edredon Bleu tamely eats Polo-mints out of Knight's hands. Best Mate is fresh and hard to hold and is controlled by Biddlecombe.

'They thought I was crackers last year when I said he'd improved by a stone,' he says. 'Well, he's improved again over the summer. Just look at his neck muscles.' But it is not the neck that stands out; it is the beautiful head, and the way he carries it. This is a horse that knows his status in the yard and revels in it.

There is a strong thread throughout the book that fate brought Knight, Biddlecombe and Best Mate together, each now helping the other to achieve their potential. What else could explain the random set of circumstances that culminated with Biddlecombe being stopped in his tracks at an Irish point-to-point on a wet March afternoon four years ago, when he first saw Best Mate?

Superstition will be paramount in Best Mate's attempt to emulate Arkle and Cottage Rake as the only horses to win the Gold Cup three times. Like last year, Knight will send him out for just two races beforehand – the Peterborough Chase at Huntingdon and the King George at Kempton. Like last year, she will back the opposition ante-post. On the day itself, she will get out her blue suit and lucky pearls and Biddlecombe will dust off his battered old hat. After that, it is in the hands of God, and Jim Culloty.

Sunday Telegraph, 9 November 2003

My Rooney Interview Was No Child's Play

The competition winner from Surrey, along with her nine nephews and nieces, put the long journey behind them and bounced out of the minibus, goggle-eyed at the prospect of being coached by Manchester United's *wunderkind*, Wayne Rooney. The venue, Bobby Charlton's Soccer School in the Egerton Youth Centre near Knutsford in Cheshire, was unprepossessing but their enthusiasm could not be dimmed and, indeed, contrasted nicely with the hard-bitten cynicism of a couple of members of the Fourth Estate waiting for a promised interview.

We gathered inside for Rooney's arrival, scheduled at 2.00pm. The children changed into their kit and watched a video of David Beckham, the most famous graduate of Charlton's school. I had been sent to do the interview by this newspaper to offer a perspective from a different sporting sphere on England's new superstar and I asked one journalist what the form was. 'You'll get ten minutes face to face. By the way, how are you going to get around asking about the sponsor?'

'Who is the sponsor again?'

'Pringles.'

'Would that be the crisps or the sweaters?' It turned out to be the crisps, but I gather the sweaters are back in fashion and footballers are nothing if not fashionable.

It was now 2.55 and Rooney was already fashionably late, but there was still no sign. Alex, a representative from his agency, came over looking formidably efficient in a pin-striped suit. 'Don't worry,' she said. 'They've been held up at Carrington [United's training ground] and he's got a bit of a cold and had to see a doctor.' The extra training, the day after United's multimillion-pound strike force drew a blank against Manchester City, seemed understandable.

'Will you want pictures?' she asked.

'Just a couple during the interview and then one outside where our photographer has set up.'

'Well, we don't want any inside. Just some posed ones with the kids outside.' There did not seem much point in arguing.

Twenty minutes later, Alex's phone rang. She turned positively translucent as she whispered into it: 'Tell me you're joking, right?'

Evidently, the caller was not joking and Alex scurried off into the kind of huddle Michael Vaughan routinely holds before each session of play. We feared the worst.

Then the news we dreaded. 'I'm really sorry, he's not coming. Got food poisoning, can't keep anything down.' Obviously the cold really had taken a turn for the worse in the last half-hour – surely nothing to do with his reported celebrations at Dwight Yorke's 33rd birthday party the night before? His agents later said it was a 'viral infection'. One of the photographers whispered: 'Happens all the time with 'em, you know.' Was he talking about PRs in general, or footballers? I assumed the latter.

The children, by now, had been taken out on to the football pitch, and in the fading light they kicked a ball around, cold but still excited and unsuspecting. On the motorway, at four o'clock, I rang the sponsor's representative. 'How did they take the news?' I asked.

'We're just about to tell them.'

Earlier, one of the parents had noticed an ageing ex-cricketer in the building and he had encouraged the children to get an autograph. That day, I'm sorry to say, it was all they left with – along with a promise to meet Rooney another day. Strange world, football.

Sunday Telegraph, 14 November 2004

My Lewis Hamilton Moment

The thing about sport is that it is just about the most powerful truth serum there is. Young sportsmen find themselves surrounded by all kinds of helpers, from agents to PR executives, all of whom are on hand to try to polish a certain image and act as a buffer between the sportsman as he is and the sportsman as others would like to see him. But out in the arena, you are on your own, every move watched by dozens of intrusive cameras and millions of prying eyes. Sport delivers, time and again, a brutal truth and a sportsman's essential nature will out – like it or not.

There have been enough examples already in Lewis Hamilton's brief career to know that behind the polished smiles, the PR guff and the copy-approved interviews is a ruthless operator. His long-running feud with Fernando Alonso, which included wilfully over-riding team orders in Hungary in 2007, should have told us everything we needed to know about him.

Those who line up to crucify Hamilton are doing so not because he has failed to live up to his own standards but because he has failed to live up to the expectations of others that have been created for him by a pushy father, an agency keen to milk the holy cow for all it is worth and a Formula One team for whom disappointment is measured in millions of dollars rather than the tarnishing of an image. Everything that Hamilton has done on the racetrack has projected a different image, so the reaction to the events in Australia says more about our gullibility than it does about him.

What is it with the British and our sportsmen? It is a curious nation that falls in love with Andrew Flintoff and despises Kevin Pietersen. One, a good cricketer who has produced the odd great moment, whose popularity soared after a post-match hug with an opponent and didn't diminish despite a whitewash in Australia and an episode with a pedalo; the other a great cricketer, whose preparations are never less than perfect, but who is damned for a few ill-chosen comments and a perception that, like Hamilton, he puts himself before the rest. But bat – or wheel – in hand, you're on your own so you'd better make damn well sure that you are prepared for everything that will be thrown your way.

There is a deeply moral thread running through our attitudes to our sportsmen. It is not enough to win or to try to win, everything must be seen to be completely above board as well, even though everybody who has played sport knows that rules, laws or conventions are pushed to the limit and often beyond. This morality is a hangover from the days of empire, when sport was seen as essential to the building of moral character, which was, in turn, seen as essential to empire-building. The biggest crime of all is not losing but not playing fair.

For a short period in 1994, accused of ball-tampering and fined, not for ball-tampering, but for lying to the match referee, I felt exactly how Hamilton is feeling right now: embarrassed, hurt, foolish, hunted and on my own. There are some similarities between the episodes: an initial mistake – Hamilton allowing Jarno Trulli to pass, me keeping one side of the ball dry by using dust from an old pitch; the confession – Hamilton in an immediate post-match interview, me in the dressing-room at teatime; then the panic – how do we get out of this one?; the cover-up – Hamilton to the stewards, me to Peter Burge, the match referee; the punishment; and then the press conference.

The last bit was probably the hardest. I can remember, as if it were yesterday, the small chamber in the inner sanctum at Lord's that doubled for the press conference room on that sweaty, humid Sunday evening 15 years ago. What I did not know then, amazingly because nobody had bothered to tell me, was that the conference was going out live and what theatre it must have been to those watching: a young, hitherto untarnished sportsman as uncomfortable as he could have possibly been, with Jonathan Agnew clambering all over me and Fleet Street lapping it up.

It was an episode that had a permanent effect on me. Pursued for two weeks afterwards with the kind of intrusion usually reserved for corrupt politicians, I was never trusting or open in front of the media again. I did not worry about the effect on my image – unlike the Hamilton camp now, by all accounts – because I had, in my own mind, no image to speak of at all, or certainly not one that had been carefully manicured. But I knew that it would be a permanent stain on my career and an inevitable chapter in my sporting obituary.

Do I worry about that now? Not one bit. Nor should Hamilton because there is nothing he can do about it. I look back now at an immature 26-year-old who made a mistake (albeit hardly a heinous one), who paid a small penalty in financial terms but a bigger one as regards reputation, who then endured some ferocious criticism, handled it badly and went and scored 99 in his next Test innings under extreme pressure. I learnt a lot about myself during those two weeks.

Given a chance to reflect, Hamilton will have learnt a lot about himself this week, too. And us? The Australian Grand Prix told us nothing we did not already know about him if we had bothered to look carefully enough at his actions on the track and beyond the spin. It told us, once again, that he is a genius of a driver and that he is a flawed human being. It is only the first bit that sets him apart from the rest of humanity.

The Times, 4 April 2009

How an Evening without Mike Tyson Unfolded

I went to the Civic Hall in Wolverhampton feeling uncharacteristically charitable, I really did. It was an interview on the telly that got me all warm-hearted.

Interviewers-cum-autocue readers keep shtoom about Charlie Kennedy's drinking, for example, but as soon as a boxer pops up, albeit one with a dodgy reputation, then bam! No punches pulled. When Dermot Murnaghan asked Mike Tyson about the death of his four-year-old daughter after an accident this year, the question seemed not so much direct and tough as callous and gutless.

There are many victims in Tyson's extraordinary story: the countless boxers smashed to smithereens in the ring (of one, Tyson said: 'I wanted to hit him one more time in the nose so that the bone would go up into his brain'); Robin Givens, his manipulative first wife, who also felt the power of Tyson's fist; his sleeping six-year-old brother, whose arm Tyson slit with a razor; the sister-in-law of one of his trainers, Teddy Atlas, whom Tyson molested; Desiree Washington, whom Tyson was convicted of raping; and countless others who have crossed him.

But there is no doubt that Tyson himself is a victim of sorts. Born to circumstances few would escape from without deep scarring – born, in his own words, to 'an alcoholic and a pimp'.

Great wealth came and great wealth went, so that before his second fight against Evander Holyfield – which was to be a $30 million (now about £18 million) pay-day – Tyson felt compelled to say: 'I've been taken advantage of all my life. I've been used. I've been dehumanised. I've been humiliated and I've been betrayed.'

Tyson laid flowers at the grave of Johnny Owen this week, but it has always been Sonny Liston, the great heavyweight who died with needle marks in his arm, whom Tyson has associated himself with most of all.

It is almost as if Tyson is becoming the victim of a self-fulfilling prophesy. The great estates in Nevada, Ohio, Connecticut and Maryland now but a memory, he finds himself on the after-dinner circuit at the Civic Hall, Wolverhampton. Nothing against the Civic Hall, you understand, but it's hardly Caesars Palace. 'It's an odd place to find Tyson, wouldn't you say?' I said to the man to my right. 'Yeah, it's nice and low-key.'

Still, he drew a crowd, of sorts. An hour before the event there was a handful of autograph hunters and a solitary snapper, when years before you would have been blinded by the flashlights. But half an hour after the doors had opened, three quarters of the venue was full. Two thousand, three tops, most of whom had paid £25 for the privilege, with a few hundred VIPs (the MC would refer to them throughout the night as not VIPs but vips), who had shelled out £200.

It was a sympathetic audience. When, at the beginning of the evening, the MC described Tyson as 'a complex man with a heart of gold' and a 'lovely, lovely guy', there was a murmur of approval.

It was 8.30pm by now. I looked at my ticket again: An Evening with Mike Tyson; doors open 7.00pm, show 7.30pm. Suddenly, we were confronted with a boy band from Wales called 4th Street Traffic who emitted an incomprehensible sonic boom, that had the vips, just metres from the speakers, wondering if they had made the right choice after all.

Now it was time for Ken Buchanan, a great former champion who has had enough troubles of his own, to shuffle up on stage. 'Sit yourself down here!' roared the MC, patting a stool so hard that clouds of dust were sent into the air. Dapper in a waistcoat, Buchanan was given a respectful welcome.

Next, Alan Minter, another great champion, who came on blowing kisses to the audience as if he was about to get going at Madison Square Garden. He was forgetful at times; the years, and bouts, have caught up with him.

The crowd were getting itchy now, their mood not helped by the news that it would not be Tyson next but a tribute artist called Miss Understood. Two heavyweight vips at the front of the room began to foxtrot as Miss Understood thundered out her tunes – this was turning into a bizarre, even grotesque, evening.

It was 9.45pm now and the organisers were beginning to misunderstand the crowd's mood. Slow hand-clapping, catcalls and no Mike Tyson. The MC blundered on, dragging to the stage half-a-dozen auction items – 'unique opportunities for your boardroom, ladies and gentlemen!' – which were flogged off for hundreds a time. The mood was beginning to turn ugly. The MC called a break at 10pm – just a short one, you understand. Only five or ten minutes for our comfort. By 10.30 the crowd were becoming visibly angered.

Did Iron Mike turn up? I could not tell you, because three and a quarter hours after the show was due to start, I had to catch the last train home. I did ring the man sitting on my right, who had brought his father, hoping to give him a night to remember. He said that shortly after 10.30pm, more auction items were flogged off, and then those vips who hadn't had their promised photo with Tyson were whisked away. At 11.04pm, Tyson appeared and spoke for 40 minutes. 'He was enigmatic but very listenable, too,' my neighbour said.

Sports fans tend to be charitable to their former heroes. They are like the newspaper editor in Ring Lardner's story, 'Champion', who did not want his reporter to write about the boxer knocking down his mother and disabled brother. Why? Because he was the champion. But it pays not to take the piss.

There are many victims in the extraordinary story of Mike Tyson. There were a few in the Civic Hall, Wolverhampton, on Wednesday night, too, and it would take someone of an extremely charitable mentality to say that Tyson was one of them.

The Times, 6 November 2009

Open: An Autobiography by Andre Agassi

It is usually a dread day when a ghosted sporting autobiography lands at your door. The 'life' story, say, of a 22-year-old who has no wide-ranging experience of his sport, never mind life, written by a hack with one eye on the deadline and the other on the cheque.

But the multiple grand-slam winner Andre Agassi is no ordinary sportsman, and Pulitzer Prize-winning author J.R. Moehringer is no hack. The result is an engaging, thrilling and only sometimes scarcely believable autobiography. If 'image is everything' (the advertising slogan that linked Agassi and Canon throughout the 1990s) was the *leitmotif* that ran through Agassi's career, then this book is his attempt to open the aperture a little wider and throw some light on some wild and hedonistic years that tennis fans, with Boris Becker, Pete Sampras and Agassi all in their prime, will remember as equally special.

The serialisation of *Open* in this newspaper, and the furore that followed, centred inevitably on Agassi's admission that he had taken the drug crystal meth at the height of his career, and that he subsequently lied about it cravenly to escape censure. This revelation is not insignificant, and there may yet be some fallout, but it forms a minor strand of the book in which the grand themes are the nature of fatherhood, the often difficult relationship an athlete has with his sport, and the search for meaning and maturity in an otherwise gilded life.

The early chapters are dominated by Agassi's domineering father, Mike, who dreams only of tennis greatness for his youngest child. The rest of the book is a journey to cast off the demons imparted by this man who built a tennis court and ball-feeding machine in the desert, whose idea of a childhood for young Andre was a diet of non-stop tennis, who thrust speed down his son's neck before a junior match and who held a shotgun level with his son's nose during an altercation with a driver.

Even at the moment of Agassi's ascent to greatness, his father cannot bring himself to share his son's joy. After winning the 1992 men's title at Wimbledon, his first slam, Agassi phones his father excitedly: 'Pops? It's me! Can you hear me? What'd you think?'

Silence.

'Pops?'

'You had no business losing that fourth set.'

Agassi's father did not attend his son's second marriage, to Steffi Graf. Largely as a result of his father's pathological ambition, Agassi hates tennis. It is one of a number of cues, another being the ongoing rivalry with Sampras, that Moehringer comes back to time and again. Every new character we are introduced to – and Agassi surrounds himself with an eclectic mix – is introduced through this admission. 'I hate tennis,' he tells his soon-to-be-trainer-cum-surrogate father, Gil Reyes. 'You're kidding, right?' 'No, I hate tennis.'

This particular admission will come as no surprise to professional athletes. Everyone, at some stage, comes to hate their chosen (or, in Agassi's case, non-chosen) sport. Punished by his father, orphaned off to a tennis academy at 13 and then spending a lifetime dealing with the extreme mood swings that come with winning and losing, is it any surprise? It is only when he meets Graf, after his divorce from Brooke Shields, that he finds someone who understands. 'I hate tennis,' Agassi says, to which Graf merely rolls her eyes as if to say, 'Doesn't everyone?'

Nor will professional athletes be surprised by the anti-climactic feelings at the moments of his greatest triumphs. After reaching the No 1 slot in the world rankings for the first time, Agassi writes: 'I tell him [the reporter] that it feels good to be the best I can be. It's a lie. It's what I want to feel. It's what I expected to feel. But in fact I feel nothing.' Later he muses, 'If being number one feels empty, unsatisfying, what's the point?' In the end, every athlete comes to understand that the glory is in the doing, the competing, and not the wallowing in adulation afterwards.

If these episodes carry the unmistakable whiff of authenticity, then others smell clearly of exaggeration on Agassi's part that Moehringer was ill-qualified to question. As someone who has suffered from a chronic back condition for years, Agassi's Lazarus-like recovery from immobility to winning pulsating five-setters stretched my credibility. If true, I wish that I'd had a bad back like his. Likewise, every fast bowler who has ever torn a rib cartilage will tell you that you simply are not able to go out and take a set off Sampras with such an injury.

But these are minor quibbles about what is a superbly written book. Moehringer knows well enough that extended match reports from Agassi's glorious career would have bored readers senseless, so he sticks to pithy gobbits from vital games and caustic observations about Agassi's rivals. Fans of Jimmy Connors ought not to buy this book; nor should Agassi's former coach Nick Bollettieri, painted as orange-coloured, grasping and a bit of a fraud, nor Shields, who Agassi sees as little more than a vapid clothes-horse. The present tense, used throughout, gives the narrative an added sense of urgency and authenticity.

Although it is well written, it is formulaic in style, and as such requires a Pauline conversion, as most of these autobiographies do. Moehringer lays down certain road signs: we are told, for example, how Agassi puts down a nest egg for the education of a child of the owner of his favourite restaurant, and the joy that this brings him. 'This is the only perfection there is,' he writes, 'the perfection of helping others.'

And so to the Andre Agassi College Preparatory Academy in Las Vegas – unquestionably Agassi's greatest achievement. And what an achievement it is, this top-class educational establishment in a run-down area of Vegas, that provides a first-class schooling to those in need.

Maybe the financial needs of the Academy are the reason for this curiously timed book. Agassi can hardly require the money, nor the hassle that may well come out of the drug-taking revelations. But ours is not to reason why: we are thankful that the mature educationist can look back on his lava-hot-panted, hair-pieced younger self with wry detachment. The best sports books are not really about sport – and *Open* is no exception.

The Times, 14 November 2009

Captaincy: John Terry Doesn't Know the Half of It

Amid the present hysteria [regarding John Terry's private life and alleged abuses of his position as captain], it is possible to wonder what the response would have been if the England football captain had excused himself from duty because of exhaustion after a year on the job, as the England cricket captain did recently. A bout of sniggering, perhaps – all that action, no wonder he needs a rest!

– followed by incredulity? After all, alongside members of the European Parliament, the captaincy of the England football team is one of the biggest non-jobs (con jobs?) going.

When Andrew Strauss pulled out of the tour to Bangladesh that starts this month, the reactions of dismay or understanding explain neatly why the John Terry affair has only a passing relevance to England's chances in this summer's World Cup finals in South Africa.

Dismay because everyone who has had the honour of leading out the England cricket team knows how central the captain is to everything that goes on; understanding, because it is, as Nasser Hussain said, a 24-hour, 7 days a week, 12 months a year job and exhaustion follows (usually after longer than a year, it must be said) as inevitably as night follows day.

When the England cricket captaincy was offered to me in 1993, it came with certain terms of reference, the first being that the ECB wanted to 'restore the authority' of the captain after a period in which it was perceived that the coach had too much influence. It was made clear that it was not a role to be accepted lightly. First thoughts were not of exploitation but of certain small sacrifices to be made: of time and of privacy, mainly.

So the early days, until those terms of reference were changed abruptly, involved being the main voice in selection, ringing those selected and – more angst-inducing this – those who had been dropped; having a say in schedules of tours on the distant horizon; dictating tactics; giving team-talks; helping to run practice and making decisions on the field. The last bit was the easy part. All this before you have even thought about your own performance. Since the advent of a tidal wave of support staff, the duties have become somewhat lighter of late, but the point stands.

Not being close to the football scene, and embarrassed about encroaching upon the patch of Patrick Barclay and Oliver Kay, soundings have been made this week to those who are in the know as to what exactly the England football captain *does*, apart from shake hands with the opposition at the toss and decide which way to kick off. One said he organises 'things'. What exactly? 'Laser shoots, and the like. You know, team spirit things.' Another talked of understanding the game – although one hopes that is a minimum requirement of any international footballer. Another talked of leading by example and of his symbolic importance.

If symbolic is too strong a word, then it gets closer to the point than most. If not a symbol then he is a reflection, mainly upon Fabio Capello, and to a lesser degree on us. This is why 'Il Capo' has to act. As Bobby Moore was for Alf Ramsey, so Terry is Capello's representative on the field and, in a welcome development, Capello has shown in his short time in charge that he will not put up with the kind of puerile nonsense tolerated by earlier managers; that the normal standards of decency, respect and discipline are as much a part of his regime as you would expect in any professional side.

The England captaincy can never be a popularity contest, and the manager cannot treat it as an audition on *Strictly Come Dancing*, with the public voting according to every passing whim. But when there is this level of revulsion aimed at a man so obviously lacking in class (of the human, not social, kind) and decency, and devoid, as he clearly is, of any sense of responsibility, then the man in charge must take note of the public mood. Not that it will make one iota of difference, one way or the other, to the team's chances in South Africa.

Once the axe has swung, Capello can do himself and his team a favour before the tournament by refusing to appoint a permanent replacement, picking simply on a match-by-match basis. A fluid, flexible approach would confer immediate advantages: there would be no single figure for the media to focus on, no single figure trying and failing to live up to the kind of standards expected by a society that is deluded enough to expect sportsmen to act as 'role models'.

In the absence of a permanent captain there would be no one to exploit the honour, as Terry has tried so miserably to do. If the only meaning to the England football captaincy is, as Matt Dickinson beautifully reported on Tuesday, 'half a million quid', then it is time that particular junket was capsized. In the absence of one focal point, England's footballers may learn that the best teams have not just one leader on the field but many.

If Capello takes this course of action, Terry's final indiscretion, in the end, may be the best thing that has happened to the England football team.

The Times, 4 February 2010

Perfect Storm Throws up Lesson for Cricket

The Bangladesh mini-series had many shortcomings, but in one respect it was entirely satisfactory: the absence of the Decision Review System (DRS) allowed for the return of the natural rhythms of the game. Wickets were celebrated with immediacy and emotion; there were no pregnant pauses while captains, wicket-keepers and bowlers conferred over the possibility of an appeal, and batsmen lingered only momentarily before accepting the authority of those paid to make decisions.

The DRS was not missed at all. It is true that there were no howlers to outrage those who would have a game free of human error. Alastair Cook got a couple of leg-before decisions that, though out at first glance, were probably a little too high, and one or two of the Bangladesh tailenders were on the receiving end of the kind of decisions that tailenders have moaned about for decades.

This interlude was a precious reminder of what cricket will lose if and when the ICC and host broadcasters come to an agreement over who should pay for the toys. Once they do, the interests of paying spectators will be ignored and spontaneity at the fall of a wicket will again be replaced by delay, dithering and debate as the players become decision-makers too.

Interestingly, in the same week that cricket found it could do without an increase in technology, baseball was having an internal debate of its own. And the argument raged over something that, for baseball fans, was a little more important than an erroneous leg-before decision against England's vice-captain.

For those of us who watch sport, the flaws are often the most interesting aspect of performance and performers, but the search for perfection is at the heart of any professional sporting endeavour. It is usually unattainable. Occasionally, though, it is: snooker players can score a maximum 147 break, jockeys can do a Frankie Dettori and ride a card of winners, gymnasts used to be able to achieve the 'perfect 10' until the sport's scoring system was overhauled in 2006.

In baseball, the 'perfect game' is awarded to a pitcher who throws 27 straight outs, sending his team to victory before any opposing player reaches base. Since 1880, this has happened only 20 times (three of them, interestingly, within the past 12 months, which suggests that baseball may be going in the opposite direction from cricket, where batsmen are dominating like never before). It should have happened again last week in a game between the Detroit Tigers and the Cleveland Indians.

Detroit's Armando Galarraga was a hitherto journeyman pitcher enjoying a perfect night. He needed one more out to join the ranks of those who had pitched a perfect game – in 83 pitches, fewer than anyone else since 1908 – when he threw to Cleveland's Jason

Donald. As Donald sprinted to first base, it was clear that it was going to be tight, but that he was going to fail to make his ground – just.

Jim Joyce, the umpire at first base, was the only man in Comerica Park who thought otherwise. He called Donald home and, because replays are not a part of baseball, he denied Galarraga his place in history. No matter that Galarraga has been asked to donate his kit from that evening to the Hall of Fame. His name will not be added to the roster of perfect pitchers.

Many of the pundits thought it should be. Mitch Albom, of the *Detroit Free Press*, one of the most celebrated sports columnists in America, called on Bud Selig, the commissioner of Major League Baseball, to overturn the call and to introduce technology to ensure that such an injustice does not happen again. There was a shared sense of outrage in Detroit.

But then something strange happened. Galarraga, whose reaction to the umpire's decision had been admirably restrained and limited to a quizzical smile, refused to add to the opprobrium heaped on Joyce.

'I would've been the first person in my face, but he never said a word to me,' the grateful umpire said. In the immediate aftermath of the decision, Galarraga's reaction was equally phlegmatic: his next pitch was perfect, too, so that, he quipped, he is now the only man to have thrown a 28-out perfect game.

Joyce handled the situation like a man. He apologised, first, and then admitted to his mistake. 'I just cost that kid a perfect game,' he said, 'I thought he [Donald] beat the throw until I saw the replay.'

His error happened on the Wednesday, in the middle of a three-game series, and Joyce was given the option of missing the final game the day after his howler. He refused to hide, though. 'I couldn't have faced myself,' he said. The day after one of the biggest blunders in baseball history, he made his way to first base again.

He was not sure what kind of reaction he would get from the crowd, though, and while there were boos, there was also a large measure of support. The men were brought together at the exchange of teams, where Joyce's remorse and Galarraga's maturity were again in evidence. The match passed off without incident; Joyce, according to observers, had a good game.

Selig has said that he will not overturn the decision and so Galarraga's name will not take its place in the list of immortals. He will be remembered, though, as a man who, in a critical moment, recognised that there were more important things in life than statistics. Joyce will be remembered as an imperfect man on a perfect night, but one who handled his imperfections honestly and with courage.

And the lesson for cricket? This came, strangely, from Hugo Chavez, the Venezuelan President, who praised his countryman Galarraga for his nobility of spirit. 'The umpire was wrong,' Chavez said. 'But, well, the umpire is the umpire.'

The Times, 10 June 2010

England Footballers Can Learn from the John Wooden Gospel

England's footballers do not need a football coach, they need a life coach. Until yesterday [when they beat Slovenia 1–0 to qualify for the next phase of the World Cup] they had appeared out of touch, pampered, bored, disgruntled, disjointed and unable to cope with pressure. As would most technical coaches, Fabio Capello looked lost when asked for the reasons why.

Once they reach a certain level of proficiency, elite sportsmen do not need to be told whether to play 4–4–2, or 4–4–1–1, or how to play a forward defensive or a cover drive, they need someone to help them to become rounded human beings – a necessary first step to becoming better performers at the highest level. They need someone like John Wooden. Trouble is, he died two weeks ago, on the eve of the World Cup.

Little-known in Britain because he coached basketball in a city better known for its navel-gazing celebrities rather than its sportsmen, Wooden could lay claim to being one of the greatest sports coaches. Known as the 'Wizard of Westwood' – a moniker he detested – Wooden coached University of California, Los Angeles, basketball team to ten national titles in 12 years [between 1964 and 1975], eight more than any coach has achieved before or since. In that period, one of his teams achieved an 88-game winning streak – a record still – and his teams overall had a win–loss ratio of 664–162.

He did it with simple, homespun philosophies, Jimmy Stewart-like morals and a broad focus. Like John Buchanan, the former Australia cricket coach, his aim was to help his players become better human beings as well as better sportsmen; one could not come without the other.

His methods worked: with small teams – his first championship side was tiny by basketball standards – and with big egos. The bigger the ego, the greater the eventual loyalty so that, three decades after he had stopped coaching, some of the greatest players in history still referred to him as their mentor, their teacher. Many kept in touch; there was a steady stream of acolytes to his humble condo throughout his final years.

When I say that England's footballers need to become more rounded human beings before they can become better footballers,

I don't say it out of some inbred arrogance that footballers are worse human beings than other sportsmen – although they often give us cause to think that. It is simply that, by the very nature of their existence, the vast majority of professional sportsmen are self-absorbed, narrow-minded, fretting obsessives who often fail to cope with the pressures – and do not let anyone tell you otherwise – of international sport.

Not that many of the managers in the World Cup are coping much better. In fact, as those on the pitch have failed to ignite, the most interesting narratives have concerned the coaches: Dunga's battle to combine ruthlessness with the beautiful game; Sven-Göran Eriksson's attempt to turn a colourful African team into a colourless northern European one; Raymond Domenech's horror story; the challenge to Fabio Capello's dictatorship; and Maradona's permanent high-wire act, balancing between madness and brilliance.

All of them, players and managers, could do with a small dose of John Wooden:

'I have always tried to make it clear that basketball is not the ultimate. It is of small importance in comparison to the total life we live.'

Often, when things go wrong in major tournaments, it is not that players (or managers) want success too little, but that they want it too much. According to those following the England team in South Africa, the campaign has been thoroughly joyless. The hardest thing in professional sport is to play as if winning is the only thing that matters, with the knowledge that it does not matter at all. It is what Andy Flower, the England cricket team director, was trying to achieve when he took his team to Ypres on the eve of the Ashes [in 2009].

'Failure is not fatal. Failure to change might be.'

With a small team, Wooden incorporated a little-known zonal press defence to win his first three national championships. Success brought recruitment of better players and when the 7ft 2in Lew Alcindor (later known as Kareem Abdul-Jabbar) joined the team, Wooden altered his tactics completely and built his team around a man who was to become an all-time great. In team selection and tactics, stubbornness is not a sign of strength but weakness.

'I'd rather have a lot of talent and little experience than a lot of experience and little talent.'

Some coaches are afraid of big-name players and big egos. Wooden was not. He saw it as his job to manage those egos and integrate them into the team. In Alcindor and Bill Walton, Wooden had two of the most difficult to handle. 'I wanted to give them something to aspire to beyond statistics in sport,' Wooden said. Alcindor credited Wooden with his decision to convert to Islam; Walton wrote the lessons he learnt from Wooden on his sons' school lunchboxes. Both visited him shortly before he died.

'The main ingredient of stardom is the rest of the team.'

Wooden never forgot, though, that no man was bigger than the team. He had strict rules on personal conduct and standards of dress. One day Walton turned up with a full, straggly beard and when Wooden insisted he cut it, Walton refused, saying, 'It's my right.' 'That's good, Bill,' said Wooden. 'I admire people who have strong beliefs and stick by them, I really do. We're going to miss

351

you.' Walton went to the barber's straight away; there might be an absence of fit centre-halves at the moment but John Terry should be wary.

'Be more concerned with your character than your reputation because your character is what you really are, while your reputation is merely what others think you are.'

We know that Terry spent the morning before his press conference reading the papers to give himself some idea of the mood before attempting to undermine Capello [by revealing his own thoughts on selection issues and other matters]. This is a bad sign. Ignoring popular, and even informed, opinion is easier said than done, but no good ever comes from wasting time reading about what others think of you or your team.

'Adversity is the state in which man most easily becomes acquainted with himself, being especially free of admirers then.'

In other words, failure is sometimes a good thing because you get to learn a lot about yourself and team-mates in difficult times. The French learnt plenty in this tournament, namely that they did not care enough about their team or nation to put personal animus aside. England's players will also have learnt a lot about themselves this week and, to judge from their reaction yesterday, it is not too late to hope that some good may come of their troubles: to climb high you have to have fallen low. To recognise the peaks, you have to have known the troughs.

John Wooden was not a charismatic figure. He lived a humble life, in a small condo in a suburb of Los Angeles; he took a low salary for much of his coaching days and was married to his childhood sweetheart, to whom he continued to write letters for years after her death.

He abided by strict personal morals that were 'real easy to follow', according to an American sportswriter who knew him well, 'as long as you lived in a convent'. But somehow this oddity got the best out of starry-eyed young athletes.

He was a teacher rather than a basketball coach, and a teacher who clearly inspired a generation. Another of his former players, Gail Goodrich, has this to say: 'Over the years, I came to realise that he really taught us lessons. All the things he talked about in basketball apply to how you raise your kids and how you live your life. Outside of my parents and my family, he's the most important person in my life. He's been my mentor.'

How many, I wonder, will say that of a coach who is interested only in the minutiae of sport?

Wooden died on 4 June, aged 99, but his teachings live on, through his books. The Football Association could do worse than ship a few to South Africa – it may help the boys to kill a few of those tedious afternoons about which they are so fond of complaining.

The Times, 24 June 2010

11

The End of an Aura

One of the least enviable aspects of punditry involves prediction. Knowledge and experience is one thing but, especially in a sport with so many variables, prediction quite another. For what it was worth, my own forecast-cum-guess for the Ashes 2010–11 was 2–2.

I felt that England were a marginally better team, especially in the bowling department where I would not have swapped one Australia bowler for an England bowler, but that home advantage would count for something, especially in Brisbane and Perth, the two venues where the pace and bounce of the pitches has traditionally hampered England.

In fact, home advantage counted for little. The only surface with anything like the pace and bounce of previous Australian pitches was Perth, where England were duly slaughtered, but other than that, the wettest and coolest Australian summer for decades played into England's hands.

What one could not have predicted was how clueless Australia's selections were — made so, for sure, by the pressure put upon them by an outstanding England team — and how out of form their main players would be. In hindsight, it seemed to me that the key indicator should have been the age-profiles of both teams: whereas the majority of England's players were bang in the prime of their cricketing lives, many of Australia's players were either right at the start of their journey, or near the end.

Australia made life hard for themselves by having stuck with the same players who lost the 2009 Ashes. Instead of introducing a young batsman such as Usman Khawaja 18 months before the series, they stuck with Marcus North, who had already showed himself to be a journeyman by Australian standards. Khawaja was not the only one given his debut in the toughest series of all.

There were other remarkable selections, too, which suggested that Australia's cricketing cupboard really was of the Mother Hubbard type. Xavier Doherty, a callow left-arm spinner from Tasmania, was selected for Brisbane and duly shown to be ordinary. Cue the remarkable selection of an unknown called Michael Beer from Western Australia. All the while, Nathan Hauritz was scoring runs and taking wickets for New South Wales, his non-selection a clue to the unrest that had run through the Australia dressing-room during the previous months.

England's build-up to the Ashes, meanwhile, had been smooth. A settled, winning team, well led and meticulously prepared, arrived in Australia and immediately set about their task by beating Western Australia and Australia 'A' in two of the three warm-up games – the competitive, 11-a-side nature of them a pleasing contrast to four years earlier.

England clearly meant business. There were few bad days thereafter: they trailed on first innings at Brisbane, and were thrashed in Perth, but the other three Tests saw them run out comfortable winners by the margin of an innings and plenty each time – the first time that such a humiliation had been suffered by Australia in a five-match series.

England's game plan was simple: score massively in the first innings (which they did in Adelaide, Melbourne and Sydney), attack with the new ball, defend with the old, strangling Australia's batsmen in the process, rotating three seamers from one end, allowing Graeme Swann to weave his magic from the other. Disarmingly simple in theory, but tougher to implement.

It helped that many of England's players were in prime touch. Only Paul Collingwood fell short of the high standards set by the rest. Andrew Strauss played optimistically and led the team superbly; Alastair Cook enjoyed the series of his life; Jonathan Trott proved himself to be the number three England had long searched for; Kevin Pietersen scored a double hundred in Adelaide and Ian Bell looked the classiest player of all.

Of the bowlers, Jimmy Anderson led the attack to the extent that he took more wickets than any England fast bowler in a five-match series since Frank Tyson, one in the eye for those who felt he would flatter to deceive on unresponsive pitches and with a Kookaburra ball; Steven Finn took 14 wickets in three games until omitted for Tim Bresnan, who showed himself to be far better than the journeyman he had been taken for. With Chris Tremlett announcing himself on the international stage with superb performances in Perth and Melbourne, it was clear that Australia would have been thankful to have any one of England's reserve bowlers – Monty Panesar included – a measure of England's advantage.

The Ashes were retained in Melbourne and the series won in Sydney, the first time both had happened in Australia for 24 years. It was a memorable triumph for England, the first time for many years it could be said that they were a demonstrably superior team to Australia.

Stench of Fear Reigns on Aussies' Big Parade

Some years ago I was asked to help select a Rest of the World XI. The task was approached diligently, although some would say with little skill because the World XI were mauled by Australia, who themselves had just been beaten by a mid-ranked England team.

I learnt one important lesson, though. The matches took place a matter of weeks after the famous Ashes series in 2005. At least I was sure the Ashes series had just taken place, because I had commentated on it, written about it, even presented the urn to the England captain at The Oval. I knew I had not imagined it, yet there was no evidence in Australia that the series had happened.

For sure, there was no reason to gloat or to engage in the kind of triumphalism that gripped the England team. Australia had lost, after all. But they were not wallowing in self-pity, either. There was no Schofield Report and no hand-wringing or soul-searching. They simply got on with things. They picked the same team, went about things the same way and duly delivered a spanking to the World XI.

Australians do not usually do introspection. Certainly, their players have the same doubts, the same nerves as everyone else, but once a thing is done, it is best forgotten and the future faced with a certain confidence, bravado, even. In cricket, maybe this is born out of deep faith in a system that, by and large, has served them better than any other nation. Anyhow, it is a country that looks forward optimistically; not that there is much history to look back on.

How strange, then, to have landed in Australia this week and to sense in the air real doubt, gloom and English-style angst. There is the smell of fear, even. The French have already nipped off with the Melbourne Cup and the rugby has gone badly. Worst of all, the Poms are here to give us a stuffing. Greetings are extended with a shake of the head and an apologetic air as if the series is a foregone conclusion. A seasoned observer likened the early weeks to touring New Zealand, such has been its tameness.

The local press has already turned its guns inward; even Malcolm Conn, the legendary Pom-baiter from the *Australian* newspaper, managed only a half-hearted whinge about the multinational make-up of the England team. No one else I have spoken to here thinks the home team a goer. The mood is grim and it is catching: Leonard Cohen, the morbid crooner, has been performing in Hobart. It is said around these parts that he's the voice of optimism.

The glass, usually half-full, is definitely half-empty. The selectors have been pilloried for picking a 17-man squad. Utter confusion, people say. Never mind that this can easily be read as a quiet, two-fingered salute from the selectors to Cricket Australia's absurd marketing department, which wanted a glitzy affair at Circular Quay in Sydney and got a deserved damp squib instead.

There was plenty to be gleaned from this nonsense, but it was not that Australia's selectors are clueless, or indeed that they have no idea what is their best team, rather that Cricket Australia has begun to get its priorities mangled. It used to be cricket before money; now it is the other way round, as Mike Hussey found out when he wanted to jump ship from the Champions League to join his Australia team-mates for Test preparation in India, but was told to stay put.

Suddenly, it is the flaws that are highlighted, never mind that Australia still has some good players to choose from: Mitchell Johnson's 11 wides in a one-day match for his club side, Wanneroo; injuries to speedsters such as Mitchell Starc, Steve Magoffin and Josh Hazlewood; the continued mauling of Nathan Hauritz and Steven Smith at the hands of state players and the lack of spinning alternatives; Michael Clarke's dodgy back; Hussey's age and lack of form, and Marcus North's very presence. Not so much baggy greens as saggy greens.

Critics have noticed a Pommification of local cricket, not that this is regarded as a good thing. A full-time selector, Greg Chappell, has been appointed, the first in Australia's history. Like high-profile former England captains who became selectors – Raymond Illingworth and Ted Dexter spring to mind – the media are attracted to him rather than the low-key, low-profile lawyer-cum-convenor of selectors, Andrew Hilditch. Chappell has plenty to say and is quoted as saying that Australia will play a spinner at the Gabba. What if it is a green top? Chappell was a great player, but his lack of success in management has been noted.

Like the Poms, Cricket Australia has turned to management-speak. Whereas Steve Waugh took his team to Gallipoli, Cricket Australia now employs a corporate team-building company called Afterburner. They use ridiculous phrases such as 'pre-missions', 'debriefing', 'task distractions' and 'flawless execution'. At great expense, it encourages Ricky Ponting's men to sit around and speak openly at the end of a day's play to each other without recriminations. Straight talking from Australians used to be a given.

A cricket writer of long standing here, Robert Craddock, wrote a piece recently dissecting Australia's cricketing ills. The players are too soft; they are paid too much; young players are too mollycoddled, too much too soon; the selectors are too conservative; the game is losing popularity among the young. The system is broken. It could have been written by any English cricket writer of the past 20 years.

This lack of confidence is catching: a local politician recently called iconic areas of Sydney, Darling Harbour and the Olympic Park, 'urban failures' and 'dead and lifeless'. Australia used to be no country for old men; it is growing old and pessimistic before our eyes.

It was left to Peter Roebuck, the former Somerset captain and the pre-eminent daily cricket writer here, to sound some sort of a rallying cry. 'For twenty years Australia has been the teacher,' he wrote. 'No shame lies in becoming student again. At present, England is a step ahead, but the locals have a wonderful opportunity to learn things from them. Of course, it is possible to beat them at the same time.' Not Churchillian, I grant you, but at least he's not waving the white flag. The irony is not lost, of course, that he is a Pom.

Maybe the mood in the Australia dressing-room is different. Let us hope so. In any case, the first Test is still a week away. There is time yet for the locals to lift the mood and approach the series with their usual optimism and confidence. It is the contest that counts. Come on, Australia, it's still 0–0, the game is on, there is a series to win. It is a fair dinkum Australia we want to beat, not Australia in English clothes. Next thing, Dame Edna will stop cracking jokes and start delivering sermons.

The Times, 18 November 2010

Leader of the Attack Who Prefers to Take a Back Seat

Mark Taylor, the former Australia captain, tells a story about Glenn McGrath which, when you think about it, tells you a lot about the present leader of the attack, Mitchell Johnson. It is the story of the 1995 West Indies tour and how McGrath came to play a defining role in the series that led to Australia displacing West Indies as the world's champion team.

At the start of that tour, Craig McDermott was the leader of the attack and McGrath was a little-heard-of first-change bowler who had been in and out of the Test team and had played with no great success. One day, Taylor went running with McDermott who, jumping off the sea wall, ruptured his ankle ligaments.

Before the opening Test, Taylor had to break the news to McGrath that he would have to take the new ball. After he had done so, McGrath stared at Taylor and said: 'About bloody time, mate.' McGrath grabbed that ball out of Taylor's hand and he never looked back. He led Australia's attack with distinction for the next dozen years.

The contrast with Johnson, a supremely talented performer – the man Dennis Lillee once called 'a once in a generation cricketer' – but one with a rather more reticent personality, could not be more profound. No cricketer should try to be something he is not, but it is clear that Australia are crying out for someone to lead the attack and while Johnson is the natural choice, he seems reluctant to do so.

Despite Ben Hilfenhaus having played only one Test match in Australia, and despite Peter Siddle and Doug Bollinger returning from injury and despite Johnson being a 166-Test-wickets performer, he is unlikely to take the new ball when Australia get their first crack at England's batsmen at the Gabba. After you, Claude.

Johnson comes into the first Test in decent enough form, having scored a hundred and taken five wickets for Western Australia in his final dress rehearsal before Thursday. But he did not take the new ball in that game, just as he has been reluctant to do over the past 12 months for Australia. He feels more comfortable coming on first change, he says.

Of course, there is history here. Johnson came to England in 2009 with a huge reputation but left with it deflated. He has said that watching England receive the urn at The Oval was one of the worst experiences of his life – Ricky Ponting forced his players on to the outfield so that they would remember the pain of the loss.

For Johnson, the pain was more acute because he knows that he did not fulfil his talent on that tour and his shortcomings could have been the difference between victory and defeat. When Ponting needed one final wicket in Cardiff for victory, Johnson was unable to deliver. More than that, he bowled so waywardly that it looked as though the occasion had got to him.

It appeared that way in the next match at Lord's, too, only more so. There, he suffered from as close as it is possible to get to a dose of the dreaded yips, the ball and the cut strip at times making only a cursory acquaintance. Whereas previous Australia teams had been led by fast bowlers who were lions, Johnson gave the impression of being not so much lion as lamb, an impression underlined by his uncertain performances in front of the media.

He was on relaxed and personable form yesterday as Australia paraded all their Test players, but no matter how hard he tried, Johnson looked and sounded like a man who needed convincing of his own mental strength and abilities and that the memories of Lord's have been banished to the farthest reaches of his mind. He talked of being delighted to 'get through' subsequent tours such as New Zealand, where the crowd 'copped him plenty'. 'Getting through' used to be a bare minimum for an Australia Test cricketer rather than the limit of his ambition.

It did not help matters, perhaps, that Johnson spent the first few minutes answering enquiries about his newly minted tattoos. 'It's a Japanese-style koi with some cherry blossoms that have the meaning of luck,' he said. 'I had three sittings for them. The last bit was done only two weeks after I had the previous bit done. That hurt. It wasn't as bad as the one on the side. That killed me.' Like listening to a warrior talk us through his flower arrangements before battle.

Still, on more serious matters, he was happy to lay down the gauntlet. He talked, in the way that fast bowlers do, of targeting Andrew Strauss. 'They really look up to Strauss and if we can get him to crumble, then their players will start thinking negatively.' How is he going to do that? 'We've had a look at him with the short ball. He's OK with the one that's chest height but if you get it on the money, he really does struggle with it,' Johnson said. Of course, it may help to have a go at an opener with the new ball, too.

Kevin Pietersen was the other object of Johnson's attention, the more so since the memories of a verbal spat between the two just prior to the start of the Cardiff Test in 2009 still linger. 'There was a little bit going on in the Cardiff game and it got a bit heated,' Johnson said. 'But sometimes KP feeds off all that so I didn't really look him in the eye and I don't think I'll be saying too much. It's important to keep my emotions in check.'

Whether Johnson's past waywardness has been mental, technical or a bit of both is a matter of speculation. Johnson thinks the former and that he is over the problem. 'I am mentally stronger now,' he said. 'I struggled at Lord's but I've definitely improved that side of my game. I was getting bashed in the media and I copped it left, right and centre, but I've come through some pretty tough series since then and showed I've improved.'

Yet the suspicion remains that his action is faulty and, under pressure, prone to short-circuiting. Technique is important in cricket only because it helps your game hold up under the sternest scrutiny. Johnson's arm is so low that, to bowl accurately, there is very little margin of error on the timing of his release. Pressure, such as all the players will feel on Thursday, is likely to have an impact on that.

So there he goes, this wonderful performer, a man capable of ripping through the opposition as well as smashing the ball out of sight. There he goes, Australia's enigmatic and potential match-winner; the man who wants to target England's opening batsman but does not want to take the new ball; the man who wants to get under KP's skin but does not want to engage him directly; and leader of the attack who does not want to lead. All the while muttering to himself, 'I am mentally stronger, I am mentally stronger, I am mentally stronger.'

The Times, 23 November 2010

England Pair Remorselessly Expose
Home Frailties as Mitchell Johnson Toils

Australia have had nearly four years to get over the retirement of two of the game's greatest bowlers, yet on days such as yesterday a certain wistfulness hangs in the air. Oh, my Shane Warne and Glenn McGrath not so long ago. Instead, yesterday Ricky Ponting had to make do with a rookie finger spinner and a strike bowler suffering an identity crisis and, on a pitch as flat as the Nullarbor Plain, my, how England took advantage on a day that must rank alongside their very best in Test cricket.

The visiting team began it deep in the red and finished it with their account showing a glowing profit and there were very few shocks to the system along the way. Only one wicket fell, that of Andrew Strauss, but not before the England captain had put two singles in front of the nought he made in the first innings. This was a performance of a man with an iron constitution, for walking out to bat on a pair in the first Ashes Test of a five-match series is no picnic. His stock, already high in England, will have grown a notch or two in Australia where, before today, he had never posted a score of note.

The runs were important, of course, but it was the way Strauss scored them that sent a message of confidence, conviction and optimism ringing around the Gabba. He did not set about reducing England's deficit by putting his nose to the grindstone, rather he went after Australia's bowling as if the thought of defeat had never entered his mind; and more than that, as if victory was still a possibility. His hundred came up in 184 balls, a decent lick given the circumstances.

It was clearly a message that resonated with the team. When Strauss departed, stumped after skipping down the pitch to Marcus

North, England's forward momentum did not stall. Any stand between Jonathan Trott and Alastair Cook has the potential to reduce the scoring rate to a crawl, but they, too, rattled along, their hundred partnership coming in only 165 balls. Anybody visiting the Gabba yesterday for the first time in this Test match would have been hard pressed to nominate Australia as the team in the ascendancy.

Strauss took the lead in this regard, driving the ball through the off side as fluently as he can ever have done, and, a nod to Mike Hussey's treatment of Graeme Swann this, refusing to allow Xavier Doherty to settle. Strauss has never been a natural down-the-pitch player of spin, nor a particularly good hitter over the top, but he did both in the left-arm spinner's opening spell and when he back-cut the spinner in the afternoon to bring up his hundred, he let out a roar that revealed what the innings meant to him. Normally a phlegmatic soul, Strauss has been unusually emotional in this game, badgering the umpires, reacting with disbelief to the occasional decision and engaging in a little chit-chat with Brad Haddin.

His desire rubbed off on Cook, who played as well and as securely yesterday as he has done for two years. His back-foot play has never deserted him in times of drought, but now he is moving smoothly into the ball; feet, head and body working as one again rather than battling against each other. The word is that Cook has abandoned much of the tinkering to his technique of the past few months, and gone back to a method that feels more natural and instinctive – further evidence, if evidence was needed, of the dangers of over-coaching.

Theirs was a significant partnership, in the course of which Strauss and Cook became the most prolific of all England opening combinations, overhauling in aggregate terms Hobbs and Sutcliffe. When Cook brought up his hundred, also with a cut, it was the first time for 72 years that both England openers had scored hundreds in the same innings against Australia.

If a measure of a team is how they respond on difficult days, Australia held up less well than England had the day before. Their bowlers eked out no response from the conditions and by late afternoon they looked like a team devoid of inspiration and ideas. Doherty looked little more than a journeyman left-arm spinner, lacking variation and bowling too quickly for the conditions, and the seam bowlers found no swing and were unable to sustain pressure for any length of time.

Catches went down, Cook being dropped at fine leg by Siddle on 105, and Trott at point by Michael Clarke on 34, although this last, at full stretch, would have been a wonderful snare. Even Ponting's use of the Decision Review System was questionable, calling in desperation for a review against Trott shortly after Clarke's drop.

It was the kind of day, toiling for no reward and, more than that, never looking like getting any, that brought to mind the Cambridge University team of my vintage. To keep spirits up we used to have a fines session at the end of each day's play. There was always a fine for a 'non-con', for the person who contributed least to the day's play – and in this match Mitchell Johnson is winning that award hands down. He went wicketless in England's first innings, scored a tentative blonger when he batted and he remained wicketless at the close of the fourth day's play. He left the field smiling with his team-mates in close attendance, in a kind of faux bonhomie, but it fooled no one. He has had a bad match so far.

After he put down a fairly straightforward opportunity at mid-off when Strauss had scored 69, the famous line about England in 1986–87 sprang to mind: there's only three things wrong with Johnson, he can't bat, bowl or field. This, of course, is grossly unfair on a man who two years ago was named the international cricketer of the year, who began the year the No 2-ranked bowler in the world and stands at No 6 in that list. Yet at the moment, Johnson is Australia's greatest problem.

He wasn't exactly overused by Ponting. Remember Cardiff? In the opening Test of 2009 when Ponting needed a wicket to win the Test he turned to Johnson even though the left-armer had been misfiring. Gradually, the captain's confidence in his speedster seems to have ebbed away, so that he is now low down on Ponting's list. More a 'shy away from' man rather than a 'go to' man. He was given only five overs in the first session, six overs in the second and five in the third.

At one stage during the afternoon, he began to go through his stretching routine at cover as if sending a message to his captain that he was still around. But Ponting's reticence is understandable, because Johnson is clearly unsure of his role: is he a speedster, a swing bowler, a defensive, holding bowler or an attacking option? His bowling reflects his confusion, being neither one thing nor the other. There is time yet, of course, for him to fire; in the absence of you know who, he needs to take centre stage.

The Times, 29 November 2010

1st Test. At Woolloongabba, Brisbane, on 25–9 November. Toss: England. Match drawn. England 260 (I.R. Bell, 76, A.N. Cook 67, P.M. Siddle 6–54) and 517–1d (A.N. Cook 235*, I.J.L. Trott 135*, A.J. Strauss 110). Australia 481 (M.E.K. Hussey 195, B.J. Haddin 136, S.M. Katich 50, S.T. Finn 6–125) and 107–1 (R.T. Ponting 51*).

Myth of the Baggy Green Is Past Its Peak

There has not been much talk about 'aura' in Australia lately. Instead, Ricky Ponting awoke to the headline 'clueless' in Brisbane's daily rag the morning after the first Test match. And for those of us who saw Doug Bollinger play for Worcestershire some years ago, the next day's headline, 'Unleash Bollinger', was one that we never thought we would come to see. Send in the pooch!

Slowly, year by year, Test by Test, session by session, selection by selection, the accretions of myth built up over a long period of time by the Australia cricket team, and their sycophantic admirers in the local media, are being washed away. If the second half of the Test in Brisbane was the less interesting in some ways, as bat totally dominated ball, it was also the most revealing. As England's top three ground on remorselessly, Australia's bowling and catching revealed them to be, well, just like anybody else.

When Ponting caught Alastair Cook at short mid-wicket on 209, observers doubted the veracity of the catch because of his subdued celebrations. The Australia captain knew he had caught the ball, even if the third umpire didn't, but his downbeat reaction was not because of his uncertainty but because the scoreboard said 457 for one. No matter who you are, no matter who you play for, it is hard to celebrate maniacally when the scoreboard reads like that.

West Indies under Viv Richards possessed the most powerful 'aura' of any team I knew. It was based upon fear, pure fear. A generation of England cricketers had grown up under West Indian cricketing domination and nightmarish stories of their fast bowlers were handed down from year to year. Michael Holding bowling to Brian Close and John Edrich at Old Trafford in 1976; Mike Gatting having his nose smashed by Malcolm Marshall in the Caribbean in 1986; Andy Lloyd's one and only Test match ending with permanent eye damage two years earlier. These images were real, not imagined.

Their effect was twofold. They diminished the opposition and gave what educationalists would call 'value-added' to everything

West Indies did. Suddenly, West Indies' warm-ups looked more dedicated and more professional than anyone else's and when they hugged and high-fived at the end of them, the opposition saw a side who were utterly united, an impression strengthened by a captain who played with hatred – especially against England – in his eyes.

Australia's aura was based not upon fear but upon a myth. The myth of the baggy green cap that adorned the head of generations of Australian cricketers, but one that, until Steve Waugh became Australia's captain, had not been so venerated. Recognising the importance of mythology and ritual, Waugh elevated the cap into something that previous generations did not recognise. It coincided with the period of Australia's greatest domination and most observers, encouraged by Waugh and his lieutenants, put two and two together.

Justin Langer, one of Waugh's closest acolytes, said that bringing the baggy green back to life was his captain's greatest legacy. Waugh described the power of this mythology: 'As far as the Australian team is concerned, the traditions that we uphold are an important element used to develop pride, camaraderie and morale that will hopefully give us a mental toughness when we are challenged,' he said.

When Australia walk out for the first session of a Test match in their caps, think of it as the equivalent of the haka for the All Blacks.

Everybody needs props in professional sport to help them cope, but when members of the Australia team went to Wimbledon to watch Pat Rafter in their baggy greens, the suspicion was that they were indulging in something that smelt suspiciously not of myth but of bullshit.

Certainly, Ian Chappell, another former Australia captain, thought as much. 'It's a five-dollar piece of cloth,' he said of the baggy green. 'There is too much made of it. It is a cap, a nice cap, but it has only become more than that since Steve Waugh started to jump up and down about it. I don't need to look at a cap to remind me of what I did.' Chappell does not have one to this day.

But mythology can be a powerful thing in sport and as Australia enjoyed a period of dominance that coincided with it, so the cap, rather than the cricketer underneath it, began to take on special significance. Everyone seemed to buy into it: the cricketers, the public, the media and, at times, even the opposition. Over the years the myth was repeated so often that the non-believers were scornfully dismissed and it came to be accepted as historical fact by mere repetition, as these things often are.

The most significant thing about the latter half of the Brisbane match was to blow these myths away once and for all. If the doubts were not already there, they are now.

This week it was the turn of Michael Clarke to undergo a forensic examination of his technique by England's bowlers and then, in the days building up to the Adelaide game, as his one-on-one practice session with his captain took on extra significance, by the media. Whereas young Australian batsmen were once held up to be role models of technical purity, now Clarke was forced to talk about the adjustments he is making, about trying to stand tall at the crease to help him cope with England's short-ball ploy.

This loss of aura spreads, so that the decisions made by selectors, for example, start to be queried, even the selectors themselves. At the moment they have certainly got themselves into a bit of a hole of their own making. Since Shane Warne retired they have used nine spinners of varying degrees of effectiveness but have not yet settled on his long-term replacement. Only the most optimistic observer, or perhaps a member of the Doherty family, would consider the latest spinning incarnation to be the answer.

There is a reason why, alone among Test-playing nations, Australia has produced generation after generation of wrist spinners. It is because the conditions here do not really favour finger spin, unless that finger spinner is exceptional. It remains to be seen how Graeme Swann's tour pans out but the early signs from the Gabba were that even he may find things tough. What chance, then, Xavier Doherty?

Having witnessed Ian Bell maul Steven Smith in the match against Australia A in Hobart, nobody in their right minds would say that Smith is a ready-made replacement for Warne or anywhere near the finished article. And yet surely there is more upside, more long-term potential in Smith?

Smith looks like the type of player that Australia needs right now: young, optimistic and energetic with an occasional fizzing leg spinner and an unorthodox style that could well irritate England before the series is done. Yet he is not even in Australia's squad for Adelaide, a squad that is full of seam options now that Ryan Harris and Bollinger have been added.

Australia have a good team and some outstanding players and will still be tough to beat, but the period of dominance coincided with a fortuitous moment in time when a handful of great players came together all at once. England's players know that now, and it helps to know that you are playing 11 cricketers, and occasionally flannelled fools, rather than gods in baggy greens. The baggy green? It's just like religion.

The Times, 2 December 2010

James Anderson Gets Deserved Rub
of the Green to Leave Australia in Dismal State

The opening moments of any Ashes Test are always pregnant with tension – anxiety and nervousness, as well as excitement, being the overwhelming emotions of any cricketer involved, regardless of age or experience. These heightened sensations bring opportunities for the team and the individuals best able to channel those feelings into something resembling normality and, yesterday, that team was England and the individual was Jimmy Anderson.

Australia's attack leader might be sitting this game out but there is no question about the health of England's. Anderson has taken to his responsibilities superbly so far and he led an outstanding all-round display from England, with the ball and in the field, so that on a blameless Adelaide pitch, they bowled out Australia for 245, an outcome beyond even the imaginings of this confident team.

After Anderson's luckless display at the Gabba, it felt just that the wheel of fortune should turn so quickly here. It turned almost before the echoes of the pre-match national anthems had stopped reverberating around the stadium, Ricky Ponting and Michael Clarke victims of Anderson's accuracy and late movement with the new ball, once Simon Katich had betrayed the home team's nerves by being run-out in the opening over without facing a ball. After that start, Anderson continued to probe, adding Shane Watson, driving loosely to gully, to his bag just after lunch, and Peter Siddle, with the second new ball.

Four wickets in all and nothing less than he deserved. One man's work though is easily squandered, and yesterday was a day of collective excellence from England's bowlers, only Steven Finn not quite hitting the zone, leaking a boundary an over in his opening spell.

Finn aside, England's bowlers went at 2.4 runs per over, an outstanding effort on a good batting pitch against a team that, while low on confidence, likes to keep the score rattling. Only Mike Hussey and Brad Haddin, the heroes of Brisbane, broke England's shackles to any degree. Australia would have been in an unholy mess without these two, Hussey building on his wonderful start to the series at the Gabba with another telling contribution here, and

Haddin, playing selflessly and left stranded by a tail that, without Mitchell Johnson, looks feeble.

Haddin was the last man to go, hooking high into the deep, with just the last man for company. There was an uncanny resemblance to Hussey's performance at Brisbane, in the small amounts of good fortune he needed before he had reached double figures and then in the utter conviction with which he played. He was dropped by Anderson on his follow-through when he had scored just three, a return chance that, while tough, was within the bowler's range and capabilities – if only because he is one of the most agile fielders in world cricket and because England set such high standards of themselves in that area.

Yesterday was another example of that, too, the athleticism and ground fielding at times better than any England team in recent memory, each moment of individual excellence visibly appreciated by the rest with ostentatious displays of touchy-feeliness.

Every catch bar Anderson's half-chance was taken and two run-outs effected, the second by Strauss at mid-wicket to send back Xavier Doherty a perfect example of the kind of panic that athletic and aggressive fielding can impart upon an uncertain batting team. England have worked furiously at this aspect of their game, and they enjoyed the rewards yesterday.

Apart from one further driven edge that fell just short of Swann at second slip, Hussey played flawlessly. At his best, and now that he seems to have erased the pre-series doubts from his mind, there is something relentless about his game, the way he strides purpose-fully to the crease, the busy nature with which he attaches himself to it and, when set, the seeming inevitability about his journey towards three figures.

It was a journey cut seven short of its destination by Swann who, until that point, had come off second best in the duel. Swann did what finger spinners have to do on the opening day of an Adelaide Test; that is to say, he bowled accurately and, with the mercury nudging upwards, he allowed his seam-bowling mates plenty of rest. He also bowled a more teasing length than in Brisbane, and it was one such delivery, floated high and tempting outside off stump, that encouraged Hussey to drive into the hands of slip.

A ball later he was on a hat-trick, although Ryan Harris, leg-before, could be justifiably upset that the third umpire decided to ignore the evidence of an inside edge. Hussey's wicket was the perfect adornment to the most dramatic start to an Ashes Test in living memory. You have to be long in the tooth to remember a worse start for Australia – 60 years ago, to be precise, in Brisbane where they found themselves three down without a run on the board. Yesterday, they were three down in a flash, although a brace of runs had come from Clarke's bat by the time that he, Ponting and Katich were all contemplating their fate from the sanctity of the dressing-room.

Katich's dismissal put in train a sequence of events scarcely believable. Anderson's fourth ball scooted off Watson's pad into the leg side, whereupon the opener set off for what, by his body language, he took to be a leisurely single. Ball watching, Watson had not sensed the reluctance of his partner to move, so that as Jonathan Trott picked up the ball at square leg, both openers were dallying mid-pitch. Trott took aim at the one stump in his sights and, one direct hit later, Katich was stomping back to the pavilion.

Katich and Watson have formed a decent opening partnership, but their running between the wickets leaves much to be desired: too self-absorbed to bother about the other, grumbled one local. One ball later, Australia were 0–2. Ponting had been cheerful enough, almost whimsical at the toss, as he cast his eye over the conditions and the glory that is the Adelaide Oval, a cheery disposition reinforced when he called correctly.

But there was grass enough on the surface, which prompted him to wonder aloud whether there would be a little swing with the new ball. There was, just enough for Anderson to catch the edge of his uncertain forward lunge to second slip. For all the talk of the perfect Adelaide pitch, it was Anderson who was pitch perfect, producing a lovely, late outswinger to Clarke now, whose stiff-legged forward push also ended up in the hands of Swann. Only six deliveries for Clarke, but long enough to reveal again his discomfort to the short ball – Stuart Broad producing one that rapped the batsman on the glove – and how terribly out of sorts he appears to be.

For Clarke, read Australia on day one. Ponting knew it, too, as he walked off grousing with Strauss at the close of play. His demeanour, in contrast to that at the toss, was thundery. His team's bowling had caused him pain at Brisbane, now the batting. This was Anderson's and England's day, convincingly, and a bad one for Australia.

The Times, 4 December 2010

2nd Test. At Adelaide Oval, on 3–7 December. Toss: Australia. England won by an innings and 71 runs. Australia 245 (M.E.K. Hussey 93, B.J. Haddin 56, S.R.Watson 51, J.M. Anderson 4–51) and 304 (M.J. Clarke 80, S.R. Watson 57, M.E.K. Hussey 52, G.P. Swann 5–91). England 620–5d (K.P. Pietersen 227, A.N. Cook 148, I.J.L. Trott 78, I.R. Bell 68*).

Resurgent Mitchell Johnson Leaves England in Tatters

Whether Mitchell Johnson ever thought it would happen again so quickly, having been dropped for the first time in his Test career in Adelaide, only he knows. But at three o'clock Perth time, with the sky a piercing blue, the sun beating down unrelentingly and a gentle easterly blowing across the ground, he held up a 62-overs-old Kookaburra ball to every corner of his home ground and soaked in the applause of the crowd.

He had just taken his fifth wicket for the seventh time in Tests, that of Chris Tremlett, who had his off stump flattened by a ball that was fast, full and swinging, the final confirmation that Johnson's career, which had threatened to unravel during this series, was back on track, and with it Australia's Ashes challenge.

Moments later, the bowler had his sixth, that of James Anderson, a wicket that pleased him doubly, since the two had engaged in 'pleasantries' the day before. He led his team off then, the king of the WACA ring once more.

Ryan Harris picked up three wickets and Peter Siddle one, but it was Johnson who answered Ricky Ponting's call at this, the most desperate of times. When, in the opening thrusts of the day, Andrew Strauss edged Harris on 16 and watched the ball sail between wicket-keeper and first slip, then when England's openers breezed to an opening partnership of 78 within the hour, it was clear to everyone at the WACA that Ponting's captaincy was on the line. But that his players play for him has never been in doubt, and Johnson's stirring response at least gave the Australia captain some breathing space – an 81-run first-innings lead that was precious indeed after the recent drought.

It was another rousing day's play of real cut-and-thrust cricket, occasionally bad-tempered but always on the right side of that, as we have come to expect in the Ashes. There was a hint of desperation, too, about Australia's batting in the final session, as they played frenetically to stretch their lead against a keen England attack that sensed the moment. Anderson was especially vocal, in the way that an opening bowler is to batsmen, rather than as a father is to a newborn child.

Australia's batting has never looked more vulnerable in recent times, with a technically suspect opener, one great player on the decline, another key middle-order player out of sorts, and a rookie No 6 who is one place, maybe two, too high in the order. England sense this, which is why the deficit did not faze them and why Australia rarely gave the impression in the final two hours of a team out in front.

Phillip Hughes got past Tremlett's new-ball spell this time, but not much farther, as Steven Finn ran one across his edge; Ponting, too far across his stumps as he was in Brisbane, gloved down the leg side for a solitary run, waited for the review and left the stage to near silence; and Michael Clarke, never more frenetic and obviously unsettled by pace, chopped an attempted cut on to his stumps.

It was left to Australia's firefighter-in-chief, Mike Hussey, and Shane Watson, characters and cricketers as different as chalk and cheddar, to take Australia to the close, their partnership a purposeful 55. Hussey owes Australia nothing this series, not that such sentiments will temper his ambition, but Watson owes his captain and his team something substantial and when he passed 50 late in the day, his cursory acknowledgement suggested that he was well aware of the fact. He knows the pitch is still playing well, and recent fourth-innings scores here have been high, the past four of 300 and more.

Still, this was Australia's day, the more so after the stinging criticism of their efforts the day before and that of the selectors in fielding an unbalanced team. It was a day that Australian cricket needed, and badly. They got it through Johnson, a cricketer who recently had looked not so much a 'once a generation bowler' as a ten-a-penny performer.

Left-arm speedsters who cannot swing the ball back at right-handers are fundamentally handicapped; no matter how quick, they rarely succeed at the highest level, especially if batsmen are disciplined enough not to go chasing the ball, as England were with Johnson in Brisbane.

But any hint of swing immediately puts doubts in the batsman's mind and awakens the interest of the umpires. Suddenly, the possibilities are endless: the stumps become genuine targets, as are the batsman's pads, and even the harmless deliveries outside the off stump are tempting, given the dangers of leaving a ball that may swing back. Swing, then, to a left-armer is essential and until yesterday morning for Johnson, it had been infuriatingly elusive.

How does something as mysterious and mercurial suddenly return as quickly as it disappeared, especially because he had done little in the intervening period other than spend some time in the nets and gym? Peter Roebuck once wrote a book on the game, with Ian Botham – ironically, given their present enmity – called *It Sort of Clicks* and the suspicion with Johnson is simply that; that some time in the middle of a nine-over morning spell from the Prindiville Stand End something clicked.

Thank goodness for Australia that it did, for with it came the first stirrings of life since England's batsmen had smothered Australia's attack so effectively in Brisbane and beyond.

There were other factors, possibly. The breezy half-century he scored in Australia's first innings may have been important for a man whose confidence levels seem to rise and fall as quickly as the FTSE. As could the mini-spats with Anderson and Strauss, which helped to raise his hackles and which may have put him squarely in the match situation and the moment rather than thinking esoteric thoughts about his technique. Who knows; whatever the reason, it was the Johnson that England have never seen before who bowled Australia back into the match.

Not that there had been many signs of what was to come in the first two overs of his morning spell, but in the next there were stirrings, as two balls moved fractionally away from England's left-handed openers. In Johnson's fourth over, Alastair Cook was the first to go, pushing half-heartedly at a ball that started two stumps wide and curved the width of another, the thick edge just carrying to Mike Hussey at gully.

Johnson was staring at England's in-form right-handed middle order now, a far less daunting prospect once the ball started responding to the messages sent from brain to arm to fingertip. Jonathan Trott, Kevin Pietersen and Paul Collingwood succumbed in similar fashion, leg-before to full, fast inswingers, Trott to the eighth ball he faced, Pietersen to his third and Collingwood, on review, to his seventeenth.

A ship that had been sailing along in a gentle breeze at 78 for no wicket suddenly found itself taking water on board in the middle of a violent storm at 98 for five, once Strauss pushed at Harris and was caught behind. Johnson is a game-changing cricketer, and this was a game-changing spell.

The Times, 18 December 2010

3rd Test. At WACA Ground, Perth, on 16–19 December. Toss: England. Australia won by 267 runs. Australia 268 (M.G. Johnson 62, M.E.K. Hussey 61, B.J. Haddin 53) and 309 (M.E.K. Hussey 116, S.R. Watson 95, C.T. Tremlett 5–87). England 187 (I.R. Bell 53, A.J. Strauss 52, M.G. Johnson 6–38) and 123 (R.J. Harris 6–47).

Andrew Strauss Revels in a Day of Perfection

They came in their tens of thousands, not quite in record numbers, but many tens of thousands nonetheless, sore heads and all, flocking down by the Yarra, through the Birrarung Marr, over the William

Barak footbridge and into the 'G', and they came to see what they had been assured was a resurgent Australia team. Instead, they left thoroughly disillusioned, many thousands of them before the end of play, the day's events confirming beyond all doubt that Perth was an aberration rather than a return to normality.

This was England's day – all lock, stock and two smoking barrels of it – another day when the remarkable vulnerability of Australia's batting was exposed for all to see by a bowling unit that rose rather than fell to the grandest of occasions. The scale of the demolition was that, in being bowled out in 42.5 overs for just 98, this was Australia's lowest total against England at Melbourne, lower even than the 104 scored in the first Test between these two teams here in 1877.

Andrew Strauss could not have penned a more perfect script: winning a good toss, then making the right decision; standing at slip and having to do little other than orchestrate some bowling changes – which brought rewards with unerring accuracy in the morning – as his bowlers delivered to order, and then watching the sun come out to take the sting out of the pitch just as he and Alastair Cook set about England's reply.

For Ricky Ponting, though, there was only the unhappy reminder of how things have changed, for himself and his team. He failed again with the bat, unfurling a couple of trademark swivel pulls but making only 10 before he edged a lifter from Chris Tremlett to slip. Later in the field, he could only hope and pray for another Mitchell Johnson-inspired miracle, but there was no swing for the left-armer, only a wonky radar, one waist-high full toss that fizzed past Strauss a reminder that for such a bowler there will always be as many bad days as there are good.

Whereas Australia could not muster a hundred between them, Strauss and Cook breezed to a three-figure partnership, so that within 30 overs, and with still an hour of the day to go, England were in credit on first innings. It was as if all the drama had been played out in the first half of the day, because they were virtually untroubled. Cook was forced to send for help on 27 when given out leg-before to Ben Hilfenhaus, and he did so with such a knowing smile that it was no surprise when the review showed a clear inside edge. Occasionally Strauss was ruffled by the short ball. But other than that their passage was as calm as Australia's had been rough.

The morning conditions were favourable for bowling to be sure. The pitch was green-tinged and the cloud cover heavy and near-permanent throughout the session, but that no Australian batsman scored more than 20 was testament as much to their own failings as the excellence on England's part. All 10 wickets fell in the arc between the wicket-keeper and gully, as England mercilessly exploited a series of flawed strokes, Matt Prior cheerfully accepting the lion's share with six catches, all of them regulation.

England's bowlers were excellent, led by Jimmy Anderson who, in a nine-over spell from the Members End either side of lunch, found the kind of sweet rhythm that comes to bowlers all too rarely and often only in their dreams. Twelve rhythmical paces to the crease; lithe and whippy in his action and with masterful control, he reduced Australia's batting line-up to rubble, taking the key wicket of Mike Hussey on the stroke of lunch and adding Michael Clarke, Steven Smith and Johnson just after. There was no way back for the home side from that.

He was assisted superbly by Tremlett, who bowled quickly at times with disconcerting bounce, and by Tim Bresnan, who was preferred in the morning to Steven Finn. Tremlett added four more wickets to his haul at Perth, starting the rot by taking the shoulder of Shane Watson's bat, ending Ponting's stay and hoovering up the tail. Bresnan did precisely the job he was selected to do, which was to act as a sponge and dry up the runs, so that England bowled 16 maidens in all, more than twice as many as they bowled in the first innings at Perth, in slightly more than half as many overs.

Finn, no doubt, would have reckoned to do a decent job as well and he would have been rightly frustrated not to have been given the opportunity, but there was no denying Bresnan's accuracy or suitability for the job; a very English bowler, for unusually English-style conditions. He picked up a couple of wickets, too, that of Haddin, who played a curiously twitchy innings, and Phillip Hughes, who, if he continues to play as he is, will be looked upon in time as something of a curio himself. How, people may ask, did such a technically inept batsman ever come to open for Australia?

Hughes had fought hard for an hour, both against England's new-ball attack and his own instincts, when he launched himself at the kind of delivery an opening batsman really should regard with disdain. Three stumps wide, and two feet short of being a half-volley, he threw his hands at the ball from a stiff-legged base, only to see it slice to gully, where Kevin Pietersen, who had already put down a difficult chance when Watson toe-ended a cut, accepted gratefully.

Hughes's dismissal was the most egregious example of poor batsmanship, but it was by no means the only one. Clarke, Smith and Haddin were all guilty of pushing hard at balls that were well outside their eyeline, so that any bounce or late movement, of the kind on offer during the first half of the day, was bound to bring their downfall. Haddin's brief innings, full of wild swishes and swipes, hinted that the batsman's earlier indiscretions were having a knock-on effect. Steve Waugh, watching on in the crowd, must have wondered at the generosity of it all.

With three early wickets, Australia's innings took on a familiar pattern, until the failure that is of Hussey. Called upon to fire-fight in each of the three Tests so far, it was inevitable, perhaps, that he would fail to answer the call at some stage. It took a good one from Anderson to get him, though, a full, curling delivery that took the edge before the batsman's feet had found their intended position. Anderson's delight, and his team-mates', knew no bounds.

From making the right call with the team and the toss, to batting staunchly at the end, there is not much the England captain is flunking right now. He was right about Hussey, too: when asked before the game how they were going to get him out, Strauss had shrugged and said, simply, 'he's due to nick one'. It sounded a little hopeful at the time, but he was, and he did. Maybe Strauss can turn his hand to the national debt next.

The Times, 27 December 2010

England Consign Years of Hurt to Distant Memory

It was six minutes to noon when Tim Bresnan, an honest Yorkshire toiler seemingly transformed over the last two days into a latter-day Frederick Sewards Trueman, produced the wicket that retained the Ashes for England the first time in 24 years. More than five sessions and a Test match were remaining in the series, the early destiny of the urn a measure, then, of the visiting team's dominance. It was time to sup.

The moment was regulation: Ben Hilfenhaus pushing half-forward, Matt Prior, the wicket-keeper, accepting a straightforward chance; the celebrations, though, were euphoric, as England's players got together in the tightest of huddles, the massed ranks of England supporters in the Great Southern Stand saluting them. Brad Haddin, as flinty an Australian as it is possible to meet, dropped to his haunches, undefeated in a personal sense, but also a member of a team that had been overwhelmed.

Australia's resistance was risible. Mitchell Johnson fell to the eleventh ball of the morning, Chris Tremlett squeezing one through via bat and pad, and he left the field hurriedly, never a man about whom it could be said that the contest is everything. Thereafter, and probably for the first time on this tour, England got ahead of themselves, so that there were some sloppy moments, notably when a couple of outside edges off Graeme Swann eluded Paul Collingwood at slip.

Haddin, as proud as his bat was straight, offered some cheer for Australia as he went past fifty, but he could only watch as Peter Siddle skied Swann to long-on, and then Bresnan mopped up Hilfenhaus, the last man. It is with warriors such as Australia's wicket-keeper that their path must be taken, Haddin one of only two men – Mike Hussey being the other – who have played well enough to make a combined XI selected from both teams.

England's players went first to Australia to shake hands in the time-honoured way, then to their supporters, who have witnessed some horrible moments at this ground in recent years. Four years ago a great Australia team eviscerated inept opponents on the way to a whitewash; four years before that they had to sit through a double century from Justin Langer, now the Australia batting coach, as he powered them to another victory; and eight years before that, on this very day, they had to genuflect before Shane Warne as he celebrated an Ashes hat-trick.

Memories for players and supporters are important because they provide context and give each encounter meaning and significance. Four years ago, on New Year's Eve, it was hard to walk around Sydney without bumping into England supporters who had shelled out their hard-earned and who felt short-changed and badly let down by the performance of Andrew Flintoff's team. This time they were rewarded with the kind of memories that last a lifetime. Sport is about losing as much as winning, the experience of the first sweetening that of the second.

For players, great memories reinforce the reasons for playing; sour ones provide the motivation needed to ensure that the contest is ongoing, for it is in the dark moments that some kind of rejuvenation must be planned. On the past two occasions in England, Ricky Ponting urged his players to watch England receive the urn at The Oval, the better to motivate them for the next encounter.

But once the handshaking had been done, there were no Australians on the outer this time, although it is at Sydney that the urn will be presented. Ponting, for sure, will not be around for the next series and there are question marks over his participation even in the next game, although he hinted that, fitness permitting, he wants to lead the team there.

But this may be some kind of watershed for Australia, the moment when the realisation hits home that the slide in the world Test rankings is a reflection of reality and not some wheeze dreamt up by a nerdish statistician.

For England, as they shimmied around the MCG to the tune of 'We Are the Champions', it was no time to reflect, rather a time to enjoy. To hell with cold explanations and cool analysis, and even the staid clichés about the match still to come, it was time to enjoy and to soak in the kind of experience granted to few. After all, what is all the training, all the practice and all the nervy nights for if not for this?

Only four times since the Second World War have an England team returned with the urn until now, this squad joining those revered names from 1954–55, 1970–71, 1978–79 and 1986–87. Winning in Australia, against any Australian team, is a significant achievement and Andrew Strauss becomes a very significant captain now that he has backed up the triumph of 2009 with this. That will not be enough for him, though; he will want to become a winning England captain in Australia.

It will be tempting at this juncture to highlight the weaknesses of the home team: a batting line-up with more holes in it than cellar cheese; an unbalanced, injury-prone bowling attack; and an ageing side. But they would have been good enough to give most England teams of the past 30 years a good game.

It is not that Australia have been very poor, but that England have been exceptionally good. They have looked the best-prepared, best-drilled, most motivated team of my lifetime. The planning was evident in the selection of Tremlett for Perth and Bresnan here.

The attention to detail was evident in two run-outs in the Melbourne Test. The near run-out of Jonathan Trott who saved himself on 46 with a full-stretch dive, and the run-out of Phillip Hughes, who did not dive, the throw from Trott gathered up by Prior in front of the stumps to save a fraction of a second. The fractions count in top-class sport and the fractions throughout this series have gone to England.

A triumph, then, for all members of this squad, from Andy Flower to the lowliest of the back-room staff. But never forget that it is the players who must take the ultimate credit, for it is they who must deal with the nerves, the pressure and the expectation, and they who must deliver. And what a series they had: only Collingwood struggling for form and looking as though he did not belong, and even then setting new standards in the field.

One who covered himself in glory was Trott, the man of the match in Melbourne, and long after the last of the Barmy Army had left the stadium, the field empty save for two white sheets

The End of an Aura

covering the end pitches and a security guard at each corner, out he came, pushing his baby in a pram.

He pushed it out to the middle, stopped at the pitch – no, he did not scrape his mark at the crease – and paused to look around and remember the scene. It was the kind of day that he will recall to his daughter in years to come, the kind of day that will be talked about for a long time. It was a day when heroes – of the sporting kind you understand – were made.

The Times, 30 December 2010

4th Test. At Melbourne Cricket Ground, on 26–9 December. Toss: England. England won by an innings and 157 runs. Australia 98 (C.T. Tremlett 4–26, J.M. Anderson 4–44) and 258 (B.J. Haddin 55*, S.R. Watson 54, T.T. Bresnan 4–50). England 513 (I.J.L. Trott 168*, M.J. Prior 85, A.N. Cook 82, A.J. Strauss 69, K.P. Pietersen 51, P.M. Siddle 6–75).

How Andrew Strauss Made Sure
That His Side Played Follow the Leader

The first person that Andrew Strauss thanked in his on-field post-match interview was Andy Flower, the calm and cautious man with whom he has formed the closest of relationships since the messy divorce between Kevin Pietersen and Peter Moores. Maybe, instead, he should have thanked Flower's predecessor, Duncan Fletcher.

In his autobiography, *Behind the Shades*, Fletcher said that after he had chosen Andrew Flintoff instead of Strauss to captain in Australia four years ago, he turned to Strauss and said: 'Someday you will thank me for this.'

Yesterday was that day: instead of going down in history as the captain who led England to a whitewash, Strauss has become only the fifth England captain since the war to leave these shores with the Ashes. He has joined a select group.

Imagining alternative narratives is always fraught with danger, given that it requires only speculation and opinion over fact. But given the injuries and other setbacks England suffered four years ago – to Marcus Trescothick, Michael Vaughan and Simon Jones, for example – given that Fletcher himself was nearing the end of the road and given that England's victorious 2005 team had taken their eye off the ball, it is difficult to see how Strauss would have made much difference had Fletcher chosen differently.

For sure, it is hard to imagine that England would have been such an ill-organised rabble had Strauss been in charge. It is likely that England would have worked harder and been better prepared, but those who think that a different captain in that series would have brought a different result overestimate the value of captaincy in cricket. It is not much good having the best skipper if the boat is full of holes.

After all, Ricky Ponting, the man now threatened with becoming only the second Australia captain to lose three Ashes series and a man criticised to the heavens over here, was in charge of the opposition when that 5–0 thrashing was handed out. Is he really so much worse a captain now than then? Of course not. It is the players, stupid.

Nevertheless, captaincy is not unimportant and this England team carry all the hallmarks of their leader. They are diligent, committed, intensely competitive and incredibly well organised. It is in the disciplined batting of Jonathan Trott and Alastair Cook, rather than the flair of Pietersen, that Strauss's England can best be sighted, a discipline that has extended to the bowling throughout this series from, principally, Jimmy Anderson, but latterly Chris Tremlett and Tim Bresnan. Not that jokers, such as Graeme Swann, are undervalued.

Few doubted Strauss's ability to succeed here, because this tour has not necessarily been his hardest challenge. Thrust into the job at short notice after a couple of periods of babysitting, he had to work in the opening few months to create a culture of self-sufficiency. It is ironic how this tour has come to be seen as the apotheosis of the culture of coaching, but Strauss's first message to the players was to tell them that they had become too soft and too reliant on outside help. That was necessary, though, because seeking help is one thing, taking responsibility quite another.

Last year came a test of a very different kind when he was forced to become diplomat as well as leader as the Pakistan crisis threatened to engulf the late summer. Those close to him say it took a toll – the late nights and the long meetings – but it was never apparent from the calm manner in which he dealt with the issue and the impassioned response that came from his players.

And so to Australia, where most things that Strauss touched turned golden. Practice games were treated with diligence and professionalism, so that state games were won and the first Test in Brisbane approached with confidence; players were encouraged to be relaxed and relatively sociable during the build-up and have remained so ever since; selection conundrums were settled effectively, the bowling choices in Perth and Melbourne proving to be canny; while his judgement at the toss in Perth and, especially, in Melbourne was sound. His batting, if not quite purple of touch, was good enough, especially in the second innings at Brisbane, where the aggressive way he played sent a message of startling confidence.

It was clear that England had plans for all Australia's batsmen, plans that were not set in stone. Initially, in Brisbane, they fancied to get Ponting on the hook, but when it became clear how much he was moving across the crease, settled for something more orthodox with the occasional chancer down the leg side. Good fields, straight and deep, with a deep-set gully, were set for Shane Watson.

Michael Clarke was bombed initially to create the self-doubt that manifested itself throughout the series. It took them time to find something for 'Mr Cricket', but they eventually did so, bowling full to a short extra cover in Melbourne. Of course, plans look good when the bowlers are pinpoint accurate and when the opposition batsmen are out of form or not good enough, but a captain needs clarity of thought and communication to demand what he wants.

He has exuded a calmness and confidence that has rubbed off on his players: no panic after the heavy defeat in Perth, no naughty-boy nets or deviation from the plan, formulated a long way out, to give the players a four-day break before the Melbourne Test. Equally, now there will be no respite once the sore heads have worn off: 'now is the time to redouble our efforts' was the message before they began their celebrations. After all, he has said all along, his team have come to beat Australia, not just to retain the Ashes.

So he joins Sir Len Hutton, Raymond Illingworth, Mike Brearley and Mike Gatting as the men to leave these shores with the urn since the Second World War; three Middlesex captains now to two Yorkshiremen, something that will not go down well in the Dales. Something tells me, though, that there is more of Illingworth in Strauss than Brearley. There are no great tactical flourishes, no words, spoken or written, that place Strauss in the Brearley mould. Rather a pragmatism and parsimony, attributes that the Yorkshireman would have appreciated.

If there is a warning to be had from the select band he has joined, it is to be found in the roly-poly figure of Gatting. After he had won here 24 years ago, Gatting might have assumed that the days of strawberries and cream would last forever. But his team played little together thereafter; a combination of a rancorous tour to Pakistan, a rebel tour and some odd selections put paid to that. Gatting himself did not last that much longer as captain, either, the glory of 1986–87 overshadowed by the Shakoor Rana contretemps and some salacious material in the red-tops. He never added to the two victories he achieved here as captain.

There is always something around the corner to keep you honest and humble – something Strauss will no doubt be reminding his players of, as he bids to become one of the few England captains to beat Australia home and away.

The Times, 30 December 2010

Alastair Cook's Welcome Triumph for Mind over Matter

It was Walter Winterbottom, the former England football manager, who nailed most succinctly the difference between talent and skill. Talent, he suggested, was the ability to do the things that most footballers should be able to do: pass the ball, shoot, dribble, tackle and any other activities that passed for the daily rate. Skill, though, was trying to do those things when 'someone is trying to boot you up the arse'.

What Winterbottom was talking about, when you really think about it, was both temperament and achievement. The ability to transfer born-with talent into something more meaningful and lasting, the kind of achievement that has to be worked and sweated for and sometimes even dropped for. It is this kind of achievement, rather than any notion of pure natural talent, that Andy Flower, a modern-day Winterbottom, is looking for.

English sport is obsessed with the talent myth. Those who possess exceptional gifts poorly exploited are the subject of far more curiosity than the modestly endowed who achieve time and time again. It is an understandable fascination because failure is often more interesting than success, but it misses the point entirely. In sport it is achievement, not talent, that matters. Just ask Alastair Cook. Or Paul Collingwood, for that matter.

Both these players are at the opposite end of the sporting spectrum. Cook is in the form of his life, batting with such sublime freedom and ease of movement that he has scored more runs on a tour to Australia than any other Englishman bar one. He is on a journey that may, just may, end with him breaking all run-scoring records for England. After all, he is only 26 and he already has 16 Test hundreds.

Collingwood is at the end as a Test player. He decided to pull the plug on his Test career before the start of the fourth day in order to go out on his own terms and on the grandest of occasions. Even though, on a personal level, his career ended with a shortage of runs, he retires from Tests knowing that he has achieved a substantial amount.

The two have something in common. Both have been regarded as moderately talented players who have achieved more than or to the limit of their abilities. Batsmen are often split into roundheads and cavaliers: the natural assumption is that cavaliers are more talented and Cook has always been regarded as a roundhead. Collingwood, for his part, acknowledged his limited gifts implicitly when on the eve of this Test he laid out his legacy by saying: 'If, at the start of my career, someone had offered me three Ashes series wins and ten Test hundreds, I would have bitten their hands off.'

An unlikely source forced us to re-evaluate the nature of their talent at the end of the second day here in Sydney. James Anderson is paid for bowling and he is bowling better in Australia than any England quick bowler in recent memory, so no criticism of him should be inferred when I say that an Anderson press conference is rarely a place where column material can be found. But he surpassed himself this time when he suggested that Cook was more talented than Kevin Pietersen, who for so long has been regarded as the most gifted player of this and many other a generation.

Anderson's analysis could have been born out of mate-ship (he and Cook are particularly close) or the absolute admiration a fast bowler feels for a good blocker like Cook. The last thing a foot-weary fast bowler wants to see is an egomaniac giving his wicket away on a whim when a doze on the couch is calling. Cook has given his bowlers plenty of rest on this tour.

But Anderson's analysis is shrewd in another sense because it suggests that talent comes in many shapes and sizes. For sure, there is the talent to do outrageous things, such as the shots that Pietersen plays on a day-by-day basis. But we have seen on numerous occasions with him – Jamaica and Edgbaston (against South Africa) readily spring to mind – that outrageous talent can be costly, too. The kind of talent that is at the heart of a good team, suggests Anderson, is not the one-off eye-catching stroke or the occasional wonder ball, but the ability to reproduce a performance time and time again in a variety of conditions and under testing circumstances.

When Collingwood is finally sent to pasture, he can rest easy in the knowledge that he has managed to fathom out some of the more difficult aspects of a professional sportsman's life. The ability to give the whole of himself on every day that England have played and trained is a talent in itself, especially when you consider how much of a rabble England were here four years ago under the leadership of an incomparably more gifted all-rounder. His role in England's revival, his ability to provide the nuts and bolts that hold things together, has been underestimated.

Cook's special talents, too, have become obvious under the Australian sun. The talent to recover from career-threatening technical malfunctions; the talent to concentrate; the talent to be greedy for runs when you have already scored more than enough for most men; the talent to keep your ego in check, so that you maintain the same disciplines that carried you far into the sunny uplands in the first match of the series. The talent, in other words, to work out exactly what your talents are.

Whether the 2010–11 Ashes become known as Cook's Ashes, in the way of Botham's Ashes or Flintoff's Ashes, remains doubtful because English sport is often infatuated to a ridiculous degree with 'characters' and 'personalities'. Cook is neither, although he has character in abundance, but it is achievement that counts and his achievements in this series bear comparison to the best that England have had to offer in this historic contest. By his deeds and not his words shall we know him.

For too long, the notion of the 'lost talent' has been allowed credence. Certainly there are cases where a talent might not be fulfilled because of a tragedy of one kind or another. We shall never know how far Ben Hollioake's special talent would have carried him but for a rainy night, a slippery corner and a fast car. If Mohammad Amir never plays Test cricket again, that would be a tragic waste of talent, albeit of an entirely self-inflicted kind.

But there is less sympathy for those 'wasted talents' who were given opportunities in abundance. Those who would flatter to deceive with the arresting stroke or brilliant delivery that would bring forth the promise of greatness, only to be followed sooner or later by the inevitable 'if only'.

England's success in Australia has been based not, as Winterbottom would have expressed it, on talent but on skill. It is an achievement formulated around many different notions of talent, but as much around the nature of Cook's and Collingwood's as that of the supremely gifted Pietersen. As a fellow *Times* scribe said to me yesterday as we watched Cook grind on remorselessly: talent talks; achievement walks.

The Times, 7 January 2011

A Foreign Field Falls to England

Two hours after play, with the last remnants of the celebratory ticker-tape blowing around the Sydney Cricket Ground, the Ashes in safekeeping and the series secured, the England players and their families made their way out of the changing-rooms. The SCG belonged to them, and to English cricket.

Andy Flower held hands with his daughters and walked them to the middle; Matt Prior lay on the floor for a photograph with his little one; Andrew Strauss strolled around the outer with his two boys; and Kevin Pietersen cradled his son in his arms. An impromptu game of cricket then started between those sons and daughters old enough to play but too young to sup, as the players retired to celebrate some more.

The blood and thunder were done, all emotion was spent and there was time now for gentle reflection with those who have to live with the nerves, the bad moods, the ups and downs and the frayed tempers that are a regular part of any professional sportsman's life.

Two hours before, after Chris Tremlett had wrapped up the victory by replacing Beer with champagne, Strauss had been presented with the Ashes for the second time in two years, Alastair Cook accepted award upon award in recognition of his achievements and the lap of honour was begun – past the half-empty Brewongle Stand and towards the Victor Trumper Stand, where the bulk of England's supporters had gathered.

They were proud of their team. Not just that Strauss's players were winners, although clearly after 24 years the victory was important, but that they were so obviously a team united in a common cause, something bigger than themselves.

Four years ago, when England lost here 5–0, it was not the defeat that hurt those who follow the team so much as the manner of it. That is always the case, I believe, with England supporters, which is why someone such as Paul Collingwood, who finished as a Test player in the grandest style imaginable, will always be fondly remembered. He typifies the best face of English cricket.

This team, too, showed the best side of English cricket: the discipline, the professionalism (in the true meaning of the word) and the sense of hard but fair play. Those of us who have worn the England cap can be thankful because they have restored faith in the English game in a part of the world that had come to look upon it with scorn.

I have made eight trips to Australia in various guises and this is the first time that England have emerged victorious; the first time, almost, that there has been a contest to treasure. The English game is suddenly looked upon in a different light: to paraphrase one local journalist here, this place of cold pies and warm beer really does still know something about the game it invented. The lions and the crown on those blue caps suddenly glint a little brighter.

Special days, then, for those who thought they might never see England win in Australia again. One such is a friend of mine who came to Adelaide four years ago. It was a bad trip for two reasons: one, because England snatched defeat from the jaws of a draw, and two, because he found out he had cancer. He said then that the chances of his ever seeing England win in Australia were remote, probably nil. Well, he is still here and England have done what he thought impossible. This is for you, Stephen. No doubt there are countless such tales; it is what sport can do.

How does it feel to win here? Time to quote the cricket writer Matthew Engel the last time England won in Australia: 'Even at this time of triumph it is important to remember the verities of cricket between England and Australia. Winning is not what matters: the Ashes are about renewing old friendships in a spirit of sporting endeavour between two nations with a common bond. But, by God, isn't it great to beat the bastards?'

The Times, 8 January 2011

5th Test. At Sydney Cricket Ground, on 3–7 January. Toss: Australia. England won by an innings and 83 runs. Australia 280 (M.G. Johnson 53, J.M. Anderson 4–66) and 281 (S.P.D. Smith 54*). England 644 (A.N. Cook 189, M.J. Prior 118, I.R. Bell 115, A.J. Strauss 60, M.G. Johnson 4–168).

Index

Index